Charred Souls

A Story of Recreational Child Abuse

Trena Cole

Oberpark Publishing Inc

Printed in the United States of America by:
United Graphics Incorporated
Mattoon IL 61938

Second Printing 2002

Published by Oberpark Publishing Inc
55 Monument Circle Suite 1422
Indianapolis IN 46204

ISBN 0-9723535-0-X
Library of Congress Cataloging-in-Publication Data
LCCN 20021110471

Publisher's Cataloging-in-Publication Data
(Provided by Quality Books, Inc.)

Cole, Trena.
Charred souls : a story of recreational child abuse / Trena Cole. -- 1st ed.

p. cm
LCCN 2002111047
ISBN 0-9723535-0-X

1. Cole, Trena. 2. Adult child abuse victims--United States--Biography. I. Title.

HV6626.52.C65 2002 362.76'092
QBI33-703

Dedication

This book is dedicated to all seven of us kids
and three other very important people in my life.

My beautiful son, Joey, who I love more than I can say, the purest joy in my life.

My best friend, Bea, who I love dearly. I don't know what I would do without her.

and

Dr. Madelaine Pinkus-Rohn, Ph. D., L.C.S.W.

What can you say about Dr. Mady?
How about, a/k/a
Dr. Mady, P. A. (Professional Angel)

Acknowledgement

I would like to thank all the nice ladies at Oberpark Publishing Inc for their hard work and the faith they placed in me to get this book published.

Foreword

As a therapist for many years, I have come to deeply understand through some of my clients, the impact on children of crushed, degraded, humiliated and charred souls. Although there is nothing typical about the victims of abuse, children who have been relentlessly and sadistically tortured frequently evolve into the perpetrators of abuse or continue in relationships where they are abused and victimized. Those who are willing to participate in long-term therapy, typically diagnosed with post traumatic stress disorder, suffer again as they explore and relive all the tentacles of their personality and how each tentacle touches and reflects early and painful life experiences. As therapists, we try to help our clients remember. Unfortunately, they often relive the early life feelings and trauma they suffered. The courage to continue this exploration is a credit and a reflection of the client's ability to survive. Clients often ask me, "When will I get over this and put it behind me and go on?" It is not easy to face that there are certain traumas in life that are never fully left behind or gotten over. The goal of therapy is to find a way to accept the impact of childhood atrocities and have them recede into black and white memories rather than continue as technicolor nightmares from which the client cannot awaken.

This book, written by a survivor of prolonged, unrelenting and sadistic abuse, gives the reader a window into the experience of a child, and the suffering that was relentlessly endured. In many ways, the author of this book is nothing short of a miracle. She did not identify with her aggressors and perpetrators, but instead became a kind, consistent, loving, caring parent who managed her own child in a fashion wholly unlike the childhood she experienced. Nonetheless, there are residuals from her years of torture, humiliation and abuse. She struggles to allow herself any needs, lest she ever again reveal dependency, vulnerability and neediness, which she fears that others could use to devastate, control or manipulate her. She has worked very hard to learn how to love and trust. Humans were not a good experience.

Young soldiers who are survivors of combat and have post-traumatic stress disorder at least know what they have signed up for or been drafted into, and they understand that if the enemy harms them it is not for any other reason except they are the enemy. It is nothing personal, just the nature of combat. These soldiers have weapons to fight back with, strategies to protect themselves and they are viewed by their countrymen as heroic. But how does a young child rationalize enemies who are the very people charged with their care, nurturance and survival, their parents? This is personal. What weapons, rationale or defense mechanisms does the child have at his or her disposal? These children did not sign up for combat, and if they do fight back or defend themselves, their victimization may only escalate. They are totally helpless, the worst experience and feeling in the world. And unfortunately, they are not always viewed as heroic. Sometimes they are viewed, or view themselves, as weak, "whiners" or complainers who have contributed to their own misfortune. This book will give the reader new insights into charred souls that smolder on, long after the flames of abuse have seared, scarred and relentlessly exhausted these victims.

Madelaine Pinkus Rohn, Ph.D., LCSW

TABLE OF CONTENTS

INTRODUCTION

While browsing my hometown newspaper on the internet, I found some letters to the editor written by a woman who sounded like a saint. She is the mother of more than a half dozen children, quoting from the bible, preaching about how to live life in order to get into heaven when you die, condemning abortion and "the system" for not protecting children from abuse. This woman went on and on about the tragedy of child abuse, mental and emotional abuse, physical abuse and how an abused spouse has choices, but an abused child does not because of the authority an abusive parent has over a child. She spoke of the failure of the child protective services in this country due to their own incompetence and ambivalence. She cited incidents of abused children being so stressed from abuse that they finally rebel, only to be labeled incorrigible and institutionalized to be fed a diet of drugs until they breakdown and agree to return to the abusive parent. What a woman! What an expert! I know she really is an expert on such subjects because I know her personally, she is my mother.

Before you start thinking how fortunate I must be to have been her child, let me explain to you how I know first hand that she is such an expert. This woman is not a saint. She is a person of hypocrisy, deceit and lies. She is more an expert at covering her dastardly deeds and giving the impression that a light shines in her heart, when in fact, her heart, if she has one, is dark and cold and evil.

She knows all about institutionalizing a child until "it" learns to mind and not resist any demands put upon them. She knows to hire a babysitter for a week or two, after a neighbor has called the welfare department to investigate her children's environment, which she controls. She knows all about keeping children mentally and emotionally crippled with verbal and physical abuse. She knows that if you tell your children they are ugly and stupid and should have been smothered at birth, it makes them controllable. If that doesn't work you can always make them watch their brutal, sadistic stepfather shoot their dog. If that doesn't do it the first time, do it again. If you call the child names and tell them how worthless they are on the way to shoot the dog, the child will be so scared they won't know if you are going to shoot them or the dog. Very effective, if the effect you are going for is to make your child a mental and emotional midget the rest of their life.

Oh yes, there is a flip side to this woman who likes to portray herself as such a gentle, caring soul. In fact, if the same newspaper had searched their own archives they would have found that they printed a different version of this same woman more than thirty years ago, when she was arrested and charged with two felonies, assault and battery and aiming a handgun, for beating one of her own children and trying to stick the barrel of a gun up their nose to blow their brains out. That was before she realized that institutionalizing the child until “it” learned to mind could be so effective and a lot more fun for herself. This is a woman who never once said I love you to any of her children. She offered no affection to her children, the only time she touched any of them was to beat on them. She used to hit them for touching her because she didn't want their “cruddy little paws” on her. I remember the first time someone tucked me into bed and it wasn't her. I was fifteen years old and my foster mother tucked me in for the first time in my life. I was so dumb struck by it I didn't know what to do.

I was born in the mid-fifties, you do the math, and all my life I have not only felt but believed that I am ugly, stupid, dirty, inferior, worthless, unloved, unlovable, hateful and lazy, just to name a few negatives. The list could go on and on, but everything on the list is negative. I do have a good therapist, I believe she is the best in her field, and she is working with me to find some positives. I know now that I am not lazy and, in spite of my own childhood, I am a very good mother. My point is this, I was not born feeling like I wasn't fit to breathe the same air other people breathe, something happened after I was born and while I was growing up to make me feel so useless. I know what happened and I'm going to face it, deal with it and conquer it. What happened has a name, recreational abuse, and it was mostly inflicted by Alcee and Gordon, my mother and stepfather. I didn't know there was such a thing as ***recreational*** abuse until my therapist used that term. I knew about abuse, but I never put the word recreational with it.

Alcee certainly is an expert on how to work "the system" to her benefit. The same system she condemns for failure. It was like recreation for her to bait the system and then beat it. She is an expert on everything she writes about, but she cunningly writes as if she were on the right side of the issues that interest her. I do believe she knows the right side and the wrong side of those issues, and I know firsthand which side she writes about and which side she lives. She does it freely and with no worry about ever being exposed, because abused children don't tell, do they? I have no respect or love for this woman who gave birth to me. I do fear her as much as if I were seven years old and still within her reach. She is no less dangerous now than she was then. Even as an adult I shake and shudder as I write, because God help me if she ever finds out it was one of her "little ugly bastards" that wrote this. If there is ever a possibility that this writing goes beyond my therapist's office I will change names so that I can deny, to the monsters, that I told. I won't use my real name or any real names of my siblings and I won't use the real name of my hometown, but I - AM - GOING - TO - TELL.

I'm going to tell that she is not a saint, but a demon. A demon of fire that charred her children's souls beyond recognition with sadistic, maniacal and recreational abuse.

CHAPTER ONE

The Beginning of an Uphill Climb

I remember being small and young, maybe three or four years old. My mother had me illegitimately and we lived with my grandmother and her second husband. My grandmother was only in her early thirties when I was born and she was still having children of her own, she had ten, two of which were born after me. With my grandmother and my mother being so young, my mother was fifteen when I was born, and all my mother's siblings being younger and still living at home, it was party time all the time. There was always music and dancing from early afternoon until late in the evening. There was also, of course, a lot of drinking and fighting.

I remember two of my uncles picking me up and dancing with me, singing to me, teasing me and most of the time being nice to me. The others, and there were a lot of them, were not so nice. There were always people stopping by to drink, party, fight and just, in general, raise hell. I remember this one guy who wore a narrow white belt with two small buckles. He stood in front of the sink in the kitchen with his arms folded across his chest. I liked to grab his belt, climb up his legs and hang onto him. I remember him laughing at me, picking me up and holding me for a while. I would find out years later that the guy was my biological father. He had gotten my mother pregnant around her fifteenth birthday, skipped town, got into trouble and was put in prison for a year or so in another state. After a couple of years he came back and got my mother pregnant again, this time he married her and she divorced him after her second baby, Dana, was born.

When I was almost four years old the partying came to an end for the most part. That's when my mother, Alcee, married my stepfather, Gordon. He had just been discharged from military service when he started dating my mother. Since she soon became pregnant with his child, Dena, her third, at the age of nineteen, I guess they decided they should marry. As loud and violent as it was at my grandmother's house I would soon find out that it was really a picnic compared to what was coming.

I was so young that I didn't know any better when my mother told me she was marrying my daddy. She said Gordon was my daddy and that his last name was my last name. I wasn't even four yet so how would I know any different? It was years later that I found out he wasn't my real father. I remember feeling relieved when I discovered that none of his blood was running through my veins.

My first memory of any dealings with him was within a week or two of the marriage. He sent me to a corner neighborhood grocery store with a list. He said to give the list to the clerk, wait for them to gather the groceries for me and bring them home. It was only a little more than half a block away, so I guess he thought I shouldn't have any problems doing such a simple task, after all I was almost four years old. As it turned out, there were several problems with sending me to the store. The groceries were too heavy for me to carry, the sack was too big for me to handle and the half block I had to walk was all uphill from the store to home. I wasn't familiar with the area because we had just moved there, but it was a straight shot downhill to get to the store, and a straight shot uphill to get back home. After the clerk filled the order and put the change in the sack with the groceries, he carried it outside and put it in my arms, so I wouldn't have to maneuver the steps at the front door of the store. I struggled and struggled with that heavy grocery bag. I kept trying to carry it up the hill, but it was too heavy. I set it on the sidewalk and tried to drag it, but it ripped. I piled everything on top of the bag and ran home to get help. I told "daddy" that it was too heavy for me to carry and I ripped the sack. He started yelling at me and asked where the "fuckin' sack" was. I started crying and led him to the sack. He picked up the stuff and started yelling at me again. He said, "I'm gonna beat yer goddamn ass ya' little crybaby son-of-a-bitch. Ya' better run and hide 'cause I'm gonna whip yer ass!" He went on and on while I ran ahead of him hoping to get home and hide from him.

I ran into the house and saw my mother ironing, so I ran behind her and tried to hide. He saw me and started laughing in his sadistic, scary laugh voice. I clung to my mother's leg crying, but she said, "Don't run ta me to save yer little worthless ass. Ya should 'a done what ya were told. Somebody could 'a stole our groceries, 'cause you don't have sense enough ta carry a sack home." She kept pushing me away and knocking me to the floor. The whole time he was laughing so sadistically that it terrified me. He jerked me up off the floor and threw me on a bed. He pulled down my underwear and started beating my bare butt. I remember it being as terrifying as it was painful. I was so scared and I couldn't stop crying. He kept telling me to stop crying, but I couldn't. I was so scared and he just kept attacking me physically and verbally, which made me even more scared. He picked me up by the back of my shirt and threw me in a closet. He said when I "decided" to stop crying he would let me out. Decided? There was no decision for me to make. It was uncontrollable. I don't know how long I was in there, but it seemed like a long time. Finally the closet door opened and I thought he was going to let me out, but he just threw a glass of cold water in my face and slammed the door shut again. The cold water hit my face and took my breath away, I wasn't expecting it. I thought I was drowning, I thought I was dying, I remember being so frightened. I could hear him laughing and telling my mother that I was spoiled, and he was going to take it out of me. She agreed with him. When I caught my breath, I started crying again. He must have worked nights at the time, because I remember my mother eventually letting me out of the closet, while he was taking a bath and getting ready to go to work. I kept sniffling and shaking and wondering what was going on. My mother kept saying I was feeling sorry for myself and, if I didn't quit it, she would give me something to cry about. One of her favorite sayings was, "The more ya cry the less you'll piss."

Where we lived was actually an apartment that was part of a house. We didn't live there very long. We moved a lot for the first few years, living only a matter of weeks in each place, but never more than a month or so. The next place we lived was over a grocery store, not the same one that I had been sent to for groceries. It was a small upstairs apartment in an old building. An old woman owned the store and the building. She had to have heard some of the fights and beatings and arguments, but she never did anything about it. Years later, when I became a teenager, I would run into her, actually I went to see her, and she told me she didn't know what to do about "some of the things she heard" upstairs. She said, "Honey, we never knew what to do." She told me she was afraid if she called the authorities on them it would only make it worse. So she did know, but the only thing she did was yell at them to quiet down and threaten to make us move. We didn't live there very long, anyway.

I remember there was a screened in back porch type room off the kitchen. I don't know if it was a breakfast nook, mud room or back porch, but a big area of it was screened and there was a little bench built across it so you could sit there and look outside. My mother used to give me a big safety pin, like a diaper pin, and tell me to sit there and stick flies as they landed on the screen. She said to stick them, pull off their wings and throw them away. Sometimes I sat there for what seemed like hours, and maybe it was, sticking flies, pulling off their wings, pulling their bodies off the pin and throwing them on the floor. After I got what seemed like a lot, I would sweep them up and throw them in the trash. I hate knowing that I so willingly did something so mean and cruel, and I'm not making excuses for myself, but I was doing what I was told to do. I was four years old. It made my mother happy when I caught the flies. She didn't say it made her happy, but I could tell because she didn't bother me while I was doing that. It was a terrible thing to do, but I did it.

It bothers me that I have ever done something like that, but it also bothers me that I could. I remember sitting so quiet and still with that big pin in my little hand. When a fly landed on the screen I got it most of the time. I have never met a four year old who could wait for a fly to land and stick it with a pin. I'm the only one I have ever even heard of that could do that. It's not just the physical act of doing the "fly thing" that bothers me, but also, what kind of mentality must I have had? What kind of self discipline and patience did I have? That can't be normal for a four year old. It just really bothers me that I ever had such meanness in me, but it bothers me more to wonder about the shape I must have been in emotionally and mentally at such an early age.

I remember Gordon used to lie down on the bed during the day. I don't remember how often, but I remember he did lay down frequently during the day. It was summertime and we still lived over Miss Miller's store. He made me lay on one side of him and Dana, the second born by my real father, lay on the other side of him. He played with my ears and I fell asleep every time. I have this memory but it doesn't make any sense, because in the memory Gordon is laying on the bed watching TV when he makes us get up on the bed with him. We didn't have a TV when we lived there, only a radio. So why do I remember a TV? I don't have a clue. I know all we had was a radio and my mother played it all the time. I also don't know where she was, I just know that she wasn't there. Even now, if someone rubs my ears I fall asleep quickly. I can't stay awake. It bothers me that I don't remember anything except him playing with my ears and me falling asleep. Since he wasn't a warm, fuzzy guy, I figure he just wanted us to go to sleep so he wouldn't have to watch us.

Sometimes, when I did something wrong while Gordon was at work Alcee would say, "I'm gonna tell yer daddy when he gets home so plan on gettin' yer ass beat." I would be scared all day. One of the worst times was the day she caught me hiding beside the stove trying to look at private parts of my body. I know I was only four years old because Alcee was still pregnant with Dena, the third born child, Gordon and Alcee's first born. When Gordon got home

Alcee told him what I had done, it was so awful. I thought he was never going to leave me alone. He kept screaming at me, asking me, "Where did ya learn ta do nasty stuff?" Every time I whined "I don't know," he hit me. He jerked me up by my arm with one hand and kept hitting me with his other hand. I was so scared. I was like a rag doll flailing around in the wind. It seems like it went on all night. I am embarrassed about it to this day. I don't know what I was thinking or where I got such an idea, maybe that's typical behavior for a child that age, or maybe I learned it somewhere else, I don't know.

Within the first year of their marriage I can remember at least six different places where we lived. Looking back, I wonder if people did call the authorities on them for abuse and that's why we moved so much. After I got older it was almost an obsession to go back to some of those places and confirm to myself that it really did happen the way I remembered. When you are being abused as a child, from as far back as you can remember, you don't know there is anything wrong with your treatment, because you don't know anything different. If you ever do come to realize that there was something wrong with the way you were treated, you don't want to believe it. Speaking for myself, when I thought about the things that happened while I was growing up, I thought I was crazy, hazy, mistaken, anything but accurate. It is unbelievable what some people do to their kids. Even the victim doesn't want to believe it happened, so why should anyone else want to believe it? While I was struggling with my own denial of the abuse, I kept hearing from the abusers that I "had never been right" and I must have "dreamed that shit up because it never happened," BUT if it did, I never "got anything" I didn't deserve. Well yes, it did happen, and I didn't deserve it, but even after accepting the fact those things did really happen and even after people, like old Miss Miller, confirming that it happened, I gave in a little and accepted that, okay, so those things *DID* happen, but they weren't *THAT* bad. After all, it could always be worse and I am still alive, so I told myself to shut up, suck it up, don't be a crybaby and get over it. However, after years of therapy and no doubt more years of therapy ahead of me, I don't think it's possible to "just get over it."

To this day, I sometimes tell myself that maybe I wasn't the perfect model child and maybe I brought a lot of it on myself. After all, I was always told that I was a hateful little bastard, ungrateful, mean, stupid and ugly just to name a few adjectives used to describe me throughout my childhood, but thank God I have a good therapist. When I go into that self incriminating mode that I go into periodically, she asks me about my own child. She asks me what he could do that would ever make me treat him the way I was treated. It pulls me back to the reality that no child deserves to be treated the way my brothers and sisters and I were treated. I feel so shaken and shattered when she asks me that question, I just want to scream, "Keep my child out of this!" It's like, if I discuss him in the same breath as discussing my childhood I might contaminate him, but she knows what she is doing and I trust her, so I don't scream. I start to imagine someone doing something to him that was done to me and it makes me sick. I think it's so jolting to me partly because I still don't want to believe that anyone would do such horrible things to me and partly because I'm still scared on some level that they could still "get me." It makes me feel so hated, worthless and unlovable. It's so ugly and painful that I don't even want my son, Joey, mentioned in the discussion or recollection of any part of it. There is nothing my child could do to make me beat him, shoot his dog, cuss him and call him names or abuse him in any way. I have always protected him from any potential abuse from anyone. I think I worry more than normal people about being a good mother. I know almost everything you're not supposed to do to kids, but when I had Joey, I wasn't sure if I knew what you were supposed to do for and with kids. I have kept the list of "don'ts" in the front of my mind and protected my son from all of them. I feel so blessed that I didn't carry on the abuse for another generation, the buck stopped with me. My son has never been exposed to my family. He knows nothing about my childhood, except that it must have been bad because it appears that I have no family. I am proud to say that my childhood would be incomprehensible to him. I wish I could say that about my brothers and sisters and their children, but I can't. I am the only one of us who does not have addictions to food, drugs and/or alcohol. Maybe because I'm the oldest, maybe because there really are angels and a special one watched over me to preserve a hint of sanity, who knows?

One of Gordon's favorite games was to say "Come 'ere" and see how fast I would go to him. When I went over to him, he pointed to a spot on his biceps and said, "Look where a horse bit me." When I got close enough he hit me under my diaphragm with his fist and knocked the wind out of me. It was so painful and I couldn't breathe. As soon as I finally got some air and could breathe again, I would cry, he would laugh, my mother would make fun of me for crying and say he was just playing and I was being mean and hateful. Then Gordon would do it again. He would say "Come 'ere" and I would start crying, he would start out laughing and then get angry because I hadn't run over to him fast enough. That made him yell, "What did I tell ya ta do, ya thick headed little son-of-a-bitch?" He kept yelling and threatening me while I cried and slowly approached him again, I knew it would be worse if I refused to go near him. After all, where was I going to hide? Who was going to save me? As I approached his chair for the second or third time, trying to protect my stomach, I cried. He would command that I put my arms down, the whole time I was crying, and he made me look at his arm again then he punched me and knocked the wind out of me again. Then he would laugh and ask, "How many times does an idiot fall for the same trick?"

I remember him hitting me upside my head just for being "in his way" when he walked through the house. His hands were so hard and big. It felt like a skin-covered brick hitting me. Sometimes when I cried he said, "Come 'ere, I'm gonna give ya somethin' ta cry about." He had a deep, coarse voice and he sounded like a monster. There were kids in the family who were afraid of him just because of his voice. I was sobbing and tried to say "I'll stop," but I couldn't because I was crying too hard to talk. It made him laugh. He grabbed me and put me on a bed on my stomach with my legs hanging over the side. He pulled my underwear down to my ankles and made me lay there like that. I tried and tried to stop crying and, right when I felt like I could stop, he rushed up to the bed yelling, “I'm gonna beat yer ass!” I screamed and flinched and then he raised his hand really high like he was going to hit me, then he laughed and barely tapped me. Then he said, “You stay just where ya are 'til I get ready ta whip yer ass.” He loved this game. It started when I was four and went on for years, until he thought of more amusing recreational games. I was so little, you would think that a child that young wouldn't be embarrassed and humiliated about their bare butt hanging out, but I was. The whole time I had to lay there like that both of them made fun of me. My mother sang “I see yer hiney, so red and shiny” along with other made up songs for the occasion. I would go from scared to angry to confused to terrified, and I don't even know how many other feelings and emotions. Periodically Gordon came up to the bed and I screamed and flinched every time. Sometimes he just patted and rubbed my butt and talked about how much fun he was going to have “blistering” it. Then he laughed and went away for a few minutes. He always laughed this maniacal, deep, scary laugh. Then he came by and “blistered” my butt for a while by slapping it as hard as he could with his open hand. It felt like fire and the more I cried, the more he hit me. He said, "Yer a dumb little fucker ain't cha?" I don't know how many minutes or hours this dragged on because I was too little to tell time, but it seemed like forever when it happened. He just wandered around the house and made me lay there and wait for him to come back and torture me some more. I remember one time when he actually shaved while he made me lay there. He walked in and out of the bathroom and said “Here I come” to make me scream and then he laughed.

I remember, more than once, falling asleep or crying myself to sleep while hanging on the bed half naked, only to be awakened by him slapping my butt again. Sometimes he asked, “Did I tell ya ta go ta sleep, ya lazy little bastard? Did I? DID I? When I tell ya ta go sleep at night ya don't do it half the time, why do ya go ta sleep when I don't tell ya to? Answer me goddamn you!" I was four or five, what kind of answer did I have? The usual, whiny, pathetic little "I don't know." "Stay right there 'til me and yer mommy can decide if ya need yer ass whipped again." I could hear them talking. I know now that I was supposed to hear them. They talked like they were trying to keep me from hearing, but it was a game and I'm sure now that I was supposed to hear them to make me scared. Oh what fun it must have been for them. Gordon asked, "Whatta ya think Mommy? How bad was she when I was at work yesterday?" Alcee answered, "Ya know how mean the little hard headed bastard is! I don't think she'll ever learn, I don't think she can learn! Maybe she's retarded and we'll just have ta beat a little sense into her every day." Then Gordon decided maybe a belt would work better since I didn't seem to learn from a regular "ass beatin." He might have to use a belt or the flyback paddle his mother gave me as a toy, he tore the rubber band and ball off it and put it on top of the refrigerator the day she gave it to me. He said I got on his nerves playing with it and I didn't deserve it anyway. I guess he saved it for his own fun and games. Every time I heard them leaning toward hitting me again I started crying again, I tried not to, but I couldn't help it. I was already learning to cry quietly, but you know how sometimes it feels like there is a knot in your throat and chest and then it just comes out? You know what I mean? You try to hold it back but it just blurts out. I heard them chuckle when I couldn't control it and blurted out a groan or sob.

Finally, I was allowed to get up and eat supper. I kept sniffling and they yelled at me every time I did, but I couldn't help it because I had cried so hard for so long. Alcee said I was having a pity party for myself and wanted people to feel sorry for me. Sitting here today writing this, I cannot imagine what a four or five-year-old child could do that was so awful. But when I was little and these things happened, I was sure I *was* awful. I remember thinking if I wasn't so ugly they might like me better. I even thought it was my fault that I was ugly! Alcee said I cried so much that I stretched my face out of shape, so I thought it really was ***my fault*** I was so ugly. I remember wishing that I hadn't cried so much when I was a baby. She called me rubber face when I cried. She told me I was so ugly when I was born, that she hid me under the covers at the hospital so none of the other mothers on her ward would see how ugly her baby was. My grandmother confirmed that for me several times, she said I was so ugly that she wouldn't go to the hospital to see me the night after I was born, because I was so deformed and ugly that she just knew I would be dead by then.

My grandmother confused me because she would cuss me out one day and the next day tell me how I had a soft spot in her heart because I was her first grandchild. Sometimes I felt like I could count on her for a little protection, but there was always a hefty price to pay for it. As I grew older the price would get higher and higher. One time Gordon put me in the closet, of course I cried, and for whatever reason my grandma stopped by in the middle of the game. She had already decided she didn't like Gordon, and hearing me cry from a closet made her dislike him even more. She got very loud and said, "If I EVER find out that you put her in a closet again, I'll call the goddamn welfare department and have every one of these little bastards taken away from you! You better believe me. You hog headed son-of-a-bitch!" (My family was really into adjectives) He said, "These are my kids now and I'll do what I want with 'em, ya old whore. What goes on in my house ain't none o' yer fuckin' business." Grandma pulled me out of the closet. Gordon threw me back in. This went on for I don't know how long, or how many times, because I was too little to count or tell time. I remember thinking maybe I could go back to Grandma's and stay there. It was loud and violent, but I had never been put in a closet there, and most of the violence was inflicted by the adults on each other or on my uncles, I was relatively safe there from physical abuse. I didn't get to leave with Grandma and I ended up in the closet for most of the night. It was not only dark in the closet, but it was dark outside too, so the room was dark and I didn't even have any light coming in under the door. Gordon said, "I hope that snake I saw didn't crawl in that closet." Then he stuck things under the door and yelled, really loud "Watch out!"

See what I mean about my grandmother confusing me? At the time I was so happy that she took up for me, I didn't think there was anything wrong with her calling me a bastard. It was just a normal everyday way of life for people to call me names. *All* the adults called *all* the kids in the family names *all* the time. That's just the way it was. I guess I thought of Grandma as the lesser of two evils, but I was too little to recognize it as that. My uncles used to call me "smashed road kill" because my grandmother told them when I was born I looked like an animal that had been run over by a car. When they called me that I cried, then Alcee called me "rubber face." She said many times, "Ya better hope yer face don't freeze like that 'cause if ya get any uglier we'll have ta tie a pork chop around yer neck ta get the dogs ta play with ya." Then she mocked the way I cried. Sometimes she would hit me on the side of my head and say, "Now ya got somethin' ta cry about, rubber face." As I got older, I started using my ugliness to make people laugh. Alcee said if I was just a little bit less ugly I would look like Ruth Buzzi when she played the old woman in the park character on Laugh In. My family loved the fact that I didn't dispute my being ugly, because that meant they won the control game, they won the mind game, they won every game. As long as they had that feeling of victory things were only bad, anytime they felt like they lost a game, things got brutal.

They didn't just beat the kids. They beat on each other too. Alcee and Gordon beat each other up weekly, he usually had fewer injuries because he was stronger and bigger. I remember my grandmother beating her second and third husbands, and neither one of them ever defended themselves against her. She beat and kicked them and they didn't even hit her back. My whole family was very physically aggressive and spiteful. If one of the adults did something to make another one mad, they would take something that person had given to them and cut it up, bust it up, burn it, jump up and down on it, whatever it took to destroy it. They either did this in front of the person that made them mad, while they screamed and cussed at them, or they would send them the ashes or particles of the item after it was destroyed with a note saying something foul and vulgar about what they could do with the remains of the item. This occurred within days, or weeks, of the fisticuffs that started the fight in the first place. Sometimes it started over something as simple as a look. One of them would say, "I don't think I like the way yer lookin' at me," and the fight was on.

I used to be terrified that Gordon was going to kill my mother. I remember one time when he was beating her, he had her pinned against a pantry door in the kitchen and he was choking her. Her face was purple and looked puffy. I kept begging him to let her go while trying to keep the little ones out of the kitchen. She was already bruised and bloody, but she wouldn't shut up. He kept saying he was going to choke her head off, and somehow she answered him by saying in a raspy whisper, "That's okay ya whore monger. I'll die happy knowin' yer goin' ta the pen."

I didn't get to see my grandmother very much that first year after Alcee married Gordon. He tried to keep us away from her because the two of them didn't get along with each other very well. Sometimes on Friday or Saturday night Alcee would load all of us up in a cab and we went to Grandma's to spend the night. It was always in the middle of the night after Gordon came home drunk and they fought until one or both of them were bleeding. One Saturday night, after Gordon came in drunk and they had a fist fight, he left with the baby, Dena. She is the baby Alcee was pregnant with when she married Gordon. Dena was only a few weeks old and she was born in winter, so it had to be during cold weather. Alcee called a cab so she could take Dana and me to Grandma's and hide out. In the meantime Gordon had taken Dena to his parent's house. The phone calls went on and on for hours with everyone yelling and screaming and hanging up on each other, only to call them right back and scream some more. Finally, sometime in the middle of the night Gordon's parents brought Dena to my grandmother's house. They said they waited until he passed out, so they wouldn't have to fight with him, and brought her back to Alcee. The next day we all would go back home, against Grandma's advice, and everything went on as usual, even the next weekend. I remember Grandma saying, to my mother, "He'll come around here tomorrow with tears in his eyes as big as horse turds and you'll go back to the sadistic, hog headed son-of-a-bitch. What ya need to do is stay here and make him pay support on that little bastard he saddled ya with."

I knew from the beginning that Gordon didn't like me, but I guess it wasn't personal because he didn't like anyone except his drinking buddies. People used to ask me if he treated me like I was his own child. I told them, "Oh yes, he's as mean to his own kids as he is to me." I think about the time he sent me to the store to get more than I could carry and I have to believe that he knew I couldn't carry all that, especially uphill. He had to know, and if he did know then it was merely recreation for him to set me up like that. I felt like such a weak, dumb little nothing when I didn't do something as simple as carrying that sack home. And he said I was lazy! I was barely four years old, and I was small for my age. How do you know if a four year old is lazy? Can you tell at the age of four? I didn't know what the word meant, but I knew it wasn't something good. I would be called lazy again throughout the years and before I turned five years old I would know what it meant. I knew something bad was happening, but I wasn't old enough to know that it was the beginning of an uphill climb for years to come. Not only that, but the hill was going to get higher and steeper, and before I figured out how to make it through the nightmare climb and get bigger and stronger I would, instead, first get weaker and smaller.

Charred Souls

CHAPTER TWO

The Baby Factory

When Dena was just a few months old my mother was pregnant again with her fourth child. I would be five when he was born. With her being pregnant and having three kids to take care of already, I had to help her a lot. Before it was over she would have seven kids in a ten and a half year period. There was almost a three-year age difference between the second one and me, figure it out, she had five kids in seven and a half years, all single births. It seemed like every year she was pregnant, and every year I would say to myself, *I* don't want another baby. I was already changing diapers, feeding babies and taking care of them so they wouldn't cry. I would walk the floor with them, bounce them or rock them, even though we didn't have a rocking chair. I did what ever it took to keep them quiet. It wasn't that I didn't like babies, but I wasn't even old enough to go to school, and I was already taking care of them. I was tired. I was only five, but I was tired.

From what I hear, we had only lived with my real dad for a few months and then moved back to my grandmothers, because my dad was in trouble again and went back to prison. I would look him up years later in hopes that he could save me, but he wouldn't, or couldn't. That's probably why I don't remember much about bringing Dana, the second born, home. I do remember getting in trouble when she was a toddler for burning her finger with a hot spoon. My mother was making fudge, and I was supposed to stand on a chair and stir it. I would stir it and then put the spoon on the stove top. Dana wanted to watch, so she pushed a chair over to the stove and climbed up. I let her do it, I didn't care if she watched. I stirred the fudge and right when I was putting the spoon back on the stove top, Dana stuck her finger under it. She was trying to scoop some of the fudge off the top of the stove that had dripped from the spoon. My mother said I did it on purpose and threatened to burn my hands, but she didn't burn me she just hit me and cussed me for a while. Anyway, I was the oldest and Dana was the second oldest.

Dena was the third child, the first one born to Alcee and Gordon. I remember one time when I was changing her diaper, sticking her with a diaper pin. Back then people used all cloth diapers, I don't even know if they made disposable ones then, and they were thick and bulky. I was told, and showed, how to protect the baby from getting stuck, I just didn't do it that time. I was supposed to put my fingers behind the part of the diaper that the pin was going through so if anyone got stuck it would be me, not the baby. The diapers were so thick that it was hard to push the pin through, so I would push really hard and then the pin went through too fast and I would get stuck. Needless to say, I stuck my fingers a lot and they were always sore. One day I was trying to protect myself instead of the baby, and I stuck her. She screamed and cried and I could tell she was really hurt. I'm sure it did hurt, because she even bled where I stuck her. My mother came running and yelling, "Why is she cryin'? Ya dumb little mother fucker, ya stuck her with the diaper pin! Ya did that on purpose, ya mean little bastard. Ya think that's funny? Ya gonna do that again? Huh? Ya little despisable bastard, I'll kill you!" The whole time she was yelling at me she was hitting me. She asked me if I thought it was funny, but I wasn't laughing. I was so upset about hurting the baby that I was crying before she even started hitting me, not laughing. I must have already turned five by then, because I remember my mother was "showing" with Tim.

By the time Tim was born, he was the fourth baby, we would have moved to the house in the alley. I was old enough for kindergarten, but back then it wasn't mandatory, so I didn't get to go. We lived there for years, it was the longest we ever lived in one place. Tim and Dena were barely a year apart, so I had my hands full watching them and trying to keep them quiet. Frequently, in between pregnancies, my mother worked as a waitress. Back then when a woman was pregnant, she could only work until she started "to show," and then she was laid off. After Tim was born she went back to work on the evening shift, until she got pregnant again and started to show with Tom. Gordon went out drinking most nights, so I babysat. People would come by sometimes and check on us.

Tim wasn't really still an infant, but he wasn't a toddler yet either. He didn't walk yet, and I could keep him in one spot by putting him in the baby bed. I might have already turned six, because he was several months old. The baby bed was in the front room of the house. The whole house only had four rooms and a small bath room. There was the front room, kitchen and two bedrooms. All of us kids stayed in the back bedroom. The house in the alley was pretty much just a shack. There were no carpets, there were holes in the wooden floors, and it was drafty. My mother nailed coffee can lids over the holes in the floor trying to keep the mice out, but it didn't work. We had to keep pounding the edges of the can lids down so we wouldn't cut our feet on them, sometimes that didn't work either.

By the time I was six I would take care of the kids at night, feed them a snack, put them to bed, straighten up the house and iron my mother's uniform for work the next day. One night, while babysitting, I was in the front room with Tim, it was late, and I had already gotten Dana and Dena to go to sleep. I don't know *how* late, because I really had no sense of time. I had already learned that I should keep going until *all* the work was done. If I sat down or tried to play while there was still work to do, I was lazy. That meant I didn't want to help, I was selfish, ungrateful, mean and worthless. I always tried to stay up until my mother came home. Anyway, Tim was sick, and someone stopped by to see Gordon, but he wasn't there. I told him I was afraid because Tim kept throwing up, and I was afraid he was going to choke to death. The guy picked him up for a minute or two and told me he was okay. He went on and on about how I was like a little mother and how much help I must be to Alcee and Gordon. After he left, I fell asleep in the front room so I could listen for Tim if he cried or got sick again.

The next morning my mother was all over me as soon as I got up. Apparently, the guy who stopped by the night before had talked to her and told her I was scared. She was not at all happy about that. She kept hitting me and screaming at me. I asked her why she was beating on me, I told her I didn't do anything, and she started yelling, "Ya little lazy bastard, that's just it, ya didn't do anything. What did I tell ya ta do when I left for work last night?" I thought I did everything; played with the kids, gave them a snack, put them to bed, straightened the house, did the dishes and ironed her uniform. Maybe I didn't get everything done the night before because the baby was sick. I had to hold him and rock him more than usual, but I don't think that's what she was really mad about anyway. She was mad because I told someone I was afraid. She said, "Oh, ya poor little thing! Did ya want somebody ta feel sorry for ya? I heard all about how pitiful little Trena was. 'Oh the poor little thing! It was late, she was tryin' to iron yer uniform, the baby was spittin' up and she was so scared.' Bull shit! Ya just wanted some attention and tried ta make yerself look pitiful. You ain't mistreated, ya little sneakin' bastard, but ya will be if you ever try ta make me look bad again! I should 'a gave ya ta those fuckin' paper brain professors that wanted ya when you was born. I worked three fuckin' jobs ta keep you and this is the thanks I get, you stab me in the back! Come 'ere, I'm not done with you yet. Come 'ere! I ought ta kill ya!"

Not long after Tim started crawling my mother was pregnant with Tom. One night, while my mother was pregnant with him, she and Gordon fought about him going out to drink. After he left she went into the bathroom and took some pills. I thought she was sick and just taking some medicine. Years later I would find out that she took Quinine, because she heard that would abort the baby. Gordon came home in the middle of the night drunk and started beating her. He said the baby she was carrying belonged to someone else, not him. He was mad because there was a douche bag in the bath tub.

He said she was 'fuckin' somebody else. She said he was running around on her. They were so loud that they woke up the kids, fighting and throwing things all over the house. Before it was over with, the kids were crying and scared, there was broken furniture and dishes laying around, and we called a cab so Alcee and us kids could go to my grandmother's to hide out for the night.

After Tom was born I had four kids to watch. I really did not want any more kids. My mother said it was because I was jealous of them, but I don't think that was it. I was so tired all the time, and I almost never got to play. It seemed like I worked all the time, it was overwhelming, and I just couldn't keep up. I wanted somebody to say the job was too big for me and save me. When Tom was old enough to jabber he called me mama one day. My mother heard him and she didn't like it. I did not do anything to make him call me that, he was just jabbering. I was the one who took care of him most of the time so whatever he said, or tried to say, he said to me. My mother started yelling at me. She said, "What did he call you? Ya told him to call you mama didn't ya? Ya little sneakin' son-of-a-bitch. I - AM - MOMMY! Not you! Ya little ugly bastard. The only way you'll ever be a mommy is if somebody puts a fuckin' sack over yer head ta fuck you. Yer too fuckin' ugly ta fuck without a sack. These are *MY* kids!" She kept jerking me around by the arm and shaking me. She said "I'll tear yer goddamn arm off and beat ya ta death with the bloody end of it."

Before Tom was a year old my mother was pregnant for the sixth time, with Tony. I was getting pretty old by then. I was about eight years old when he was born. Alcee and Gordon fought all the time through that pregnancy, too. But by then my mother and I had a 'split up and he can't catch both of us' plan. When the fighting started she would run through the house so Gordon would follow her and, as soon as the front door was clear, I ran for it. I ran *up* the alley screaming "somebody call the police," so he would chase me. While he was chasing me up the alley my mother would run from the house *down* the alley. One of us was bound to get away, it was always my mother who got away. It was always me who got caught. Sometimes it was kind of rough until the police got there. It did help a little that he knew the police were on the way.

I think Tony was almost two when Denise was born. It's not that I didn't love my brothers and sisters, but thank God, Denise would be the last one. My mother's pregnancy with Denise was a rough one. She bled a lot and had to stay off her feet. Needless to say Gordon was no help, none of our relatives helped, so that left me. I was so tired all the time. I was puny and sick half the year with strep throat and ear infections. I was so under weight that the doctor kept prescribing this awful, nasty, liquid iron tonic to make me eat more and gain weight. It never worked, I was still under weight and sick half the time, but my mother enjoyed making me take it. They had told them several years before to have my tonsils taken out, but for whatever reason they didn't.

I remember one night, when Alcee and Gordon were fighting, he opened the front door and pushed her out. The 'split up and run in different directions' plan didn't work when he did that. She was pretty big, being pregnant again, and it was snowing, and there was already snow on the ground. I was so scared. I cried and begged him to let me go with her. I was sick, as usual, and I kept saying, "Stop it, I'm sick. I want Mommy." He said, "Ya want Mommy? Go find 'er!" He opened the door, picked me up by one arm and pitched me out. I had on a little undershirt and underwear, we rarely had pajamas so we just slept in our underwear. It was so cold. I knew from habit, that my mother went to the neighbors to call the police. Sometimes we had a phone and sometimes we didn't. It was shut off a lot for nonpayment of the bill, and sometimes Gordon just had it shut off so my grandmother couldn't call, or so my mother couldn't track him down at the bars. She used to call a cab from the neighbors phone, and take us kids from bar to bar until she found him. One time she made me go in, walk up to him and say, "Daddy, Mommy wants to know when you're comin' home." He later made me hope that she never made me do that again. Anyway, the neighbors let me in and wrapped a blanket around me. My mother was pretty beat up. The police came and gave Gordon a ride to his parents' house, the cop knew his dad. My mother called a cab from the neighbors house, and we went to Grandma's to hide out in case he came back. My grandmother let me go to bed, but I remember worrying that my medicine was at home, we forgot to bring it with us.

As usual, the next day we went back home and Alcee and Gordon were a team again. I heard them talking about how Denise had to be the last one. My mother probably couldn't carry any more full term, she said her 'play pen' was shot. If she had a hysterectomy or had her tubes tied, she would be laid up for a while, but if Gordon had a vasectomy he could have it done on a Friday or Saturday morning and be back to work on Monday. He had a vasectomy. I don't remember if it was on a Friday or Saturday, but he came home afterward and sprawled out on the bed naked. I remember seeing him laying there and being embarrassed. I also remember that it was my job to keep the kids quiet so they wouldn't wake him. I guess all he needed was a nap, because he got up and went out drinking later that night.

So by the time I was ten there was, in order of birth, me, Dana, Dena, Tim, Tom, Tony and Denise. We were all products of the *Baby Factory*. We might as well have been plastic dolls. We couldn't even have been rag dolls, because they would be too soft. We had to be cold, hard and tough like *plastic dolls*, because that is how we would live our childhoods. Plastic dolls are empty headed, pretend babies. You can throw them on the floor, or drag them around by one foot, if you want to. You don't have to touch them, and they can't touch you, because they aren't real. You don't have to show them any affection or love and it won't change their existence at all. They don't have feelings, because they are not real, they are not human beings, they are empty-headed toys. You can pick them up by their arm and throw them across the room, it doesn't matter, they won't feel it, because they ***are not real***. They are spit out at the *Baby Factory* every day for anyone who wants one. You can pick them up by the ankle, hold them in front of your face and scream at them until you scare the breath out of them. Then you can call them "little bat mouth bastards," and literally throw them into a baby bed. It doesn't matter, no harm done, empty-headed dolls 'will get over it.' They aren't little people. They are plastic toys, cold, tough and hard.

We weren't allowed to touch our mother, she always said, "Get yer goddamn cruddy paws off me ya dirty, little bastard." Then she wiped herself off where ever we touched her and made this sound, while she shuddered, like she had just been grossed out. That made me feel so dirty. I tried not to touch anyone or even brush up against anyone, because I was so embarrassed and ashamed of being so dirty that I would contaminate others. When a stranger, or anyone, patted me on the head or touched me at all, I was embarrassed. I kept thinking how mad they were going to be when they realized I had given them cooties. I used to wonder how long it took cooties to come out after I infected someone. I remember trying to crawl into my mother's bed in the middle of the night once. She said, "Huh-uh. Ya get yer little ass back in yer own bed. I don't want yer goddamned cooties. Ya ain't sleepin' with me." And God help any of us if we drank out of her glass, she said it was contaminated and threw the contents out in the yard. She said, "I ain't drinkin' it after you've had yer dirty, little bill in it. But you ain't gettin' it either ya ugly bastard!" and out in the yard it flew.

I always loved it when my own little boy climbed into my bed in the middle of the night. Sometimes, when I went to bed, he had already climbed in there and fallen asleep. He looked so sweet. I even have a note in my 'treasure drawer' that he left on my pillow one night when he went to sleep in my bed instead of his own. He was at that in between stage where he wouldn't want his buddies to know he still slept with Mom, so just in case they ever found out, it would have to be my idea. The note said, "Mom, I didn't feel good and I knew you would want to keep an eye on me so I got in your bed." I dated the back of that precious note and kept it. My son has no idea what a gift he gave me with that note. I have always loved the way he just walks up and feels free to drink out my glass or bottle of water. I admit, when he was a baby I tried to give him his own sippy cup and avoid the little 'floaties' that little ones leave in your drink. But if there was no sippy cup available, I fished out the floaties and drank it anyway. For God's sake, he's my baby, there is nothing dirty about him.

Alcee used to get aggravated when the babies cried. It was my job to keep them happy and/or quiet, but sometimes the babies just cried. Maybe they were sick, scared, hungry, sleepy or just felt like crying. I didn't always know what they were crying about, and sometimes I couldn't get them to stop. There was always more than one baby toddling and crawling around the house, and some days I did good just to keep one of them quiet and happy. Sometimes, when she got tired of hearing them cry, my mother would swoop down on one of them and grab them up off the floor by their ankle. She jerked them up high so their face was in front of hers, still holding them by one of their little ankles, and screamed in their face, mocking their cry. She looked like a big bird swooping down on them. Then she dangled them in the air in front of her face and screamed so loud that the baby lost his or her breath from fear. You know how sometimes babies lose their breath when they cry and their mouth is still open, but there is no sound coming out? Then they finally catch their breath and let out a big wahhhhh? That's what the babies did. Then Alcee would jump over to the baby bed and dangle the baby over it while she screamed, "How's that, ya little bat mouth bastard?" Then she dropped the baby in the bed and yelled, "There ya go, scream some more!" This was a common occurrence. It didn't just happen once or twice. All of the babies experienced dangling in mid air, while she screamed in their face. I used to wonder if she did that to me when I was a baby. I didn't remember her doing it to me, but since all the other babies 'flew' with the big bird, I wondered if I had flown too. I knew I flew when one of them picked me up and threw me, but I couldn't remember if

I had 'flown' as an infant.

During the summer Alcee would throw us kids outside in the morning and lock the door, so we couldn't 'run in and out.' She stayed in the house and played the radio, she liked to sing and dance while she listened to music, and us kids probably got in her way. If we had to use the rest room we banged on the door until she let us in. That used to aggravate her, she said we were running in and out, and there is no way we had to use the bath room that much. I remember one very hot summer day, she came out and told me to go up to the station and buy her a bottle of pop from the machine. She said, "Open it, because I don't have a bottle opener." I went up to the station, bought the pop and opened it. On the way back home I sipped out of it. It was a hot, dry day, the pop was cold and wet, and even though I *knew* better, I didn't *do* better. It was too tempting and I sipped out of the bottle. I didn't think she could tell if I just took a little bitty sip. It was so good I took another sip, and another sip until anyone could tell that I had sipped out of it. The level of pop was half way down the neck of the bottle, there was still most of it left, but it was obvious I had drank out of it. I got scared, but I told myself maybe she wouldn't notice. She noticed. When I got back home, she was standing in the side yard waiting for me, she had been keeping an eye on the kids while I ran to the station and back. She was so mad at me she said, "Did I tell ya ta stick yer goddamned nasty little bill in it? Did I?" I was crying by then because she was pregnant and I felt awful about ruining her pop. Even then I knew when a pregnant woman wanted something special or particular to eat or drink they should have it. I knew it was called 'craving' a certain thing. She screamed, "I don't want it now!" and she slammed the bottle of pop against the side of the house and busted it. Now she wouldn't have any of it because of me. She snapped a switch off a tree and started hitting me, mostly on the legs. She said, "Ya little greedy son-of-a-bitch! I'm gonna stripe yer fuckin' legs for ya and when yer goddamned daddy gets home you can explain why ya look like a fuckin' zebra, ya hoggish filthy little bastard. I ain't savin' ya, he can beat yer ass again.

Maybe the next time I tell ya ta do somethin' you'll do it right. Ya little fitified son-of-a-bitch."

Did I mention how all my relatives loved adjectives? Not just my mother and stepfather, but my grandmother, uncles, great-uncles, cousins, aunts, great-aunts, almost all of them loved adjectives. But it wasn't just their love of adjectives my relatives, near and far, had in common. Most of my cousins came from baby factories too. I remember one day at my grandmother's house, my great-aunt picked up my cousin by one of her arms and threw her. My cousin was less than a year older than me, and we had a lot in common as far as abuse went. Anyway, she grabbed my cousin on her forearm, just below her elbow, and swung her back and forth, while she counted, one, two, three. On the third swing she said, "Let's see how far you can fly, you mean, little son-of-a-bitch." When she let go of my cousin, her sleeve slipped off her arm. I started screaming because I thought her arm came off. I remember screaming until I lost my breath. I ran over to Grandma and screamed, "Her arm came off!" The adults cracked up, they laughed until they got tears in their eyes. Us kids were used to seeing each other being thrown across a room, but none of us had seen any of our limbs torn off. I calmed down after I realized her arm hadn't really come off. When I look back on that day, I think about how all the adults laughed about it. That was sick. I was really scared and my cousin was hurt, but us kids didn't know it was sick because that's what we were all used to. We thought everybody lived like that. How would we know any different? That's just the way it was.

I don't know how well any of us *Baby Factory* kids really made it. Over the years I've heard, through second and third hand gossip, about several judgmental comments made about every one of us kids. The thing is, I don't condone what some of us have done, but I do know why we are all like we are. Sometimes I feel guilty, because I think maybe I survived it better than some of the other kids. Sometimes I feel like I owe them, because maybe the only reason I made it was because I thought they needed me. They are the reason I didn't turn to drugs or alcohol. I was afraid if I did, they would follow my example and end up with addictions. My grandmother used to say, "You'll be knocked up or in the pen before you're sixteen, just like yer goddamned no-good daddy and mommy." I made sure that didn't happen either. In fact, I was in my late twenties when I had my son, Joey. Sometimes I feel like I somehow dropped the ball on the little ones, but by the time I was old enough to try to save them, they were too far gone. I couldn't deal with having alcohol or drugs around me. They were already into self medication, and they didn't want to give it up. My therapist said it's called survivor guilt, and that's what it feels like. She gave me a big break when she said, "Kids make lousy parents." She's right. Even though I did the best I could, I *was* just a kid myself, there was no way I *could* have been a good parent. I was just a product of the *Baby Factory,* just like the other six that were made there to become Alcee and Gordon's recreational plastic dolls. Have you ever noticed how some people take better care of their toys than others do?

CHAPTER THREE

Can't Hurt Me, I'm Gone

The house in the alley soon became more like a torture chamber than a home. There was never any peace and quiet. If Alcee and Gordon weren't fighting with each other, they were taking turns berating, cussing, screaming, beating us kids or playing some more of Gordon's sadistic games. We still did the "How many times does an idiot fall for the same trick" ritual. The only difference now was that sometimes Gordon would say, "Come 'ere and give Daddy a kiss." When I got close enough he punched me with his fist and knocked the wind out of me. I cried, he laughed, same game, same players. I asked Alcee to make him stop. She called me a little horse faced bitch, and told me that I was the most despisable son-of-a-bitch she had ever seen. She said, "He's just playin' with you, and ya have ta show yer ass. Maybe you'd like it if he acted like ya weren't even here." I finally got to the point that I could cry without crying, and I didn't ask anyone to save me. No one would anyway. I just kind of shut down, it was like I was there but I wasn't there. I have recently learned in therapy that there is a name for how I coped or toughened up. It's called dissociation. Your mind just kind of goes somewhere else, disconnects from your body. I even remember feeling like I was up in the corner of the room, near the ceiling, watching myself being berated or beaten.

There was also the "milking a mouse" game. Gordon would call us over to his chair and say, "Let me see yer hands." Then he took our ring finger and bent it down toward the palm of our hand. Then he pushed on the first knuckle until we screamed, he said he was milking a mouse. I remember it bringing me to my knees. It's very painful. He laughed and said, "Say uncle" and I said it. Sometimes my face felt like it was on fire because I would try not to cry. It's not that I never cried, but I could take an inordinate amount of pain for a kid my age. Gordon also liked to tickle me until it hurt. I would start out laughing because it tickled and I was very ticklish. He tickled me under my arms and on my ribs for so long that I would beg him to stop. He wouldn't stop, he kept tickling me until I peed my pants. Then they made me put on a diaper and walk around while they called me a little baby and made fun of me. I remember being so embarrassed and ashamed. I had to clean it up while they taunted me.

One of Gordon's favorite games was to take us for a ride in the country and dump one of us. I was always the one who got dumped because I was the oldest. I was about six when this game started. It was really scary because there were no street lights out in the country, so it was pitch black. He pulled down a secluded dirt road and said, "Who's gonna get dumped? Let's see, hum." Then Alcee said, "It makes more sense ta dump the biggest one 'cause it costs more ta feed her." Then Gordon said, "Tell the babies bye and get yer ass out o' the car. Hope the snakes don't getcha." I remember crying and shaking from being so scared, but I got out of the car. Then they pulled down the road until they were almost out of sight and turned off the car lights. When they first started playing this game I really thought they were gone. I didn't know what to do. It was so dark I couldn't see and I was afraid the snakes *would* get me. Eventually they came back and let me beg my way back into the car. Gordon had fun letting me get close to the car and then pulling away. He did this several times and I must have looked like an animal chasing the car. I was covered in dust that the car tires kicked up, I was crying and that made the little ones cry. Alcee and Gordon laughed and mocked all of us for crying. It was chaotic insanity. It felt like I had mud on my face because the dust was so thick and my tears mixed in with the dust. After a few trips to the country I started to toughen up. I remember still shaking so hard that my knees literally knocked, and my whole body shook so hard I could barely stand up after I got out of the car, but I don't remember feeling the intense fear when they dumped me. My therapist said it's because I left, I dissociated.

I think two of the others dissociated, at times, too. Dena and Tim would go into a trance when things got loud and violent. They just froze wherever they were. When objects started flying and the arguments got loud, I tried to get the little ones gathered into the back bedroom. Most of the fighting took place in the front room and kitchen. It is really scary to be knee or waist high when a brawl breaks out in your home, where you should feel safe. Dana, Tom, Tony and Denise would cry, scream, shake and run around in circles, but Dena and Tim just turned into little statues and stared straight ahead. They didn't move. They didn't make a noise. I used to try to get them into the bedroom first because they wouldn't even move to avoid being trampled or dodge flying objects. I used to take them by their hands and lead them right into the bedroom, they just walked along like little zombies when I led them. When they got to the bedroom they were quiet, but okay. It was as if they thought they were invisible until they were taken out of the line of fire. It might have affected each one of us differently, but it no doubt affected all of us.

Tim was only about three years old, maybe four but no older than that, when the effects, more than dissociation, started to show. I didn't know it then, I thought he was just meaner than the other boys because he was the oldest of the boys and seemed to get beat on more than the other two. One day we were outside and he put a puppy under a meter cover and tried to chop off its head. I don't know how he got its head under there. I was supposed to be watching him, Dana, Dena and Tom. When I got to him, he was pulling the meter cover up and slamming it down on the puppy's neck. He did this over and over and I remember, at first, I stood there and watched him. I couldn't believe it was a real puppy, but it was. I screamed at him to stop it, but it was like he didn't hear me. I went over and pulled him away from the meter. When I lifted the cover and pulled the puppy out it was pretty bad. The puppy's neck was smashed and it had mucous, or something, coming out of its mouth. It was lifeless, but I don't think it was dead yet. Tim just stood there and watched me pick up the puppy. He didn't look happy and he didn't look sad, he didn't look like anything in particular. It was like he wasn't really there. I got my mother to come and look at it. After the puppy finished dying, she threw it in the trash and beat Tim.

Throughout the coming years I would know that Tim was definitely the most effected of the boys. Or at least the most dangerously effected. He eventually developed a fire fetish which caused him to get beat often. The beatings are probably what caused him to be a firebug, and he was beaten for being a firebug. It was another no win situation for another one of us byproducts of the baby factory. I remember one day, when he was about seven or eight years old, Alcee caught him playing with matches. It was awful. She kept screaming, "Ya little sick son-of-a-bitch. So ya like to play with matches, huh? I'll beat you ta death!" She kept hitting him with a belt anywhere she could hit him. He just stood there and didn't even run, he put his arms up to protect himself then put them back down. Alcee knocked him down to the floor and he just laid there. I thought she really was going to beat him to death. I kept trying to get her off of him. I grabbed her arm and yelled, "Stop it! You're killin' him." She said, "Somebody ought ta kill the little stupid mother fucker." It wasn't five minutes later when she caught him lying under a bed striking matches again. She said, "I'm gonna beat ya ta death this time so say good bye ta yer big sissy, ya dumb little fucker!" This time Tim got up and walked outside with her right behind him swinging a belt. He didn't cry, scream, beg or talk at all. She kept hitting him and he looked so blank and pale. He looked like he was already gone, like he was just about to lay down and fade away or turn to dust. I was sure she was going to kill him this time. I was so scared. I grabbed her arm and kept screaming at her, "Stop it! You're killin' him! They will put you in jail! The neighbors are lookin'. Give me the belt! Give me the goddamn belt!" That got her attention, but I forgot to factor in her insanity and rage. She turned on me and said, "Oh, ya want the belt? Here it is!" Then she started hitting me. She said, "How 'bout if I just beat both o' you little bastards ta death and I'll have two less mouths ta feed?" I kept screaming at Tim to run and he did. As soon as I got away I went after him. When I tried to touch him he said, "Get away from me." When he got like that it was better if you just left him alone. He didn't want to be touched or babied. He really wanted to be left alone. Sometimes he scared me, but I tried to never let it show in front of him.

Dena cried a lot at night, and it was a quiet, whimpery cry. It seemed like after all the chaos calmed down for the day she could weep. I remember one time when she was just about a year old, or maybe as old as eighteen months, Gordon got mad because she wouldn't sit still and he made her sit by his feet on the floor. She kept trying to crawl away and he kept sticking his hand down beside his chair and smacking her on the side of her head. Every time he smacked her, her little head jerked back against his chair. She kept crying, she was only a baby. She screamed and cried and kept trying to crawl away, but he just kept hitting her every time she made a move. He yelled, "Sit there!" When he first put her on the floor in front of his chair her cry sounded like an angry cry, but after he started yelling at her and hitting her, I heard fear in her cry. She wasn't just crying because she had to sit there, she was scared. Most of the time she was with me and I was the one who took care of her. She wasn't used to being treated that way, *yet*. I acted like I was doing Gordon a favor and said, "I can take care of her. I can make her stop cryin'. You want me to take her?" He got mad and yelled, "I told 'er ta sit right there and she's gonna sit right there. She's gettin' old enough ta know who the fuckin' boss is around here." His hand looked like a big bear claw hooking around her little face and jerking her back every time she tried to crawl away. My mother was there, but she didn't make him stop. Eventually Dena cried herself to sleep. She looked so pitiful sitting on the floor with her little head bent sideways and back against his chair. She kept sniffling and her entire little body shook with each one. She was such a beautiful baby. I remember thinking, "Now can I put her to bed? Come on Dena, God, please don't let her wake up." I don't know how long it took Dena to learn how to 'leave,' but I'm sure she did because of her ability to trance out. I think Tim went the farthest when he zoned out, or left, I don't know where he went or how far, but it was far, far away. I think Dena zoned out more often, but didn't go as far as Tim went.

I don't know if Dana ever zoned out, or left, because she was to Alcee and Gordon, what the winged monkeys were to the wicked witch in the Wizard of Oz. She was constantly making up lies and laughing when we got into trouble. She did things and denied them so that we all got punished. One time she carved her initials in the kitchen table and then denied it. Alcee and Gordon had to know it was her. The other kids couldn't write yet, and Dana made her D's backwards. She and I were the only two who were big enough to do something like that, and God knows I sure didn't have enough time to do something like that. Gordon started out making us all stand in corners. Dana kept laughing, and Alcee and Gordon kept laughing with her. There were more of us kids than there were corners, so Gordon put Dana in the other room, and he put the rest of us in corners in the front room where he could watch us. He told me to hold the baby in my corner with me. He said, "I ought ta beat yer ass anyway, either way it's yer fault. If you did it I ought ta beat yer ass, and if one o' the others did it I ought ta beat yer ass for not watchin' 'em, like yer supposed to. If you'd been doin' yer job, the table wouldn't o' got marked up. I'll tell ya what, you hold the baby in the corner with you, and if **he** cries I'm gonna beat **yer** ass." Well the baby did cry, and kept crying, and Gordon did beat my ass and kept "beating my ass." He kept making me walk over to his chair and bend over his lap, then when he was done I went back to the corner with the baby. The baby cried again, and I had to go over to his chair again, and when he was done "beating my ass" again, I would go back to the corner with the baby. This went on all afternoon, and every time he "beat my ass" I could hear Dana in the other room laughing. Every time she laughed Alcee and Gordon laughed and whispered about how funny it was that Dana was so mean. Eventually the baby cried himself to sleep and all I had to do was hold him. It didn't really matter, after a while my butt numbed itself and when Gordon beat on it it felt more like a bruise than a sting. I was over it, I had left the building, I dissociated, toward the end of the ordeal I didn't even cry, I left. Days later I asked my mother why she let that go on all afternoon, when they both had to know it was Dana who marked up the table. She said they knew Dana lied, but it was important for her to think they believed her because she was special. It wasn't easy to not hate Dana.

Tom didn't trance out and it was hard to tell if something was bothering him. From the time he was born he was an easy going, pleasant little boy. Only occasionally would his temper erupt, but when it did it was to be reckoned with. He was a loner and kept to himself most of the time. He got made fun of a lot because he had thick glasses and was hyperactive. He was the subject of foul comments during some of Alcee and Gordon's fights, because he is the one that Gordon said didn't belong to him. He is also the one that Alcee was pregnant with when she took Quinine to abort, supposedly. I sometimes wonder if that's why his vision was so bad or if that's why he was hyperactive. He was always moving around, jingling something or pacing back and forth. When the other kids made fun of him he usually just smiled, like he could take a joke, and walked away. I don't know if he left or not. He was definitely verbal when he was scared, at least when he was still a baby.

One night, actually it was in the middle of the night, all of us kids were asleep in the back bedroom. We shared one bed. The youngest baby slept in the baby bed, I slept at one end of the regular bed with the two oldest babies, at the time that was Tim and Tom, Dana and Dena slept at the other end. I don't know what time it was, but it had to be after the bars closed, when someone started beating on the window and yelling and cussing. It was Gordon, but with him being so loud, and me being half asleep, I didn't recognize his voice. I was so scared and the other kids were too. I remember we were all screaming but Tom's scream was blood curdling. I thought something, or someone, already had him. While all this was happening, Gordon was screaming "Open the door ya bitch." Alcee was answering, "Go sleep with one o' your whores, ya cock sucker." I finally realized it was Gordon, but I wasn't any less scared. I was trying to bunch all the little ones up together so we could huddle in the middle of the bed, when suddenly the glass shattered all over us. He busted the window! He knew we slept there and he busted the window anyway. There was glass all over the bed. Our bed sat in front of that window and he knew the bottom of the window was level with the edge of our bed. I was so scared, the little ones were crying and screaming, there was glass all over our bed, and I had to be careful how all of us moved so we wouldn't get cut. Then as if things weren't bad enough, Gordon lunged through the broken window in a rage, screaming, "I'm gonna kill ya this time, ya fuckin' whore." He was screaming and crawling over us kids in the bed while it was still covered with broken glass. I didn't know what to do. It was dark, no one had turned on a light, I had found Tom and picked him up, but he was still screaming, Dena and Tim were trancing out, Dana was crying but not hard, it was a mess. I couldn't have been more than eight years old when this happened. The fist fight was on with Alcee and Gordon. They were knocking each other all over the kitchen as they screamed and cussed at each other. I couldn't get the kids out of the bed of glass *and* run up the alley for help. I just wanted to scream. I wanted it all to stop! Somehow I got all the kids out of the bed, rolled the blanket up to hold most of the glass, put the kids on the other side of the room and told them to stay there. I handed Tom off to Dana and took off up the alley screaming, "Help! Somebody call the police!"

Just like clockwork the plan went as usual. Gordon caught me and dragged me back into the house. While he was dragging me down the alley, I saw my mother running the other way toward the neighbors. Gordon was really pissed this time. He made me put all the kids on the bed in the front bedroom and get up there with them. Then he got his shotgun and sat in a chair next to the bed with the shot gun laying across his lap. He was drunk and yelling, "Let the fuckin' police come! There ain't nobody takin' my goddamned kids out o' here." I was crying and shaking and begging, "I want to go with Mommy, I want Mommy." He finally told me I could take Dana and go find my "whoreing mommy." I took Dana and ran to the neighbors. Eventually the police came and talked him out of our house and gave him a ride to his parent's house. The rest of us took a taxi to my grandmother's house to hide out. I did feel safer at my grandmother's because my uncles were mean enough to keep Gordon at bay if he came around. I remember thinking, "At least I can sleep now. Nobody will get past my uncles." Some nights were worse than others.

I don't think Tony ever left either. He was the youngest boy and next to the youngest child. He was very intelligent and, in later years, his school grades reflected how smart he was. He was the smallest of the boys, and the funniest. He had a sweet disposition, and he was a master manipulator. He got teased a lot for being thin skinned, because he got his feelings hurt easily, and you could see the hurt in his eyes when that happened. He was the most playful of the boys, but as sweet as he was, it didn't matter, his life was going to be hell just like the rest of the baby factory babies. Tony always used his verbal skills to try and diffuse situations between the other kids, it seldom worked, but he tried. If two of the other kids were arguing he would try to pick a fight with one of them so they would chase *him* in hopes of breaking up the original argument. I think because he was so smart, that he took everything in and tried to make sense of it. He let me baby him longer than any of the other kids. He would be the one to 'self medicate' more than any of us. Maybe he had to do that because he *didn't* learn how to dissociate, I don't know.

I don't think Denise ever left or dissociated either. Sometimes I wonder if the younger ones didn't leave because they had us older kids to comfort them. They still got beat on, cussed, ridiculed and humiliated, but it seems like the younger ones leaned more toward escaping through drugs and alcohol as soon as they were old enough to get their hands on some. As far as self medication, she would grow up to be second only to Tony. I really don't know how many of us 'left' or didn't leave. I know I did and that's how I survived. I think some of the others did and some of them didn't. But I don't really *know* who did or who didn't.

I know that out of the seven of us, some beat their kids, some are drunk more often than they are sober, at least one is on permanent disability due to alcoholism, six out of seven have criminal records and at least one has served time in jail on drug related charges, some (mostly the boys) still try to be close to our mother, some still try to be close to Gordon. I don't know for sure who ended up where or how they got there, if they ever want to tell, they will tell. But what ever any of us did, I know why we did it and why we are the way we are. We are all split up now, most of us never see each other, we never talk to each other, and above all, we don't tell what went on in our house while we were growing up. Well, six of us might not tell, but one of us is going to.

CHAPTER FOUR

My First Paying Job

My first year of school was first grade. As much as I wanted to go to school, first grade wasn't that much fun. My teacher was not at all warm and fuzzy, in fact, she was far from it. Maybe she had been teaching too long and was burnt out, or maybe she just didn't like kids. She wasn't very nice to any of the kids in class, but she especially didn't like me or my cousin. She was the kind of teacher who was into using humiliation for discipline. For instance, one day while she was reading to the class she caught my cousin and me whispering. She made us both go up to the front of the class and sit on her lap because we were "acting like little babies and not paying attention." My cousin sat on one of the teacher's knees, and I sat on the other while the class laughed at us. It was pretty humiliating, but at least we were in it together so we didn't cry. I hate it that I didn't get a nice first grade teacher. I think she didn't like us because I was one of the "kids that lived in the alley" and my cousin was one of the kids "from across the railroad yard." Anyway, first grade wasn't much fun, but I did have some nice teachers throughout my school years.

Back then you could only ride the bus if you lived more than a mile from the school. We lived *about* a mile from the school but not *over* a mile, so I walked to and from school. Actually, I usually *ran* because I had to get home quickly so my mother could get to work on time. Whenever she was "showing' and couldn't work I could walk home. But when she wasn't showing, I had to run home real fast after school, so she could jump into a waiting taxi and head to work. I knew all the short cuts between the school and home and I could run like the wind. Usually, when I turned the corner of the alley, the taxi was in front of the house and my mother was standing by the door with her coat and purse ready to take off. I went in the door as she went out and it was time for my shift with the kids. I would feed them, play with them, give them a bath, put them to bed and do whatever other chores I had to do. Gordon was rarely there in the evenings while my mother was at work, and I considered that a blessing.

The summer between first and second grade my mother was showing with another pregnancy, so she couldn't work. She would be at home all day and all night with us kids, while Gordon was out drinking and doing whatever it was he did most nights. One thing that bothers me is that we shouldn't have had to live like we did. Gordon made a lot of money, but he drank and gambled it away. Sometimes on payday he went out drinking and gambling from work before he even came home, and by the time he did get home he was broke. He would lose his whole pay check some weeks before he even made it home. There were a lot of fights over that, but then there were a lot of fights over everything.

That summer I actually got a paying job at a restaurant at the end of the alley and across the street, which was only open from late morning to early afternoon. They catered to the workers from the nearby factory for the lunch crowd. There were only a couple of restaurants close enough for the factory workers to go to for lunch, this one was right next to the factory, so it was practical for them to be open for the lunch crowd. I didn't ask for the job. The old man who ran the place, Raymond, stopped by my house one day and told my mother he could use me to help out during the lunch rush. He said I would just be cleaning off tables, putting the empty pop bottles in the back, keeping the pop cooler full, just light weight stuff to help out, and he would pay me fifty cents per day. He lived in our neighborhood so he wasn't really a stranger. Our house actually sat at the intersection of two alleys. One alley ran the same direction as the two streets at each end of the other alley. The front of Raymond's house was on one of the streets and his back yard ran out to one of the alleys, the one that ran along side of my house. The other alley ran in front of my house.

My mother did ask me if I *wanted* to work up there and help her out. I didn't realize it then, but I do now, she really manipulated me. She said, "Well, ya are old enough ta help out and I can use the money. You'd be helpin' Mommy buy groceries. It's just a few hours a day, if ya wanna work up there and help me out, I guess ya can." I was so excited, I had my first job and I felt like my mom was proud of me. She said 'I would be helpin' her' and she had never said I helped before. I started to work the next morning at ten o'clock and I got off at two or three in the afternoon, depending on how long it took us to clean up after the lunch rush. There were only three people working there, the old man, Raymond, an old lady named Flo and me. Sometimes the owner stopped by, but she would only be there for a few minutes and leave. I thought I was a working woman, so big like Mommy, working in a restaurant.

The first week was fun, sometimes Raymond got a little grumpy with me, but I didn't mind, I was used to a lot worse. The factory workers gave me a lot of attention and teased Raymond about his 'new help.' A lot of people smiled at me every day and called me names like honey and sweetie and cutie. *ME*, they called *me* those nice names. Then after work every day Raymond gave me fifty cents and boxed up a bunch of left over food from that day's menu to give to my mother. It was always enough to feed all of us that night and still have some left. Raymond loaded the boxes in the back of his car and drove me and the food down the alley to my house. I felt like I was helping a lot by working up at the restaurant. Not only did my mother not have to cook every night, but she didn't have to spend the fifty cents on groceries! I felt so good every day when I gave her the fifty cents. I didn't have any realization of how much fifty cents was, I was only seven, but it seemed like a lot because my mother was always glad to get it. And really, back then fifty cents went a long way.

One afternoon during the second week, Raymond told me, after Flo left, that he was going to have to fire me. He said he didn't want to let me go but the owner told him I was a boy and she didn't want a little boy working there. He said she thought I was boy because my hair was so short. I said, "But my mommy needs the money." Raymond said he could get the owner to let me keep working there if I proved to him that I was a girl. Flo was gone, the lights were off and he locked the doors. He walked toward me and I backed away, I was so scared. I didn't know what to be scared of yet, but I knew I felt scared. He talked really nice to me and said to come to him so he could prove to the owner I was a girl. That's how it started out. For a few days he kept saying the owner still didn't believe I was a girl and he had to get more proof so I wouldn't lose my job. It was always after Flo left and the lights were off. It was daylight, so I could see, but people weren't able to see in. It looked like nobody was there.

I didn't know what to do. If I told my mother I would lose my job, and I knew somehow it would be all my fault. Things got progressively worse and worse. Raymond did things to me and he made do things to him. I don't remember how long it went on, I know it went on for weeks, but I don't remember how many. I was so scared. After the first couple of days Raymond started threatening me. I started saying, "I don't want to" and Raymond said, "By God, you're goin' to or I'm gonna tell your mommy what you been doin' and she'll whip your little ass." He said, "Now you come here or I'm not gonna take the leftovers to your mommy. What's your mommy gonna say when I tell her?" Every day I was more scared than the day before, I didn't know what to do, I was seven. Everyday Raymond threatened to tell my mother what I had been doing and was still doing, or threatened to fire me because the owner thought I was a boy, or both.

After a long time, I don't know how many weeks, I started trying to get out of going to work. I would say I was sick, I had a belly ache, my foot hurt, anything to get out of going to the restaurant. It only worked one day, after that my mother said I was lazy and I just didn't want to help her. The one day it worked, Raymond still showed up with left overs from the lunch rush. I remember being so scared, he looked at me so mean. He said really hatefully, "If you ain't comin' back to work, I'll have to find another little girl that wants the job." I was so scared that he was going to tell my mother what I had been doing. Alcee said, "She'll be there tomorrow. I think she was just playin' sick today. There ain't nothin' wrong with her but meanness and laziness."

I started to cry every morning before I went to work. And every morning Alcee yelled and screamed at me for being lazy and worthless. She said, "I worked three fuckin' jobs after I had you so I could keep ya, and you don't wanna help me out at all. Yer a filthy, lazy, little no good bastard." She would go on and on and on. She said, "How much do I ask you for? Ya said ya wanted ta help me, ya lyin' little despisable son-of-a-bitch! What am I supposed ta feed these kids today? You ain't too good ta help me and yer goin' ta work! If ya didn't want that job ya should have said so before ya took it!" It just kept getting worse and every morning I cried and begged, "Mommy, I don't want to go up there. I'll get another job. Please don't make me go up there. Raymond's mean and he yells at me." She just said, "You think everybody's mean to ya! You don't know what mean is. Turn off the water works and get yer ass up there, ya little snot nosed bitch."

People, the customers and Flo, must have noticed a change in my behavior because I remember them trying to get me to smile. The customers said things like, 'where is that pretty smile you used to have' and 'what's the matter sweetie?' Raymond always piped in about how I had been bad and my mommy had to spank my little butt. He had an excuse every day about me being different so I didn't even try to come up with one, I just kept quiet. I was embarrassed that these people, who used to like me, would now think I was bad. Looking back, I think Flo was figuring something out. She wasn't really nice to me but she wasn't mean either. I think I might have been in her way more than really helping her, and maybe I got on her nerves. She started taking her time cleaning up after we closed every day, it was like she stalled until Raymond and

I got all of our work done. I didn't realize that's what she was doing, and I don't know for sure if that *is* what she was doing. I know that she and Raymond started snipping at each other when she was there late. He told her he would finish up but she would insist on staying and doing it herself. Maybe she had figured out what was going on and was trying to save me, or maybe she just needed the hours. At the time I didn't know it, but looking back now, I think she knew and was saving me. One day Raymond was yelling at her to get her work done and get out. She just kept lolly gagging around, finding things to do. Finally, he started loading up the boxed leftovers in his car like we were leaving. We all three went out the back door, Flo got into her car, I got into Raymond's car and right when Raymond was opening the driver's car door he said, "Damn, I forgot something" and he went back in. I was still in his car and Flo left. After she pulled out, Raymond opened the back door and motioned for me to come back in. When I went in, he was mad and asked me if Flo had been questioning me about him having to find out if I was a boy or girl. I told him no, and she hadn't been. He said, "If she does you better tell her how nice I am to you. I've been good to you! If you don't, I'll tell your mommy what we like to do to each other. She'll whip your little ass. Now come here. You're my girl. Oh yeah, you're a girl and I'm a boy. By God, I'm gonna tell the owner that you are too a girl and I'm not gonna fire you!" He smelled so bad and he was so disgusting and scarey. His hands were hard and bent up from arthritis, and he was so awful. I can't even think of words to describe how awful and disgusting he was.

The next day Flo asked me if we left when she did the day before. I was so scared. Raymond was looking right at us, but he couldn't hear us. He was out front and we were in the kitchen. I was so afraid, I can't even describe how scared I was. She asked me again, "Did you and Raymond leave when I did yesterday?" I said, really quiet and low, "No, Raymond forgot some of the leftovers and we had to come back in and get them. My mommy needed them to feed the kids. Raymond is nice to me." I remember my voice quivering and how I almost started crying, I thought I was going to pee my pants. It was from fear and shame. Thoughts just started racing through my head. What if Flo found out what I had been doing? She would know how awful I was. What if she told my mother? I remember thinking, "Oh my God, what am I gonna do?" I wondered if Raymond told her, I wondered if she knew how awful I was, I didn't know why she was asking me questions. Raymond didn't tell her because he told me not to tell her, so why would he tell her? He wouldn't, oh my God, what if she had been watching us? Did she see us? Now what am I going to do? She must have seen us. I thought, she knows what I have been doing and she's probably going to tell my mother! Then she will tell Gordon! I thought I was in so much trouble that I would be killed for this. I knew what had been going on all summer was wrong, but I didn't know what to do about it. After the lunch rush was over Raymond and Flo got into an argument, because Flo said she would take me and the leftovers home. Raymond said no, he would. They got loud and I got scared because they were fighting. I didn't know if Flo knew about us, and I was afraid Raymond would think I had told her if she did. It ended up with me and the leftovers in Flo's car. She pulled down the alley and my mother came out and got the boxes of food. I didn't leave Flo's side while they were unloading the boxes because if she had told the secret I was going to deny it. My mother asked her why she brought me home instead of Raymond, and she told her that he was still busy at the restaurant. After Flo left, Raymond pulled down the alley and asked my mother if everything was okay. He just kept glaring at me. I was just sure he was going to tell, but he didn't.

I couldn't take it anymore. The next morning I was hysterical at the thought of going back up to that restaurant. I cried and begged, and carried on and on and on about not wanting to go up there. I promised my mother that I would go out pop bottle hunting every day until I found fifty cents worth of bottles. I told her that I could find them and cash them in at the store in less than the hours that I spent at the restaurant. I promised I would find even *more* than fifty cents worth so she would have even more money. I told her I would be home earlier to help her with the kids. She said, “Don’t gimme that shit! Ya don’t care anything about these kids or you’d help me! Ya got yer ass fired didn’t ya? Ya probably don’t even have a job ta go to, do ya? I ain’t never been fired from a job! I hope nobody finds out one of my kids got fired from a goddamned job. I couldn’t look ‘em in the eye.” I told her I could make more money finding pop bottles. She asked me, “What about all the leftovers I’d be out if ya quit?” I told her she wouldn’t need them because I was going to make more money for her, I would find lots and lots of pop bottles and cash them in every day. Finally, she said I could do that instead of the restaurant job. She said she was ashamed of me because I said I wanted that job and then quit. I didn’t care. I just wanted out of there. I mean, after all, I had been called a lot worse things than a quitter and she was ashamed me of me anyway.

I kept my promise and went pop bottle hunting every day, even if it rained. I went up and down all the alleys in the neighborhood, up and down the railroad tracks and over by the railroad yard where my cousin lived. I went anywhere that someone might have thrown down a pop bottle. At the time they were only worth two or three cents each, but I found more than fifty cents worth every day. I found as many as I could carry and took them to the store to cash them in. Then I went back out and found some more to cash in. I wondered why people threw them down instead of cashing them in at the store like me. I guess two or three cents didn’t mean that much to some people, but it meant a lot of money for me. After I got *more* than fifty cents and was done hunting pop bottles for the day, my mother sent me to the store to get something for supper with the money *I* made. She could be ashamed of me if she wanted, but I still thought I was doing a good job. My new job was better for her, too, whether she admitted it or not, because I could take one or two of the kids with me and she didn’t have to watch them. I didn’t take them all the time, but sometimes I did. Whenever I went out hunting I always tried to walk past my cousin’s house so we could say hi to each other.

For years, as long as we lived in the alley, I was scared of Raymond and also scared that he would tell. Sometimes when she sent me to the store, my mother said, "Run up the alley, it's quicker." That meant I had to walk past his back yard. Whenever he saw me running through the alley he stomped his feet and yelled like he was chasing me. I screamed and ran as fast as I could. A few times I tried to sneak past his house by running really quiet, I would try to go fast without letting my feet hit the ground hard, my feet had to hit the ground real softly. I really thought I could run so fast that my feet didn't hit the ground. I thought it worked sometimes because he didn't yell and stomp his feet. Other times he would jump out from nowhere and yell and stomp and scare the life out of me. When he did that I thought he was going to catch me because he was closer to the alley when he jumped out of nowhere. It was like he knew I was coming and he hid and waited for me to go by. Now, looking back, I realize that the times I thought 'running quietly' worked were probably times that he wasn't even there. Sometimes when Alcee told me to 'run through the alley' I asked her if I could go up to the street and take the sidewalk if I ran extra fast. She said, "What - did - I - tell - you - ta - do? Did I tell you to take the sidewalk? No! Did I tell you ta take the alley? Yes! Do *what* I tell you ta do, the *way* I tell you ta do it and *when* I tell you ta do it, ya little fitified mother fucker!" I told her I was afraid of Raymond because he yelled at me and was mean to me. She said I thought everybody was mean to me but I didn't know what mean was.

All those years I was so scared of him and that he might tell on me. I think the hardest part for me to take from all this, was what happened when I was around fourteen years old. I was walking into a super market with my grandmother and Raymond was walking out. As we passed him he said, "Hi Frankie, how ya' doin'?" She said, "Fine, how 'bout you, Raymond?" She knew him? I couldn't believe Grandma knew him. I asked her, "Grandma, do you know him?" I couldn't believe what she told me. She said, "Oh yeah, everybody in town knows *him*. He's a child molester. He's been arrested for it I don't know how many times. In fact, it worried me to death the summer yer mother let you go up to that restaurant and work for him. I told her, I begged her, I said, 'Alcee, don't let that youngin' go up there with that son-of-a-bitch, ya know what he is.' He never bothered you did he, Trennie?" I thought I was going to pass out. The store seemed like it was spinning. I felt like I was in the corner of the ceiling watching myself. I couldn't walk, talk, hear or even move. I could see myself totally frozen, mute and everything was spinning, not fast, but turning and distorting. I don't know how many seconds or minutes or what amount of time passed, but my grandmother had a hold of my arm shaking me. I could see the whole thing from above, from the ceiling. I saw her grab me. I know that is physically impossible, but that is what it was like. She said, "Trennie, what the hell's the matter with you? Are you crazy? Speak to me, what's wrong with you? I asked you if that old cock sucker touched you, did he? *DID HE TOUCH YOU?"* She had raised her voice and people were looking at us. I said, "No he didn't touch me. I haven't eaten today and I think I almost fainted. I just don't feel good. I feel weak or something." She said, "Well, goddamn it when I'm talkin' ta you I want an answer! Speak ass, mouth won't! Don't you ever ignore me again!" My grandmother was in a panic. I wonder if she really cared and was worried out of love that Raymond had gotten to me, or if she was just angry that he might have touched some of her property. She was so loud, not screaming but loud, and demanded an answer so quickly, I sometimes wonder if she would have chased him down in the parking lot to take up for me. If I had told her and she didn't confront him, I think it would have killed me. I think I would have shriveled up and blown away like dust.

It wasn't just pain I felt when I found out my mother knew all along. I felt stupid, used, worthless, dirty and I don't even know how many other feelings I had, but I certainly felt betrayed. I was working to *help her* and she knew what he was doing to me, and when I cried and begged her not to make me go back she called me lazy.

I think, out of everything that has happened in my life, that has to be one of the most, if not *the* most, hurtful moment in my life. All those years I had been terrified that my mother would find out about Raymond and me, and she knew all along. She *had* to know when I cried and begged her not to make me go up there, when days earlier I had been so proud of my job. My grandmother had told her not to let me go up there because they all knew about him. My God! She knew! My mother was pimping me out at the age of seven. I had been a seven year old prostitute *for fifty cents a day!* How could she do that to me? If a heart can really break, mine did. My heart has been broken many times throughout my life, but that is by far one of the most painful ones. If I live to be one hundred years old I will never forget that sick, hurtful feeling I had that day. I've heard people talk about child abuse and molestation cases that were printed in the newspaper or that they have heard on the news. I have actually heard some people say, "Well, the kids were pretty young. They might not even remember it when they grow up." I just want to scream at them, "Bet they do!"

Not long ago, I went back to the alley. The old shack we lived in has been torn down, but the alley and Raymond's house are still there. So is the building the restaurant was in, there is a church office in it now. Isn't it ironic? They have no idea what sins were committed under that very roof. I can't help but to believe that Alcee had to hear me scream when he scared me the way he did. When I was little the alley seemed so big and it never occurred to me that she would have heard me scream, but looking at it as an adult, I see that the alley was not that big and his house was not that far away. I think she *had* to hear me, but I don't *know* that she did. Thinking about what my grandmother told me, the way I cried and begged not to go up there, the obvious change in my behavior and the fact that I was so little she *had* to have seen signs from my clothes when she did laundry, *I know* she knew. I would say that my heart is still broken over everything that happened, but it breaks a brand new break every time I think about that summer. It's like my heart is *still* broken over it, and even though I think it can't feel any worse, it breaks again and again, every time I think about *My First Paying Job.*

CHAPTER FIVE

Grandma Fagan

My grandmother, as I said earlier, confused me. One minute she was crazy about me because I was her first grandchild, the next minute she would say I'd end up no good just like my "goddamned no good mommy and daddy." She was full of left handed compliments, for instance, one time she told me I wasn't *really* ugly I was just homely. She said there was a difference and, when I was 'well groomed' I wasn't *"that bad."* She said, "somebody will probably have you someday." As confusing as she was I did love her, and I think maybe I still do. She was a wealth of information, although I will never know how much of it was true and how much was not. She threatened to hit me a few times but she never did. She shook me a few times and let my uncles hit me sometimes, but she didn't. Grandma was kind of like Fagan in Oliver Twist, and Fagan wasn't *all* bad. At times she was protective of me, but there was always a price to pay and she was *always* on the best end of the deal.

She lived at the intersection of two alleys, too. Both of the alleys where she lived had gravel. She had a mean bulldog named Brute that she kept tied up by the water meter in back of the house. She kept him tied there so when the water company came out to shut off the water, and they frequently did, the man couldn't get to the meter. She acted like she wasn't home and that would buy some time. After the man left she sent my uncles to the gas station to fill up big trash cans with water. It took two of them to carry it, one on each side. By the time the water company sent someone back out to shut off the water we had some stored in the trash cans. I remember one time the utility man came to the door and asked her to move her dog. She told him to "go to hell." He called the police and they told her to move her dog or they would shoot him. Grandma liked to dance, drink and party loud and often. She did cook almost every day and made sure all the kids had plenty to eat. I always liked staying at her house more than I liked staying at home.

Grandma's brother, the same great uncle who told me they tried to 'smother me at birth,' babysat us kids a few times when Grandma went out. He was basically a hobo and frequently traveled with carnivals when he needed money. He was in and out of jail a lot, usually for alcohol or battery related charges. Whenever he came through town he stayed at my grandmother's house until he hooked up with another carnival or went back to jail. Before she left Grandma would always tell us kids to be good, and she always told him to be nice to us kids. Well, he wasn't very nice. He didn't have any kids of his own and he didn't really like any of us. One night after Grandma left he was supposed to cook and feed us our supper. He was drinking and being his old hateful self. He was fixing hamburgers for us and he was angry because he didn't want to cook. He kept yelling at me and my aunt, who is about my age, until he made us both cry. Then he made fun of us for crying. While he was frying the burgers he said, "You little bastards want hamburgers, huh? How 'bout if I fix ya ham-boogers?" He stuck his finger in his nose and wiped his finger on our hamburgers. He yelled and screamed at us and made us eat the sandwiches. He was drinking the whole time. My aunt and I were crying and choking down the sandwiches, we were around six or seven years old. I knew when my grandma heard about this she would run him off, but she wasn't there right then.

That was the same night he told me that my mother and grandmother tried to smother me when they brought me home from the hospital. He said they tried to give me away but I was so ugly that nobody wanted me. He said, "What the fuck are you cryin' about, ya ugly smashed road kill little bastard? Come here baby, I didn't mean ta hurt yer feelings. Come 'ere baby." He said it really nice. When I got over to him he said, "I didn't mean ta make ya cry. It ain't yer fault, you cain't help bein' ugly!" And he laughed at me. When I started crying again he said, "I'm just kiddin' you! Get the fuck out o' my sight, ya little fittified idiot or I'll feed ya ta the fuckin' dog! If the dog'll have ya. Yer ugly enough ta scare the goddamned rats away! Boo hoo, boo hoo! I'll rattle yer friggin' skull!" I was right. When we told Grandma the next day she ran him off. She said, "You ain't mistreatin' these kids! I don't care if ya are my brother. Get your fuckin' ass out o' my house!"

Grandma beat on some of her own kids, some of my uncles, but she never hit *me.* From what I heard and witnessed throughout the years, she never beat any of her daughters and was selective about which of her sons she beat on. I remember one night when I was little, maybe four or five years old, one of my uncles was going to a school dance, maybe the prom, with his girlfriend. He had a job to make his own money but he gave Grandma most of it. He was getting dressed in a white sport coat and a pink carnation. There was a song popular at the time about a white sport coat and a pink carnation so I guess that was the current fad. My uncle kept trying to get dressed while my grandmother followed him around the house yelling, "You ain't goin' to that fuckin' dance with that little whore you been a runnin' with." He kept saying, "Yes I am." He was whistling, and singing the song about the white sport coat while he was getting dressed. I think grandma was mad because he had been "knocking down." That's when you lie about how much money you made and "dark hole" some of it for yourself. My uncle didn't have a car so his girlfriend was picking him up, I don't know if she was driving or if someone drove her over to our house. After his girlfriend got there she came up on the porch to wait for him. My grandma started yelling about her being a little whore and she grabbed the dish pan, which was full of dirty dishwater, from the sink and threw it on my uncle. He went outside to talk to his girlfriend. When he came back in he was crying. He was one of them that was nice to me and I was sad that he was crying. He picked me up and carried me upstairs where he put on some dry clothes, then he carried me back downstairs and left. I cried because he did. I wasn't very old but I remember feeling so sad for him. I don't know if they made it to the dance that night, but he eventually married that girl.

I remember another time when she beat up one of my other uncles. She called him 'a queer' because he had been running around town with a guy that was homosexual. He had his own job, too. He had also been knocking down and dark holing money for himself and Grandma caught him. She said "You ain't leavin' here so you can run all over town with that queer!" My uncle said not only was he going to leave, but he wasn't coming back. My grandmother hit him on his arm with a hammer as she screamed, "That's right! If you leave here, ya ain't comin' back! See how much that queer likes ya when ya got no place to go!" I heard my other uncles talking later, they said Grandma broke his arm when she hit him with the hammer. His friend took care of him and he never came back there to live.

I only remember one other uncle getting beat on. Grandma made him stand on a kitchen chair with his pants down and beat him with a belt. Sometimes he jumped off the chair and tried to run away, but my other uncles, the ones who were never beaten, held him down across the chair while my grandmother finished beating him. I always cried when any of my uncles got beaten. It was really scarey to watch, maybe that's why I cried, and I was pretty little when all that took place.

I don't know what made Grandma tick like she did. Maybe she loved me and maybe she didn't, I don't know. Maybe she was the least of the evils that surrounded me. I just know that whenever I was forbidden from seeing her, and I frequently was, I missed her. I missed the information I was able to get from her and I missed the left handed compliments. I was too little to know they were not *really* compliments, so I thought she was being nice to me, and I missed her.

I was in second grade when I found out Gordon was not my *real* dad. Alcee denied it and said Gordon was my real dad. After hounding Grandma for the truth she finally confirmed it for me. Some kids on the playground told me. One day at recess two kids, who were brother and sister and only one grade apart, made fun of me on the playground and said, "My mommy said your daddy isn't really your daddy. Your real daddy is in jail. Your mommy had you before she was married." I don't know why they were mad at me, maybe I didn't give them my swing or something, but they must have been mad at me about something. I told my mother what they said and she said they were lying. They said it several times when we were outside at recess or on our way home. One day my teacher heard them and made them stop. She talked to them both, I don't know what she said to them, but it stopped. By the way, I had a wonderful second grade teacher, as well as wonderful third and fourth grade teachers. Nice teachers do make a difference.

Whenever I was alone with my grandmother I asked her why those kids said those things to me. At first she kept saying I would have to ask my mother, but I had already asked my mother and she said they were lying. I didn't believe her. I started going through dresser drawers and boxes of papers while my mother was at work and I found something. I found some newspaper clippings and a divorce paper, and it had Alcee's name in it. I couldn't read all of it, but I knew the words divorce, Alcee, children, Dana and Trena. I wasn't old enough to put it all together, but I did wonder why my mother, Dana and I were named in that paper. I asked my grandmother again and she explained it all. She said I could never tell my mother what she told me, and I didn't.

Grandma told me how, when I was born, it broke her heart that my real dad got my mother pregnant when she was barely fifteen, and how she insisted my mother keep me instead of adopting me out. Even as ugly as I was when I was born, she still wanted to keep me because I was her first grandchild. She told me about my real dad being in and out of prison, but she said he was a likable guy. She said I used to climb all over him whenever he came around, but that was before Alcee married "that hog headed, jack-o-lantern lookin' son-of-bitch she's married to now." I told her I remembered a guy with a pink shirt and narrow white belt with two buckles. I was so excited when she told me that was him, that was my real dad. She told me how he used to lean on the sink and let me hang on his belt and climb up his leg. She said he used to pick me up and say, "She's a cutie ain't she, Frankie?" Grandma said he was crazy about me! I wanted to find him and tell him what Gordon did to all of us. If he liked me as much as Grandma said he did he would take us away from Gordon! I remember being so excited to find out that he was out there somewhere and maybe he would come back. Grandma said he was Dana's daddy, too. So Gordon was *not* my real dad and I felt happy that he wasn't. There was no way I could get to my dad though because he was in prison again. Grandma said that's where he was most of the time. She said he just kept getting into trouble, but whenever he was in town he always came by to see her and ask about me and Dana. I asked her if she would tell me the next time he came by. She said she'd think about it.

I never told my mother what Grandma told me, but one of my uncles did, and it got really ugly when she found out that I knew. My uncle was running away from Grandma, his mother, because he was mad at her, so he told Alcee everything Grandma said so she would hide him out from her and the police. I could tell he enjoyed the ranting and raving about Grandma being so mean and rotten. Alcee and Gordon said I could "never see that old trouble makin' bitch again." Alcee said, "Yer goddamned daddy ain't no good. He's a jailbird! Why would you want to see the son-of-a-bitch anyway? He gave me two black eyes when I was pregnant with Dana! He's a no good son-of-a-bitch! He's been in trouble since he was eleven years old. They might as well have sent him straight from Boy's School to prison! He ain't never put a bite of food in yer mouth." She went on and on and on. "That old bitch lied if she told ya anything else!" She pointed to Gordon and said, "He's yer daddy! He's the one that puts food on this table that ya don't mind eatin'! He's the one that buys yer fuckin' glad rags! If I ever know o' you speakin' to that old bitch again, I'll kill you! If ya think the old bitch has any love for ya, you ought'a ask her why she tried to make me give ya away when you was born."

Grandma said my mother wanted to give me up for adoption when I was born, but she wouldn't let her. My mother said Grandma tried to make her give me away when I was born, but my step grandfather stepped in and forced my grandmother to let her keep me. To this day I don't know which one lied. Over the years I would hear many different tales about who wanted to keep me and who didn't. One of my great uncles, the one that made us eat 'ham-boogers,' told me that my grandmother and mother tried to smother me the day I came home from the hospital. He said he caught them and threatened to call the police if anything happened to me. I'll never know the truth. I do know that my birth records were stolen from the nurses' station after I was born. The only records of my birth are the ones that were locked up in the nursery, the ones that detail feedings, diaper changes and baths. I would find out, after my own child was born, that I didn't even have a birth certificate. The application for a birth certificate was never submitted to the state board of records and the delivering doctor didn't sign it until I was over two years old. It had a different spelling of my name and looked like it had been altered several times. I didn't know then, I don't know now, and I will never know what the real truth is.

Grandma was really angry about me not being allowed to see her or even speak to her if I accidentally ran in to her somewhere. She was also angry at my uncle for running away. Within a couple of days the police, with Grandma in tow, showed up at our front door. She told the police that her son had run away and she knew he was staying in this house, hiding from her. Back then the police picked up teenagers for being runaways. My mother stood in the front door telling the police she didn't know where my uncle was. I knew where he was, he was going out the back door and would come back later that night. I didn't tell though. I was standing by the door holding one of the babies on my hip. My grandmother told the policeman, "That one there's mistreated and somethin' ought ta be done. Look at her!" She held up her index finger and her middle finger and said "She ain't no wider than my two fingers! They work her like a goddamned slave and make her take care of all those other little bastards runnin' around here!" Alcee was yelling back, "The old bitch is just mad because she cain't run my house. She's a goddamned liar. If she's so fuckin' good why are her kids runnin' away? Did ya ask her that?" The policeman went back and forth saying, "Now Frankie, calm down" and "Now Alcee, that's no way to talk to your mother. Frankie's a good woman." My mother let the policeman come in and look for my uncle, but he was already gone so they didn't find him. This happened frequently over the years. Sometimes with the same uncle, sometimes a different one.

One night during warm weather a man came by the house. I knew he was my real dad, but I was afraid of him. I kept thinking about Grandma saying he was crazy about me, but I guess I didn't totally trust what she said because I still felt fearful. I was watching the kids and we were in the front room. I know it was warm weather because I had the big door open and the screen door locked. The man walked up to the screen and said, "Yer Trennie aren't ya?" I asked him what he wanted. He said, "I want to see Trennie and Dana." I don't know why I felt so scared because I had hoped and prayed my real dad would show up someday and take us away. But I did feel scared. I said, "I know who you are and you better go away." I slammed the big door and locked it, then made all the kids get behind the couch. I don't know why I chose the couch, but I always did whenever I felt like we were in danger. Even if it was just a thunderstorm I herded the kids behind the couch and we all sat on the floor. He went to the window and kept talking to me. He told me not to be scared, he said he wouldn't hurt me. He said he wouldn't come in, he just wanted to see me and Dana. I knew he had already caught a glimpse of both of us, while I was putting the kids behind the couch, because he identified Dana and he had already asked me if I was Trennie. I stood up behind the couch and let Dana stand up for just a second. He looked friendly and nice, he smiled and chuckled and talked softly. He kept trying to coax me into coming out from behind the couch, but no way, I wouldn't do it and he finally left. I remember wondering if Grandma knew he was there. How did he know where we lived? Maybe Grandma told him. If she did she would probably be mad at me for acting that way. I was afraid my real dad would tell her I chased him away. I wasn't allowed to see her so I couldn't tell her about it.

I look back now and wish I hadn't been so afraid that night, but I think I know why I was. For one thing Dana told everything and loved to see rest of us get into trouble. She made up lies to get us into trouble. I knew she was bound to get me in hot water over this, and she did. Another reason might be that I was so confused all the time, I never knew who was telling the truth and who was lying. Grandma said he was crazy about me, my mother said he was no good and beat her. I guess it really doesn't matter because, as it turned out, he was going back to prison soon anyway. The next day I was in trouble for standing up and letting Dana stand up so he could see us. Alcee yelled and screamed at me, kept slapping me in the face and telling me how stupid and spiteful I was. Gordon kept hitting me and shoving me while he said, "If ya want that son-of-a-bitch to be yer daddy maybe we'll just send ya to the pen with him. See how ya like that, ya little ungrateful bitch!" Alcee said, "You ain't gonna out do me for that old whore! What ever she told you was a fuckin' lie because the bitch don't know how to tell the truth." I don't think I was being spiteful. I think I was being hopeful.

I'm not sure how long it had been since I had seen my grandmother, but I know it had been a long time. At least months and maybe even a year or more. My cousin told me at school that Grandma had moved about six blocks from my house. She said Grandma told her I could sneak over there to see her when Alcee and Gordon wouldn't catch me. She said just me, the other kids might tell, so I had to sneak over by myself. I remember being so excited. I really missed her. I didn't know when or how yet, but I knew I would find a way to see Grandma. She was living just a few blocks from the railroad tracks where I still hunted for pop bottles. I felt happy that

I was going to see her again, as soon as I figured out how and when.

Whenever I went pop bottle hunting by myself, I sneaked over to Grandmas's for just a few minutes. I loved seeing her. She still screamed and cussed a lot, but she called me by my nickname and told me she missed me. I liked hearing that. She also bad mouthed Gordon a lot, and I liked hearing that too. She asked me a lot of questions about what went on at home, and I could tell her because she couldn't tell on me, we were both being sneaky. We were like a team, outsmarting Alcee and Gordon. I remember feeling like, 'Ha ha ha. I can too see Grandma,' but my ha ha ha wouldn't last long.

The same uncle who ratted me out before, one of them that never got beat on, ratted me out again. He told my mother what I was doing and they set me up. One night, after I got home from school, Alcee said that she and Gordon were going mushroom hunting. She said they were going to take the kids with them so I could play or do whatever I wanted. I guess I must have been stupid because that was a first and I didn't smell a rat. I couldn't have been anything *but* stupid. I was young, but I was wise beyond my years and I should have known that I was being set up. As soon as they left and I had waited long enough for them to really be gone, I took off to Grandma's. I remember thinking, if they went mushroom hunting I could stay at Grandma's for an hour. I had been in her house for maybe two minutes when I heard Gordon's voice from a half block away screaming, "Trena, get yer ass out here!" I was really scared and hanging onto my grandmother. I had been caught. Gordon kept screaming, "I know yer in there, I saw ya go in. Get yer ass out here! Don't make me come after you!" It sounded like a lion's roar. Grandma said, "You better go before the hog headed son-of-a-bitch has the police out here." I stepped out on the porch and there they were, a half block down the street, looking madder than hornets. When I got to the car Gordon told me to get in. I got in and we headed out to the forest where he liked to mushroom hunt. When we got to the forest he ordered me out of the car. I was hoping he was just going to leave me in the forest, but he had other plans. He made me walk to the back of the car where he picked me up and threw me over the trunk. He started beating on me and screaming, "Didn't I tell ya to stay away from that old bitch?" I looked in the back window of the car and saw some of the kids crying. Dena and Tim looked terrified, and both of them were crying and shaking and rubbing their eyes. I have often wondered why Dena and Tim didn't zone out and turn into statues that day. They already knew how, they had done it before. Years later Dena would tell me that she thought he was killing me and was going to dump my body in the forest. She was afraid the wolves would eat me. I kept sliding off the trunk, Gordon kept pushing me back up on the trunk and beating on me as he screamed and cussed about my grandmother. They would only catch me coming out of my grandmother's house one more time. The next, and last time, went pretty much as that time did. They were going mushroom hunting (talk about being stupid) and they just happened to be driving down the street right as I walked out the front door. Imagine the luck. It resulted in another beating, the same forest, same trunk, same game, same players, and probably the same uncle. Over the years I would see my grandmother on and off, on whenever she and my mother made up, and off whenever they were fighting. But when I was about fourteen, not long after Grandma told me she and my mother had known all about Raymond all along, Grandma and I would have another plan together. We would be a team again, and we would outsmart Alcee and Gordon again.

My mother used to make me stay home from school and watch the kids, clean house or whatever else she wanted me to do. When I was around thirteen or fourteen the school truant officers got involved over my missing so much school. They didn't like my mother and she didn't like them either. They came to the house and asked too many questions. One of them even threatened Alcee with court action if I kept missing school. I kept saying, in front of my teachers, that I liked to come to school but I had to stay home and help out. The truant officers jumped right on that one. They hounded and harassed my mother every time I was out for more than one day at a time. She absolutely hated those people. I used to go to school and leave early just to get them to chase me home. And when they got to my house my mother would go around and around with them. She wanted me to come home early and help with the kids, so she had no problem at all with me leaving school. Her motto was that I didn't need a diploma. I just needed to marry one. Grandma found all the harassment amusing and came up with an idea. One day I told my mother how she could get even with one relentless truant officer that wouldn't give up. I told her I didn't like that school anyway, so if she signed guardianship papers giving my grandmother guardianship, I could switch back to my old school, in the district that Grandma lived in, and that truant officer would be out of the picture. "Of course," I said, "I would really still be living here." She signed the papers and I moved in with Grandma. Alcee was livid. She had lost control of me by voluntarily signing those papers and Grandma had outsmarted her. We would both pay for tricking Alcee. We would pay over and over. It turned really ugly and it stayed ugly for years.

While I lived with Grandma she had six kids living there, and five of us were teenagers. She had us to take turns writing bad checks. She said the law didn't prosecute minors like they did adults. We all had fake identifications that indicated we were old enough to open checking accounts. Everyday she would decide who's turn it was to write a bad check and tell us which store to go to and write it. She kept a ledger of where the bad checks were, who had written them and whether or not we had picked them up. I think I wrote the most because I never squabbled about it being my turn and I wanted to please her. She used to praise me when I did things for her. She said, "Trennie will do anything for Grandma, won't 'cha, Trennie? Me and you's tight, ain't nothin' can come between us." The bad checks we teens wrote went for food, gambling and booze. We did eat pretty good though.

Alcee started turning my grandmother in to all the utility companies so they would shut off her utilities. You see, when the utilities were shut off, or when my grandmother moved, she just had them turned back on under a different name. Alcee called them all and gave them all the aliases that she knew about. In the dead of winter our heat would be shut off. As soon as we got the heat back on, the water or electricity would be shut off. You get the picture. It went on all winter until I moved out of there and into a foster home.

My grandmother had a gambling problem, but only when she was drunk. So that meant about five nights a week, some weeks every day except Sunday. She would go out around seven or eight and come home sometime after midnight. Sometimes she took one or more of us with her. She would be so drunk when she got home that she was either extremely nice or extremely not nice. One night she came in and took everything out of the refrigerator, one item at a time, and threw them against the kitchen wall. Then she demanded that us kids “get up and clean up that kitchen!” Well, some of us had to get up and clean the kitchen. Some of her favorites ‘needed their rest’ so they got to stay in bed, her favorites being her own kids. It was a mess. There were eggs stuck to the walls, broken bottles of ketchup and pop, shreds of cut up clothes thrown all around the kitchen in the middle of it all and she was still screaming and cussing. I just told myself to shut up, suck it up and get it done. Cleaning up that mess was a big job.

She beat her second and third husbands. I only vaguely remember the fights with the second one, but the third one I remember vividly. She hit him with what ever she could get her hands on and made him sleep on the kitchen floor like a dog. Then periodically throughout the night, she would run in there and kick him. Then she went back to bed laughing. I used to feel sorry for him. But he wouldn’t let anyone stick up for him, he always took her side and said he deserved what ever she gave him. He said he asked for every scar, bruise or mark she put on him. One time she got mad at him and pulled all the wiring out of his car, under the hood and under the dashboard. Then she threw bottles at it trying to break the windows, and she did. My uncles stood there watching in case she needed them to help. If her husband even *looked* like he wanted to say something my uncles just moved towards him and he looked away. One time he said, "Now Honey, that hurts!" She said, "Shut the fuck up you bastard or I'll finish killin' you!" If he even got grumpy with one of us kids she would beat the daylights out of him. It was okay for her to tell us, "I'll beat you to death!" but no one else could look at us cross-eyed or she would be all over them.

One night she took me out with her to drink and gamble. She had been drinking for a couple of hours when she got into an argument with another woman. This other woman was big and looked mean and tough. They argued for a few minutes and then my grandmother said, "You fuck with me and I'll turn my granddaughter loose on you! She'd love to kick your ass anyway. She don't appreciate the way you been talkin' ta me!" I was so scared. I was only around fourteen years old. I thought this woman could really hurt me and there was no way I wanted to fight her. Grandma said, "Take the whore outside and kick her ass, Trennie." She kept saying, "Go on. Go on." That woman must have sensed how scared I was and took pity on me, because she walked away.

I think the ultimate *Grandma Fagan* incident was when she had my uncles dress me up like a man, put shoe polish on my face so I would look black and told them to drive me to a little neighborhood store where I used to work. The owner was legally blind but he could see shadows and shapes. I was supposed to wait for him to come out of the store after closing, grab his bag of money and run back to the car. Two of my uncles would be waiting in the car a block away to drive me out of there. Grandma said she knew I could do it better than anyone she knew. She said it was in my blood on my dad's side. I didn't want to rob that guy, or anyone else, he had been nice to me when I worked for him. I went with my uncles, they parked a block away on the next street and let me out of the car to go do the dastardly deed of robbing a blind man. I went to the street where the store was and waited for the guy to close up and come out with his money. When he came out I ran past him as fast as I could, I didn't go for the money, I just ran by and headed to the car a block away. I ran up to the car frantic and told my uncles, "He has a gun!" That scared the daylights out of them and we took off in a hurry. I was forgiven for not fighting the guy for the money since he had a gun. He didn't really have a gun, I just told my uncles that to scare them so I wouldn't have to do anything wrong to the store owner. I knew when we left the house that I was not going to rob a blind man, but I had to go through enough motions to make it look like I tried. That's what I mean about Grandma being like Fagan in Oliver Twist. She had nothing to lose and everything to gain by sending me to rob someone. She made me feel like a hero while my uncles got me disguised. She kept saying, "I always knew you was special to me, Trennie. You and Grandma's tight." I just couldn't do it. I had decided years before that I was not going to be a jailbird, a drunk, a junkie or a teenage mother.

I have said these things about my grandmother, not to be mean or hateful, but to illustrate how confusing she was to me. She used me with no regard for the consequences I would bear. Yet, I have some memories of my grandmother that are good. I remember watching her put on her make up and giggling when she made lip prints on my forehead to blot her lipstick. I loved the way she looked when she was going out, always well dressed and every hair in place. She was a small pretty woman. I remember loving the way she smelled, not when she was drunk but when she was sober, even though I can't remember the name of her perfume now. I loved making her laugh. She had a beautiful laugh that I can still hear in my head. Before she went to work, or out drinking and dancing, she primped for hours, and she let me follow her around and watch her. Almost every day while she cooked, she played records and danced all around the kitchen. She called me by a nickname that she gave me. Sometimes when others were taunting or teasing me she would say, "That's enough!" and make them stop. Other times she would join in with the taunting and teasing. It hurt my feelings when I heard her laugh the same laugh that I loved, while Alcee or anyone else made fun of me. She was superstitious and whenever there was a thunderstorm she made us all be quiet. She would hang a belt around her neck and say, "If I hear one more peep out'a you little honyocks, I'm gonna beat you to death." One time I said, really low, "peep." In her most threatening voice, she said, "I mean it, Trennie!" But I saw her turn her head and chuckle and she didn't hit me. She took me in when I had no place to go. There was always a price to pay, but at least she let me in. I'm not sure if she loved me or not, but I know I loved her.

Even though it was all like left handed compliments, she did appear to be the least of the evils that surrounded me. After she tried to get me to commit the 'robbery,' I kind of distanced myself from her emotionally. I have always wondered if she suspected that I blew it on purpose. I still needed a place to stay and I did what I had to do, but even Grandma sensed that there was a limit to how far I would go to pay for her 'kindness.' In both our eyes, we became less and less 'tight.' In Oliver Twist Fagan took advantage of the kids, but at least they were off the street at night and had food. He gave them a feeling that they mattered. Even though it looked as if he was protecting them, every one of them was disposable to obtain his goals. Just like I was disposable to my grandmother. Still, it was better than sleeping on the street in the cold. The character in Dickens' novel wasn't *all* bad, and neither was *Grandma Fagan.*

CHAPTER SIX

"You Ain't Mistreated"

Every single day Alcee found a reason to tell us that we were not mistreated. She had to tell us how lucky we were and that we didn't know what mistreated was. She even backed up her remarks with newspaper pictures and horrible stories about other kids being abused. I don't remember how old I was when she showed me a newspaper picture of a little boy sitting in a hospital bed, but I know I was still in elementary school. Both of his hands had been burned and they were bandaged from his fingers to his elbows. Alcee shoved the picture in my face and said, "Look at that! Now that's mistreated! He got in his mom's ice box and stole cheese and she held his hands over the flames on her stove. See, you ain't mistreated. Ya oughta be but ya ain't! Ya little bastard! Ya only wish you was mistreated so people would feel sorry for you. Think about that the next time ya have a pity party for yourself." I still remember that picture and the feeling I had when I saw it. He was a little dark haired boy about five or six years old. He was sitting on the edge of a hospital bed with his legs hanging over the side. His little face reflected so much fear. Maybe it was pain and fear, but he looked so pitiful and scared. It made me sad and scared. That picture is forever etched in my mind, I can see it now as plain as I did the day she showed it to me. I'm not sure what the point was of Alcee showing me that picture. I wouldn't show that to a little child. Maybe she wanted to intimidate me or maybe she really wanted me to think I was lucky. Maybe she wanted me to stay out of the salad dressing and cheese. I remember telling myself to be careful what I helped myself to in the refrigerator.

When Alcee worked at night and I fed the kids and took care of them, I used to get into the refrigerator and eat stuff that she hadn't specifically said to eat. I always fed the kids first. I couldn't eat and feed the babies at the same time, so I spoon fed them while the bigger ones fed themselves. Then after I had all of them fed, I ate. Sometimes I was still hungry because most of the supper was gone by the time I fed the others. I ate what was left and then scrounged for whatever I could find. One of my regular standby fillers was pouring salad dressing on a saucer and sopping it up with bread. I also sneaked cheese out of the refrigerator, usually at night after the kids were asleep. Then, when sometime later Alcee went to get the salad dressing or cheese, she was mad because most of it was gone. She screamed, "Who in the fuck got in the goddamned salad dressing? I didn't put salad dressing out fer anybody did I? I 'cain't' have a goddamned thing for you little son-of-a-bitches! In India they cut peoples hands off for stealin' and maybe that's what I oughta do. It'd be the last goddamned thing you'd steal!" She threw the bottle out in the yard because she said there wasn't enough left to nasty her mouth with. This happened several times. I didn't feel like I was stealing it, but I did feel like I was sneaking it. After I saw the picture I stopped stealing, or sneaking, the salad dressing and cheese. I moved on to syrup and bread until she figured out someone had been in that, too. I don't remember thinking I was malnourished, but I was so little I guess I wouldn't have known. As an adult I have some physical characteristics that indicate maybe I was. I remember the doctors giving Alcee tonic to give to me because I was underweight. I also remember my grandma talking about how thin I was. She said I looked like a stick. Sometimes she said, "You ain't no bigger than a whippoorwill." Maybe I was, I don't know. Like my therapist says, kids make lousy parents. I guess that's true even when they are trying to parent themselves, not just their siblings.

If anyone tried to do something nice for us kids Alcee accused us of trying to make her look bad. One night after dark she sent me to the store. I was sick, as usual, and it was so cold outside. I remember feeling so bad that it seemed like it took me forever to get to the store. I did get there though, and one of my aunts, by marriage, was there. The store owners and my aunt asked me if I was okay and I told them yes. I must have looked like I wasn't okay because my aunt insisted on giving me a ride home. She had to go past the alley to get to her house anyway so I didn't argue too much. I felt so bad I was just glad I didn't have to walk in the cold. She pulled up to the house and went to the door with me. She said to Alcee, "I ran into her at the store and didn't think she looked very good so I gave her a ride home. She is burning up with fever. Have you had her to the doctor?" Alcee was not happy. She said, "Yeah, I've had her to the doctor and he said there ain't nothin' wrong with her but meanness and laziness. How 'bout if you take care of yer kids and I'll worry about mine." My aunt was apologetic and said she didn't mean to cause trouble or rub her the wrong way. She said she was just worried about me and gave me a ride home, but she was sorry. You know, that was the same girl my uncle was going to take to the dance and ended up marrying. After she left Alcee lit in on me. She said, "The next time somebody brings ya home with a sad story about you, they can fuckin' have ya! I'll bet ya ate that up like candy. Poor little thing, did auntie feel sorry for you? Ya sneakin' little bastard! I'm tired o' you makin' me look bad! The next time somebody wants to help ya with a pity party make sure they fuckin' want to keep ya 'cause I'll send yer goddamned filthy ass off somewhere if they don't! There ain't nothin' wrong with you but meanness!" I must have had tonsilitis and an ear infection again because I had ear drops for my ears. Alcee turned on the oven and put the bottle on the edge of the bottom of the oven to let them heat up. She said, "Come here you poor little thing so we can put ear drops in your pitiful little ears. I even warmed them up for ya." When she put the first drop in my ear it hurt really bad. She heated them up alright, they were hot! I started crying and screaming that they were too hot. She said, "Shut the fuck up, ya should have thought about that before ya got sick. Ya probably went out without yer coat, maybe you'll think twice next time. Make sure ya tell everybody that Mommy put medicine in yer poor little ears. Make sure you tell yer auntie! Ya little spiteful despisable son-of-a-bitch!" She was furious because I got a ride home from the store. I usually turned down favors from anyone and everyone, but I was so sick that night I just didn't resist and took the ride. That is the last time that aunt ever offered any help. In fact, she acted like she couldn't stand us after that.

Another time the school had clowns in for the afternoon. I don't remember what the occasion was, but we all went to the cafeteria to see the clowns. I don't remember if I was already sick or if the smell of the clown make-up made me sick, but I know I felt very bad when I headed home after school. I got so far and just felt like I couldn't go any further. I was walking by a house with steps that went out to the sidewalk. It was across the street from the neighborhood grocery I usually went to. In fact, it was the store owners house. I stopped to sit on the steps for a minute and rest. I thought if I sat down and took a break I could make it the rest of the way home. I fell asleep! I fell asleep on the steps of that house right there on the sidewalk. The next thing I remembered was a man holding me in the doorway of our house in the alley. He said he picked me up and carried me to the grocery store across the street from where he found me, and the store owner told him where I lived. Alcee said, "Yeah, she's my kid." He handed me over to her and left. I have no idea who he was, but he seemed nice. He must have been nice to find out where I lived and carry me home. As soon as he left she turned on me. She was so mad at me. She said, "You stupid little bastard! Where in the fuck is yer mind? I don't know who that son-of-a-bitch was that dragged yer little ass home! If those people at the store hadn't seen him pick ya up he probably would have took off with ya! They would've found ya cut up in pieces in a goddamned field somewhere!" That really scared me because she had read me a newspaper story about a little girl who had been abducted and dismembered and thrown in a field. I still remember the name of the guy who did that to that little girl. She kept yelling about that story and telling me how stupid I was. She said, "If you had a fuckin' brain you'd take it out and play with it!"

There was another time that a store owner offered me a free water melon. It wasn't the store I usually went to because Alcee owed them money so I had to go to the one further up the street. Anyway, it was summertime and it wasn't completely dark yet. She sent me to the store for something and the guy that owned it said, "Hey, I'll bet you kids would like to have a water melon. I've got one I'm givin' away, would you like to have it?" I knew better than to accept favors, it made Alcee look bad, so I asked him if I could go home and ask my mom first. He said yes. I ran home as fast as I could and asked my mother if we could take the free water melon. She said, "Ya little fittified mother-fucker, go get it before he gives it ta somebody else!" I ran back as fast as I could and told him my mom said yes. He still had the water melon and he gave it to me. I' was really happy and proud about that water melon. I knew the kids were going to love it. I knew I was going to love it, too. I was carrying it home, by then it was dark, and I dropped the melon and busted it. It busted on the sidewalk and I just started crying. I cried all the way home. When I got there Alcee said I busted the water melon on purpose. She said, "Ya little spiteful son-of-a-bitch! Ya came runnin' in here gettin' these kids' mouths waterin' for that fuckin' water melon and then you busted it! You are the most despisable spiteful son-of-a-bitch I ever saw in my life!" She told the kids, "You can thank Trena for not havin' a water melon! She busted it so you couldn't have it! She promised it to ya then busted it on the sidewalk!" I felt so bad about dropping that melon. I wanted it and I knew the kids and Alcee wanted it. I knew I had let everybody down, but I did not do it on purpose. I had to go home to ask first and then go back and get it. It was dark by then and I was trying to hurry. I know it sounds like I'm making excuses for myself and maybe I am. Looking back, maybe I'm trying to give myself a break. Even though I never felt like one, I was just a little kid. Also looking back, I think that store owner wasn't giving away a melon to just anybody. I think he was being nice to the kids in the alley. Even though I screwed it up, I hope he knew how nice that was. I hope he knew how big and valuable little things like that were to the kids in the alley.

If anyone was nice to us kids Alcee took it as an insult to herself. The fact that someone offered any act of kindness to any one of us made her accuse us of 'acting pitiful to get attention' or having a 'pity party' for ourselves. She always said we were trying to make her look bad. She was always trying to make herself look good. She would go on and on about having a houseful of kids and how much it took to feed us and clothe us and how much work it was to take care of us. She did things like take food and toys to poor families. One year at Christmas she took a laundry basket full of food and toys to a poor family. She said she was doing it anonymously so they wouldn't be embarrassed, but she made sure everyone in the neighborhood, except *that* family, knew it was her that took the food and toys to them. Just like the letters to the editor of her hometown newspaper make her look good today, *maybe*. I know that there are some people in town who know what her true colors are. I know that there are some people who don't know her true colors. Some people are too young to remember, most of the ones old enough to remember are probably too old to care or are dead. I think Raymond knew her true colors and preyed on me through her. I think old Miss Miller knew her true colors and was afraid of her. I believe what she did to her children goes beyond hypocrisy. We, my siblings and I, weren't trying to make her look bad. I think we just clung to anything anyone was willing to throw our way. It was like throwing a bone to a dog, the dog will go for it ***unless*** the dog gets beat every time he goes for it. That's why we all learned early not to accept favors or kindness from people. Not only did Alcee say we were making her look bad, but she said they were making fun of us and we didn't have sense enough to know it. She said those people laughed at us for acting so pitiful because they knew we weren't mistreated.

As the little ones grew older I became the clearinghouse for accepting favors. If someone offered the kids something they came to me, most of the time *after* they had accepted it, and told me about it. As I got older I covered for them or justified it to Alcee. She still didn't like it, but it was too late, most of the time, for her to do anything about it. I told her things like, I was busy and didn't know what was going on until it was too late. I told her we took advantage of whoever was being nice and that *they* were the stupid ones. I didn't mean it. I was always grateful for anything anyone did for us. But it gave Alcee some sort of satisfaction to think we took advantage of someone and made *them* look stupid. I know it sounds mean, but I had to do what ever worked. For instance, one time when she sent me to the gas station to make a phone call because our phone was shut off. I let someone use the phone ahead of me. The factory was on strike and there was a lot of activity with picket lines and reporters. I started to use the phone and some guy said "Hey kid, I need the phone." I backed off and let him use it first. When I got home Alcee wanted to know what took me so long. I told her about it and she got angry because I didn't hold him up for a dollar. I told her that he had a camera and seemed like he was in a hurry. She said, "He was a reporter ya fuckin' idiot! Ya should 'a told him he could have the fuckin' phone for a dollar! You're so fuckin' dumb! He's probably laughin' his ass off at ya right now. He took advantage of ya. I don't know how I spawned such stupid kids!"

She used to say one of the guys who worked at the station, Wendell, made fun of me, but he was being nice. He used to tease me. He said, "There's that pretty girl with the pretty smile. What do you need sweetie?" Sometimes he said, "Hey, there's my girl! Where you been?" I was there to buy cigarettes or pop or use the phone, almost every day. I loved it when he teased me, even if I didn't feel good. I never felt like he was making fun of me, but my mother said he was. If I went in there and didn't smile he would tease me until I did. I remember not smiling on purpose sometimes so he would tease me and talk to me. Then when I smiled I covered my mouth with my hand and he said, "Aw, now quit that. Let me see that pretty smile. Your teeth are so pretty. You've got the prettiest smile of any girl I know." I remember wishing that he would take me home with him. I wanted to tell him what Gordon did to us because I just knew he would save us. I used to daydream about him wanting me to be his little girl. I wanted *him* to be my daddy, not Gordon. I wouldn't know where to begin to find him today. I didn't know his last name and the station is long gone. But just like the store owner who gave us the ill fated watermelon, he probably never knew what good he did for that scrawny, sad little girl. Just like Flo, I didn't know when she was saving me *that she was saving me* and she probably never knew that I finally figured it out. I'll bet she never knew how grateful I would be, and still am. And I'll bet Wendell never knew how much that ratty little girl loved him.

Every time someone was nice to us we paid for it. Alcee swore that we solicited pity from who ever would listen. That just wasn't true. We learned at a very young age not to tell anyone anything that went on in our house. She said, "If ya ain't out cryin' the blues why in the fuck are they so worried about ya, ya poor little thing? I ain't crazy! Do you think I'm crazy? Well, I'm not. And you ain't gonna make me think I am!" She said, "If I find out you been out waggin' yer goddamned tongue I'll cut it out! You lyin' little bastard! You ain't mistreated, you just think you are. Keep waggin' that goddamned tongue o' yers and you'll find out what mistreated is!" It was especially scarey when she was holding a knife while threatening to cut my tongue out. She said that's what they did to liars in India so they couldn't tell any more lies. Everything always happened in India. There were kids starving in India, they cut off peoples hands for stealing in India, they cut out peoples tongues for lying in India, they cut off peoples feet for running away in India, you get the idea.

One night I got up in the middle of the night and went into the front room to sleep on the couch. It was always crowded in the bed with five or six of us in it. Dana heard me and followed me in there. She wanted to sleep on the couch too. I don't know what was wrong with me that night, but I remember crying and begging Dana to go back to bed and leave me alone on the couch. Dana was just plain mean to us other kids and she said, "No. Either I sleep here too or I'm gonna wake up Mommy and tell." I kept begging and crying for her to leave me alone, but she didn't and we both ended up back in bed. The next morning Alcee made fun of me. She said, "I heard ya up in the middle o' the night cryin' and carryin' on like a fuckin' idiot. Next time I hear ya I'll get up and give ya somethin' ta cry about. If ya don't like it here I can send ya off, ya little ungrateful bastard! I don't know what ya *think* you have to cry about but you don't have a goddamned thing to cry about! YET!" Referring to my grandmother, she said, "It's probably somethin' that old bitch put in yer head! What ever she told you was a fuckin' lie so get over it!" She kept mocking me. She said, "Oh, boo hoo! Poor little me. I'm so mistreated. Somebody feel sorry for me. I'm a little ungrateful bastard."

One time I asked Grandma if I remembered things that really happened or if I just had nightmares that seemed real. I told her that Alcee said I was "a sick little bastard, full of shit and just made stuff up." Grandma said, "Alcee is the one that's full of shit and she's been a liar all her life! She don't want you to know the truth about her or Gordon. He's a sadistic mother-fucker and I told her and him both that! Me and that son-of-a-bitch has went around and around over you kids, many a times. I told him if he didn't quit mistreatin' you kids I'd kill him." She said "I don't care what he does to his own, but by God he better not touch you and Dana!" She brought up the time I was in the closet when she stopped by their house. She said she had heard Gordon had been doing that to me and she kept stopping by periodically trying to catch him. And she did. She said, "No, you ain't full of shit and you ain't crazy, but your mother is. I'll tell you one thing, they don't want to get Grandma's dander up, they don't know who they're messin' with! I'll see to it that everyone of them youngins get taken away from 'em!" Grandma said, "Don't ever let that bitch tell ya' that you're the one that's crazy! She's the one that's crazy! And don't let her tell ya' that you *drove* her crazy. She was crazy long before you came along."

Alcee was wrong. Us kids did not tell on her and Gordon. I tried it one time and paid dearly for it. I was the only one in school, the other kids were still preschool. I remember my second grade teacher taking me to the office to talk to someone about my home life. She was very nice to me. She was a nice teacher and was nice to all the kids in her class. She's the one who made those two kids stop making fun of me because my real dad was in prison. I don't know who the guy in the office was. I remember his name, but I don't know what his title was. He and my teacher said they wanted to talk to me about my mommy and daddy and sisters and brothers. My teacher said, "You can tell us and it will be our secret. No one will know that we talked." They asked questions like, does Daddy hit Mommy? Does Mommy or Daddy hit you or your brothers and sisters? Does Daddy drink beer? What did you have for breakfast this morning? What did you have for supper last night? I remember being reluctant and scared, but I must have told them enough to stir things up because Alcee found out. They had to have already known something was wrong because Gordon's name was in the paper frequently for being arrested, usually for drunk driving or assault and battery. Kids are so easy to trick. They tell things and don't even realize they have told. I was never tricked by school officials after that incident. There was obviously no secret to it, and somebody did know we talked. It was awful.

Alcee said, "I know ya told them a bunch o' fuckin' lies at school. I should have smothered you at birth, ya little mother-fucker. Where is yer fuckin' mind? Ya keep makin' shit up and tellin' people lies and they will come and take every one o' you little bastards and put you in the orphanage! Maybe that's what I ought 'a do anyway is just call the orphanage and have them to come and pick up all you little snot nosed son-of-a-bitches! I think I will! I'm tired of wipin' snotty noses and nasty little asses anyway! I'll just get rid of all you little dirty bastards." I begged her not to call the orphanage. I kept crying and begging while she kept screaming and threatening. I said, "No. No please! I won't tell anybody anything. They tricked me. I won't do it again. I wanna live here with you." She said, "Too late! I'm callin' the orphanage and they'll split you all up. Ha ha ha! Ya won't see the babies anymore. But you don't care because yer so fuckin' lazy ya don't want to take care of 'em anyway." I was still crying and begging her not to call the orphanage. I said, "Yes I do. I do want to take care of 'em. Please let us stay with you. Mommy, please let us stay here. I'll be good. I'll take care of the kids and help you. I'll be good." Alcee kept mocking me and saying she was calling the orphanage. She said, "Ya little lazy bastard! You'll earn yer keep there! They'll roll yer ass out o' bed at the crack of dawn every morning and work yer worthless little ass off 'till dark. Ya won't see the babies anymore. Ya might be able to hear 'em cry, but ya won't see 'em because they keep the babies in a different room." I was so scared. It just seemed to me like I couldn't do anything right. I was in trouble for something all the time and it was always my fault.

As bad as things were, it was still all I knew. Remember, when all you know is one way to live, no matter what that way is, it's all you know. You think everybody lives like that. The thought of not seeing the babies terrified me. I remember having all these thoughts going through my head and I was so sorry. What if they did pick us up and take us to the orphanage? It would be all my fault. The kids would hate me forever. We would never see each other again. Oh my God! Why did I open my mouth at school? Why can't I just be good? Now look what I've done. It was a mess, the whole fiasco was a mistake. I didn't think this could be fixed. My only hope was to keep begging Alcee not to send us off. I did. I begged and begged. I cried and said, "Mommy, please! Just give me one more chance! I'll be good! I swear I'll mind every word you say." Looking back now I'll bet that was a lot of fun for her. That was the last time I let anybody trick me into giving any information about anything.

My third and fourth grade teachers were nice too. They tried the same game my second grade teacher played on me, but it didn't work. I remember them telling me that I didn't have to talk to my second grade teacher and the guy in the office. My fourth grade teacher, Mrs. Jones, said, "You know you can trust me and Mrs.

Smith. We can keep a secret." Yeah right. Who told them I was that stupid? Alcee? They asked me the same questions that Mrs. White and Mr. Brown had asked the year before. I remember almost choking on my words when I told them, "My mommy and daddy are nice to us. They don't hit us, they love us. I love my daddy. My mommy said I'm a daddy's girl. He takes me to the library. Well, he said he's gonna take me to the library. He says I'm cute. He loves me." I knew it wouldn't be good enough to just not tell, I had to give them something to make it look like everything was okay. I remember smiling and acting so chipper when I told them how good things were at home. I also remember hoping they believed me because I didn't want Alcee to call the orphanage. We weren't mistreated so why did they keep asking questions? Why didn't they go pick on someone else and stop trying to get me in trouble? I was in enough trouble all the time without them adding to it. They were nice teachers, but I wasn't about to let them trick me into something that would split up us kids.

One weekend I fell in the alley and flat faced the gravel. It was winter time and the ground was frozen so I didn't get much gravel in my face, but I did scrape my face and break my nose. I was trying to ride my aunt, the one that is about my age, on a bicycle. Georgie, my aunt, was less than a year older than me. We were in the same grade at school. My grandmother was still having kids when my mother started having them. I have uncles and aunts several years younger than me. Anyway, it was icy and when the bike went down I flat faced the icy ground and Georgie fell on top of me. It hurt so bad. I was bleeding and my whole face was swollen. I thought I was dying. I was in third grade so I must have been eight or nine. We went in the house and I got in trouble for crying. Alcee said, "Shut up! Ya fuckin' cry baby! You just wanna make her feel bad! Shut up!" I stopped crying and started making fun of myself so my aunt wouldn't feel bad. Alcee had always said I had a big horse face, so I said, "I really look like Mr. Ed now. Hey, I'm a movie star! I am Mr. Ed." Alcee and my aunt laughed and, when I felt like crying, I made myself laugh, too. It hurt so bad. The next day I went to school and I was in a lot of pain. It was winter and I remember my face hurt from the cold while I was walking to school. Right after I got there, my teacher asked me what happened and I told her. She asked me if I had seen a doctor. I told her yes, but I was lying. I hadn't really seen a doctor. Then she asked me the doctor's name. I said I didn't remember. She took me to the office and got the principal. Everyone was scared of the principal, including me, he was kind of gruff and old. He was really nice to me that morning. He and my teacher took me to the nurse's office. She looked at my injuries and asked me questions about how it happened and what the doctor, I had supposedly seen, said about it. Then she talked to the principal and my teacher. Oh no! The principal said he needed to talk to my mother! He drove me home in his car and told Alcee that he insisted I see a doctor. He said he was willing to take me to one if that was a problem for her. She said, "No, no. I'll get her there."

I was in so much trouble after the principal left. Alcee accused me of going to school and 'cryin' the blues' so they would feel sorry for me. I didn't, but there was no sense in trying to convince her of that. I was in pain, she was screaming at me, and thanks to the school authorities *again*, she was sure I had been talking about our private family business. She was even more angry than usual because she had to find a way for an adult to take me to the doctor. By the time I was in third grade I was going to the doctor by myself. If I was sick Alcee called them and told them she was sending me in for a sore throat or earache or what ever. With the school authorities bringing me home, she couldn't send me by myself that time because they might find out. They could call the doctor because I had to take a doctor's statement to school to prove I had been there. She was so angry. She kept telling me how she was tired of me stabbing her in the back. She said, "I worked three fuckin' jobs ta keep you when you was born and this is the thanks I get. Yer gonna keep on actin' like yer mistreated 'til ya get yer wish! Keep cryin' wolf and when ya do end up mistreated nobody 'll believe ya!" She finally got one of Gordon's relatives to pick me up and drive me to a doctor's office. The doctor said my nose was broken and told the woman how to take care of me. She took me home and relayed the information to Alcee. She wasn't very gentle when she put cream on the abrasions on my face. It went kind of like the ear drops. Alcee said, "You are just bound and determined ta make my life miserable, ain't cha?" She just kept jerking my head around and smearing that stuff on my face while she went on and on about how mean I was. But I didn't even cry. I kept making fun of myself in an effort to make up with her. The next day I went back to school with a doctor's statement. I didn't ask them for help and I didn't cry when my face hurt.

When I look back, it seems like the school authorities who tried to help helped just enough to get me into more trouble. None of them helped enough to save me or any of the other kids. They only helped enough to stir things up. I would have been better off, most of the time, with no help at all from them. Sometimes I still can't figure out which side they were on. My uncle, the one who got his arm broken with a hammer, knew at least half the teachers at school through his work. I don't know if he told the teachers stuff about us to get them to turn Alcee in, or if he asked them not to turn her in, because she was his sister, as a favor to him. I don't think reporting abuse was mandatory back then. Even after it became mandatory, you didn't have to report what you *claimed* you didn't see.

One of my biggest fears, oddly enough, was being permanently separated from my mother and my siblings. The thought of the orphanage, where I could hear the babies cry and not be able to get to them, terrified me. I used to have nightmares about it. Alcee told me they beat you *everyday* at the orphanage, and made you work to earn your keep. She said, "You ain't mistreated! You just think the world owes ya a livin' and it don't." I didn't care if Gordon went away. In fact, I used to wish he would die and then I would get scared because I did something so mean. Alcee used to say, "Yer so goddamned mean! When ya hear chains rattlin' under yer bed some night, don't cry for me ta save yer sorry little ass. It'll be the devil comin' to get 'cha!" I never wished her dead, but I did do the 'step on a crack and you'll break your mother's back' trick on the way home from school, sometimes. I remember thinking if I just stepped on a crack and it really broke her back she couldn't get up and hit me. I remember thinking that I could carry to her what ever she needed and take care of her and the kids. That way she wouldn't be dead, but she couldn't physically hurt us either. She would still be there so we wouldn't have to go to the orphanage and I could take care of all of us. I was just a little kid and I really believed that would work. I didn't know I was just a kid.

One time my therapist asked me who was nice to me when I was growing up. Not very many relatives were nice to any of us, but there were some people that were nice. Like Flo, she saved me from having to work at Raymond's all summer, the store owner who gave us the doomed water melon, the man who found me sleeping on the sidewalk and the store owner who told him where I lived. When I was around twelve I was working in another restaurant. One night a teenaged boy gave me a one dollar tip. I was ecstatic talking about my one dollar tip. This older woman who worked there took me over to the side and said, "Honey, you go give him his dollar back. I know that kid and he'll be here when you get off work tonight expecting something for his dollar. You give it back to him and tell him no thanks." I did what she told me to do and felt so good that she cared about me. I felt so protected or something. Actually, I don't know *what* I felt, I only know that it felt good when she was so nice to me. She spoke to me so gently and kind. When I was sixteen, and living in a sleeping room, my gym teacher approached one of my friends and asked her what was going on with me. I was working at night and going to school during the day. I had lost a lot of weight and I didn't have much to start with. I must have looked pretty thin and gaunt. My friend told her I didn't eat very well because I worked at night and went to school during the day. She also told the teacher that she and her mother had taken food to my sleeping room several times. My gym teacher called me into her office and gave me money to buy food.

She said, "I want you take this and get yourself something to eat. It's not a loan, it's a gift. No one needs to know about this, okay? I want to see your belt let out, not tightened up." She said I could come to her anytime I needed anything or just to talk. I never did. I didn't want to use the favor unless I *really* needed it. There were my foster parents, who I'll talk about later. There was Wendell, my pretend daddy, who called me his pretty girl.

I have so few warm feelings to remember and hold on to. They were few and far between, but thank God I have them. I don't want to sound ungrateful because I am very grateful to everyone who threw anything my way. I can't even put into words how valuable it was to me when someone just winked at me or smiled at me. And I have talked about a lot of people who were nice to me, but if you figure in the length of a childhood they *were* few and far between. My second and third grade teachers were nice to me, but the summer between those two grades was like an eternity to me. What most kids saw as a break from school, a summer vacation, seemed like forever to me, like the summer I had to work for Raymond. Even though I didn't tell them anything, and they didn't really help, I was safer during the school year. Yes, I do have a few precious memories of nice people being nice to me. I don't know if I would have survived without them, and I am very grateful for them. My fear, and maybe a little guilt, is that all those people probably never knew how much their kindness meant to me. When I was little, and Alcee kept telling me that people were just tricking me and making fun of me, I believed her most of the time. She was my mother and I was a little girl. I think that's what little girls do, isn't it? Don't they believe their mothers no matter what they say and do? I believed that if she said we weren't mistreated then we were not mistreated. Maybe I wanted to believe her or maybe I wanted to believe *in* her. Maybe I just wanted her to like me. My God. I didn't even know what I wanted or needed. Because everything was so screwed up, I didn't know what was wrong. When I was little I didn't even know something *was* wrong most of the time. For the most part I thought everyone lived that way.

When I was a little girl I believed in angels. Even now, sometimes, I think about when I was little and believed in them. I ask myself if I still do. Sometimes I tell myself that I do, other times I feel silly. I don't mean to sound abstract, I'm not an abstract type person. I am a very practical, logical person, but think about it. I'm not saying they have to be winged, heavenly creatures that show up with magic powers. Maybe angels are merely the good part of us while we are alive, just like demons are part of some people. When Alcee said, "You look just like your goddamned daddy when you smile! Every time I look at you I see the biggest mistake I ever made," maybe that was a demon part of her. Then when Wendell said, "You have the prettiest smile of any girl I know," maybe it was really an 'angel part' of him that gave me the lift I needed to make it through that day. Maybe, if they do exist in any form, an angel caused him to say it. I have to believe that I have been touched by angels (whatever they are) throughout my life. Do you believe in angels? I think I do. How could I not believe in them?

CHAPTER SEVEN

Go Get In The Car

When Gordon said, "Go get in the car," we all knew it couldn't be anything good for us. We were never told where we were going. We were only told to 'go get in the car' and that could mean almost anything was about to happen. Gordon always drove because Alcee didn't know how to drive and it would be several more years before she learned. There were a couple of times that we went to a root beer stand and got free root beers. I don't know if Alcee and Gordon knew someone who worked there or what the deal was. Maybe it was so us kids would say we had been there if the authorities questioned us. But for us to expect something good, would be disappointing nine times out of ten. Sometimes it meant that Gordon was going fishing and we were going to sit in the car while he fished. When this happened I knew someone had called the welfare department to investigate our environment, not because I had talked to anyone, but because I knew the signs. Otherwise, we would have been left at home. I liked it better when we were left at home because it was safer and more peaceful, but as soon as the investigation was over we would be able to stay home alone again. I knew that, I only hoped it would be soon.

When Gordon and Alcee had to take us fishing with them, it was miserable for us kids. Sometimes when Alcee was working, Gordon had to take us with him alone. He would pull the car over to the side of the road at the lake and park along the bank. He and Alcee, when she was with us, got out of the car and sat on the bank to fish. All of us kids sat in the backseat of the car and watched from the window. Sometimes Gordon got mad because he said the kids were making too much noise and scaring away the fish. He yelled at me to keep the kids quiet. He said, "If them kids make one more noise, I'm gonna whip yer ass! I ain't catchin' nothin' cause all the goddamned racket is scarin' the fish away." Okay, do you know how hard it is to keep a bunch of little ones quiet while sitting for hours in the back seat of a parked car? I do. It's next to impossible. Even after Gordon and Alcee got out of the car we all still had to stay in the backseat. It was hot, we were tired and crowded, and the little ones picked on each other and made each other cry. Dana would even pinch one of the others to make them cry if things got too quiet. Sometimes Gordon reached inside the car and smacked me in the head while he cussed at me for not keeping the kids quiet. Sometimes he made me get out of the car and go to him. He said, "What did I tell you? Why is he cryin'? Come 'ere to me ya little hard headed son-of-a-bitch! Right now!" Sometimes he 'whipped my ass' and sometimes he hit me in the head and face with his big hard hands. I remember him hitting me so hard, sometimes, that I thought my eyes were knocked loose. I would get such a headache. I can't really describe it. It kind of felt like my head was cold and heavy. It felt like it had cold stuffing in it. It felt huge and tight, but not like it was swollen, just big and heavy. It hurt. But most of the time I didn't cry. It was my job to keep the little ones from crying. It didn't make sense for me to cry.

Go get in the car could also mean we were going for a ride in the country. We still played that game too; the one where they dumped me and said they weren't coming back. I remember that I still shook and felt scared, but I don't remember *how* scared I was. I shook the same and had the same fears, but somehow I turned it off. Getting in the car could also mean we were going to Gordon's parents house. When we got there he would order us to line up on the couch and sit there. He said, "Sit yer asses right there and don't move!" I held the baby, who ever that happened to be at the time. His mother told him he was being mean. She said, "Gordon, let them kids be kids. They ain't gonna hurt anything here. Let 'em play." I liked her. He said, "I know they ain't gonna hurt anything 'cause they're gonna sit right there like I told 'em to." I remember several times when she told him and Alcee that they made me watch the kids too much. She said, "She's just a kid herself and she's tied down too much with those little ones. She needs to play, too." They even got into arguments about it. Gordon always got hateful with her about it. He said, "These ain't your kids, Mother. It ain't none o' yer goddamned business, is it?" She shook her head and said, "I know it ain't, but she's too little to be motherin' those kids. She's takin' care of them babies and she's just a baby herself." Then Gordon looked at me and said, "I'll bet you're eatin' this shit up like candy, ain't 'cha?" Then in a mocking voice he said, "Poor me! Even Grandma J feels sorry for me! I'm so mistreated! Boo hoo hoo! I have ta help watch my brothers and sisters. Boo hoo!" His mother said, "I don't know when you got so mean, Gordon. Me and Daddy didn't do you like that." There were times that, in spite of Gordon and Alcee, she dumped toys out on the floor in another room and took us in there to play with them. We would sit on the floor and play. If Gordon tried to bother us, she stopped him. She said, "Leave them kids alone! I told them they could play there. Now I mean it! Let them be." I *really* liked her! She was never mean to me. Alcee hated her and would eventually forbid every one of us from speaking to her for years and years.

After I grew up, some of Gordon's relatives told me about the first time they saw me and how they used to talk about the way Alcee and Gordon treated us kids. One of them said, "I'll never forget the first time I saw you. You took to me right away, warmed up to me instantly. You were so cute and sweet. I never could get close to Dana, but you were like a little love starved puppy. And you were so tiny to be three or four years old! Your mom acted like it made her mad that you liked me." She said, "I remember thinking that you were so cute, I could have just hugged you to death." Another one said, "Trena, we always knew it was bad, but if we had known *how bad* the things were that went on in that house, we would have done something. We always thought it was strange the way Alcee made over everybody else's kids, but acted like she couldn't stand her own. She acted like it made her mad if any of us was nice to you kids or tried to make over you." She said, "If I'd had any idea, I swear I would have called somebody myself. I am so sorry, for you kids that no one ever did anything about it." She said she felt bad about it and I guess I believe her.

Alcee fought with them off and on through the years. Unfortunately for us kids, it was mostly off. We were forbidden from speaking to any of Gordon's relatives. She hated them and was always telling us horrible stories about them. She said, "If I ***ever*** know of you speakin' to any o' those mother-fuckers, I'll beat you to death! Ya speak ta them and ya stab me in the back!" She kept telling us how much Gordon's relatives hated us. She said they made fun of us and didn't think we were as good as the other kids in the family. She said awful things about them all the time. I missed them. One time, we were at my other Grandma's house and my mother told me to go to the neighborhood store down the street to buy something. I said, "Grandma J works there. Can I go to the other store?" She said, "You little fittified bastard! Which word didn't you understand? I said go-to-THAT- store! Get-what-I-told-you-to-get-and-bring-it-back-to-me!" Then she said, "I better not know o' you speakin' ta that old bitch! Georgie, you go with her and make sure she don't speak ta that old bitch. If she does, I wanna know about it." I hated that. I had to go into that store and be face to face with Grandma J and not say a single word to her. I felt like crying before I even got to the store. She had always been nice to me and this was going to be awful. Plus, Georgie was with me and she loved to cause trouble. Even if I didn't speak to Grandma J, Georgie might lie just for the fun of seeing me get into trouble. What a mess. I went into the store and Grandma J was there. She said, "Well for land's sake! Look who just walked in! My gosh! How are all you kids doin'?" She yelled at somebody else in the store and said, "Come up here. I want you to see one my grandkids." She didn't say 'step grandkid,' she said 'grandkid.' She was smiling from ear to ear, just beaming. I felt so bad, but I just ignored her. I tried to signal her with my eyes so Georgie wouldn't see, but Grandma J was crushed. She teared up and walked to the back of the store. Someone else checked us out and we went back to Grandma's. Georgie told them all that I didn't speak to the 'old bitch' and she ran to the back of the store crying. Grandma, Georgie, Alcee and my uncles started laughing about it.

They thought it was a real hoot. Georgie said, "You should 'a seen the old bitch, Alcee. She went boo hooin' ta the back of the store. It was all I could do ta keep from laughin' right there in the store!" I didn't join in the party of making fun of Grandma J, and the fact that I didn't made me look like I was 'on her side.' Georgie said, "What's wrong with you? You act like you feel sorry for the old bitch." They started making fun of me for being sad about it. Alcee said, "Ya little stupid bastard! You must be retarded. You ain't got sense enough ta know when somebody's makin' fun of ya. The old bitch don't like you! Never did! Get over it! Ya don't need any of those mother-fuckers!" Then Grandma said, "Trennie, I don't appreciate you actin' like that. It hurts my feelings that you like that old bitch like you do. She ain't never done for you like I have." Then Alcee jumped back in. She said to my grandmother, "I told ya, that is the most despisable, ungrateful, spiteful, little bastard that ever set foot on this earth!" My uncles started calling me names and making fun of me. Everybody was laughing about me making Grandma J cry. I felt like she must hate me now. She had always been nice to me and I really liked her. I felt terrible about what I had done.

Later, after I was grown, one of her daughters told me that I broke her heart that day. She said, "It broke Mother's heart that day you came in the store and wouldn't speak to her. She kind of understood why you did that because you were just a kid. But you wouldn't speak to her that day and it like to have killed her. She did say that maybe it was because you were afraid Georgie would tell on you and you'd get into trouble. But she said Georgie used to talk her leg off when she came in by herself. She wondered about that." Whenever they made up, for short periods of time, Grandma J still took up for me. Not like she did before, but some. She seemed a little more cautious about doing so, but she still did it. At the time I thought it was because I hurt her so badly. Looking back now, I think maybe she just didn't want to rock the boat and be banished from our lives again, but it would happen again anyway. Maybe that's what I want to believe because I feel so guilty about hurting her so much. I didn't want to hurt her. The same thing happened to Dena a few years later. I know she felt bad about it too. Alcee and Dena ran into Grandma J at a drug store. Grandma saw Dena and whispered "hi" to her. Dena looked at her and took off down the aisle. Dena knew Alcee had moved just far enough away to catch her if she tried to speak to Grandma J. To this day I don't know if Grandma J ever knew that Alcee was lurking around a corner just waiting to catch Dena speaking to her. I hope she knew it wasn't Dena's decision to not speak to her. Just like it wasn't mine when I went into the store where she worked that time.

When Gordon told us to get in the car it *could* mean we were going to the quarry so he could swim. He usually met his brothers and sisters there. And they usually talked him into letting us kids get out of the car. They promised to keep an eye on us if he let us get out of the car. Most of his family was nice to us. None of them were mean to us, it's just that some of them were nicer than others. Trips to the quarry always ended up with us kids being scared and crying. Mostly the others cried, usually not me. Gordon would swim awhile and then start on us kids. We weren't doing anything to bother anyone. We just played in the dirt near the car. What else can you do at a quarry? But Gordon had to pick on us, scare us, make us cry and threaten us like a monster. He loved scaring me, he did it all the time. I remember one time he threw some of us in the quarry knowing that we couldn't swim. His brothers and sisters fished us out. He told his sister we could stand on one of the rocks that was just inches below the surface of the water. It was covered with moss and was too slippery to stand on. She said, "It's too slick, they can't stand on that." Then he sat Dana and me on the rock and told us to stand up. Gordon just cackled, he thought that was real funny watching us slide around on that rock. While we were sliding around on it I said, "Daddy we'll drown." He said, "Ya will if ya don't swim!" There was an iron bar or pipe, or something like that, sticking out of the rock. We tried to hold on to it, but we slid off the rock and into the deep water. While his sister and one of his brothers fished Dana and me out, he threw Dena in. He just threw her in. He just picked her up and threw her in the water! Obviously, one of them saved her too. I think he really scared one of his sisters that day. She got so angry at him, that they got into an argument. She said, “Are you that fuckin’ crazy? You could have drowned them! Do you hate those kids that much? What if one of them had hit their head? What in the hell is the matter with you?" He said, “Hey, yer the one that wanted ta drag the little bastards out o' the car. If they was in the car where they belong, they wouldn’t even be wet would they?" He said, “They can be in the car, or they can be in the water! Their choice!" She said, “No! They're not gettin’ in the car and they're not gettin’ in the water. And YOU are gonna leave ‘em alone!" He had this menacing sadistic smile, and in his almost whispering mocking voice, he told her, “We'll see." Then he kept asking us kids what we wanted to do. He was loud and drunk. He kept laughing his deep mean maniacal laugh and asking, “Do ya wanna get in the car or do ya wanna get back in the water?" I kept telling him and his sister that we wanted to get back in the car. I spoke for all of us kids. I was afraid if she kept arguing with him, he would get us kids again. We got in the car and he and his sister kept arguing. One of Gordon’s brothers kept getting between the two of them. She was really angry or scared or both. I heard her call him a sadistic son-of-a-bitch. I didn’t know what sadistic meant, but I could tell by the way she said it that it didn’t mean anything good. I had also heard Grandma call him that. Pretty soon we left and went back home. That night I asked Alcee what sadistic meant and she said, “That's what that mother-fucker I’m married to is."

One day Gordon told me to put the kids in the car. Then he said, “Put the dog in the car, too." I remember trying to figure out why we were taking our dog. I don’t remember what kind she was. I think she was just a mutt. She had short dark brown hair and her name was Cinnamon. She was a small dog. I think she was at least part short haired dachshund. It was too early in the day for Gordon and Alcee to play ‘dump Trena in the country.’ They always did that after dark. I think so it would be scarier. I wondered if we were going to dump Cinnamon. It was the first time he told me to put the dog in the car. I knew it couldn't be a good thing, but I didn't know how bad it was going to be either.

We drove to the quarry where he usually went swimming. When we got there Gordon told me to get Cinnamon and come with him. He opened the trunk and got out his gun. I don't know if it was a shot gun or rifle, but I think it was a shot gun. We walked around a little bend and we couldn't see the car. I'm glad the kids couldn't see us either. We got out of sight and Gordon said, "Put yer dog down." I said, "No! Why do ya have your gun? What are you gonna do?" He said, "What did I tell you to do? Let the fuckin' dog go!" I started crying and said, "No you're gonna hurt her! You're gonna kill her!" I started begging him to let her run away. I said, "Maybe somebody will find her and keep her. Maybe they'll like her." He was laughing and mocking me. He started screaming at me. He said, "Put the fuckin' dog down, right now! Nobody wants 'er, she's got mange. Ya didn't take care of her. Let the dog go!" I let her go and moved away from Gordon. Cinnamon started running around, sniffing everything like dogs do. She was standing in a spot of loose dirt, not far from a big rock. Gordon said, "Call yer dog." I was crying and shaking so hard that my knees literally knocked together. I felt like I was shaking apart. He said, "Say her goddamned name. Call yer fuckin' dog right now, ya little bitch!" Maybe he was just scaring me and we were going to pick her up and go home now. I said her name and she looked up at me. She was standing kind of sideways with her head turned and tilted to one side, looking at me. The gun went off. He shot her. He shot her in her side. Her little body lifted like someone had blasted a puff of air under her. She just lifted and fell back down on the dirt like a 'poof.' The loose dirt puffed up, too, just a little bit of it, like a small cloud of dust. She just laid there motionless, so still and quiet.

I was so sad. I was so scared. I don't even know what all I was feeling. I couldn't believe it, I was having trouble believing I was there. I kept hoping I was having a nightmare. I already hated Gordon and I wanted to hate him even more, but it was like I already hated him so much there was no more hate to conjure up. I wanted to pick up her body, but he wouldn't let me. Maybe somebody will find her and save her before the wolves get to her! We weren't even going to bury her? We were just going to leave her laying there? Thoughts were flying through my head so fast, like a movie on fast forward. I started begging. I was so panicked and I remember begging so fast that I'd be surprised if anyone would have been able to understand what I was saying. I was talking so fast that it was more babbling than talking. I remember putting my hands together under my chin and pleading with him. I did that a lot. Gordon seemed to get a kick out of it when I turned into a little spazz and begged real fast. I said so fast, "Daddy, the wolves might eat her! Maybe we can take her to the dog doctor! Please! I'll take care of her. Give me one more chance! The dog doctor can save her! Maybe she's not all the way dead! Daddy please! Daddy please!" But she *was* all the way dead. And Gordon didn't even care! He was still laughing, not as loud, but still laughing none the less. He laughed like it was funny that I didn't understand. Like some people would laugh because their child said something innocently cute. Like when they say 'yogret' instead of yogurt. It was like he didn't do anything wrong and it was so funny that I didn't get it. That I was being silly or dumb or making a mountain out of a molehill. He grabbed my hair and said, "Come 'ere I think ya got mange." Then he cackled and said, "Go over there and stand by that rock. Heh, heh, heh." You know, I was scared enough, he didn't have to do that. I didn't have any idea then, but looking back now, I wonder if I went into shock. I was crying and had the strangest feelings. To be honest I don't even know how many different emotions I felt that day.

When we went back to the car Alcee was just smirking at me. She had her hand under her chin and her head was half way hanging out the window. I wasn't crying, but I had been, and she just looked at me with this smirk, like 'gotcha' or something. I don't know what she meant by it. She didn't verbally say 'gotcha,' but I felt like that's what her mouth and eyes were saying to me without words. The kids asked where Cinnamon was and Gordon told them she ran away because we didn't take care of her.

I remember feeling embarrassed later. I felt embarrassed about acting so stupid and spazzing out. I felt like I did make a mountain out of a molehill. I felt like I had acted like an idiot. I felt like Gordon was just teasing me and I couldn't take a joke. What a big baby! I was crying and begging like a little fool! He could have shot me, then I would have had something to cry about! He could have shot one of the kids. Now, that would have been mean! I remember calling myself a big cry baby and telling myself to suck it up and get over it. He didn't do anything wrong. The dog would have suffered. Talk about making a mountain out of a molehill! Where is my brain? It's a dog! He could have been a little nicer, but that's just the way he was. And if I had taken care of her better, maybe she wouldn't have gotten mange. It was really my fault. I'm the one I should be mad at. It's just that I wasn't expecting it and it caught me off guard. The only thing he did wrong was making fun of me and laughing at me for thinking it was sad. And I threw a fit over it! Alcee is right, I am despisable. How *could* anybody like me? I am an easy kid to despise. I am rotten to the bone. I remember telling myself, "You *are* a little fittified idiot! You deserve anything you get, dummy! Mommy *should* have smothered you at birth. You *are* the most despisable little bastard that ever set foot on this earth!" I told myself not to throw anymore fits like that. What a big cry baby! I was so embarrassed and ashamed of the way I had acted at the quarry.

Cinnamon is not the only dog we took to the quarry. It happened several times. The next time we took a dog to the quarry he got away. He was still a pup and he wasn't at all like Cinnamon. He was a bigger dog with shaggy black and white hair. I sort of remember how I felt the second time Gordon said, "Put the kids in the car and get your dog." I felt kind of numb and dizzy, or tingly and light headed. It was a weird feeling. I know I must have felt something because I was shaking like a leaf, but even though I knew what was going to happen, I don't think I actually *felt* my emotions. If I did feel something I didn't acknowledge it. I just had this 'oh well' attitude. We went to the quarry and Gordon got out of the car. He told me to get the dog and 'come on.' When Gordon told me to let him go, I did. The dog got away. He took off like he knew he was doomed. He ran, more like bolted, between some rocks and disappeared. Gordon made me call him, but he didn't come back. He said I let the dog go too early and it was my fault that he would suffer now. He said, "He's got mange and he'll die miserable now! We 'cain't' even put 'im out of his misery!" He said it was the humane thing to do for animals, put them out of their misery. He said I needed to know that. Uh-huh, okay. Looking back, I wonder if the dog took off like a streak of lightning because he sensed something was wrong. I might not have acknowledged any of the emotions I had to have felt, but maybe I emitted a sense of danger to the dog. Maybe he felt scared because I did, even if I didn't know it.

I don't know how many months passed, but one day a dog came to our house that looked just like the puppy that got away, only bigger. He had the same markings and the same kind of hair, only he was not a puppy any more. Gordon said, "They say animals will always find their way home no matter how far ya take 'em. Goddamn if that ain't the same dog! I swear that's the same dog. It's even got a scar on it's head." Now, if that ***was*** the same dog, he obviously didn't die a miserable death from mange. I have thought about that for years. The dog was gone the next day. I asked where it was and Alcee said, "It took off. Why would it wanna stay here? You little bastards don't take care o' anything! It took off because it's got more sense than you do!" I never saw that dog again, but I don't believe it 'took off' on it's own. I don't remember his name. I remember him, but not his name. In fact, I don't remember any more names of the dogs that we had while I was young, except for one. We had another dog that looked just like Cinnamon and we named her Cinnamon, too. I remember the names of more dogs we had after I was thirteen or fourteen, but not while I was young.

The second Cinnamon got mange too, supposedly. Gordon said there was no cure for it. We took her to the quarry to 'put her out of her misery.' It was the humane thing to do, you know. Uh-huh. This time we took dog food so we could make her stand in one place while she met her fate. We did it that way every time after the puppy got away. It was my job to go dump the dog food on the spot where the first Cinnamon died. There were a lot of rocks around, but that spot was just a dry spot of loose light brown dirt. It was like powder. I know I had to be scared, hurt, angry, who knows how many other emotions, but I don't remember feeling them. Gordon said, "Put the dog food down and get back." I put the dog food down and got back. He always said, "If ya took care of 'em like yer supposed to, yer dogs wouldn't get mange." I don't know how many dogs got mange because I didn't take care of them. I don't know how many we took to the quarry and put out of their misery. As awful as it sounds, I think I got used to it. After the first Cinnamon was killed, it would be years before I bonded with another dog. That would be a mistake too.

When I was about thirteen or fourteen we lived out in the middle of nowhere. That's when Alcee learned to drive. Her brother gave her a dog that grew very protective of her. She had to call the dog off so Gordon could get in the bedroom at night because he would growl at him. She wouldn't let anything happen to that dog. She was as protective of that dog as that dog was of her. Gordon threatened to kill it a few times and she said, "My brother gave me that dog and you ain't touchin' it, you cock-sucker!" And he didn't. THAT dog NEVER got mange! Amazing. A year or so later, her brother gave her another dog. He said it was born on my birthday. It was a cute little beagle puppy. I felt pretty good about the beagle because my uncle gave it to us. I figured Alcee wouldn't let Gordon touch this dog either. And it was born on my birthday, it was fate. I kind of warmed up to the beagle and made it my dog. She was so sweet and cute. She was mostly white with some light brown spots. I fell in love with her and gave her a cute name, Sugar. Alcee said I couldn't keep her in the house, she had to stay outside. One day Alcee was leaving and when she backed up the car, Sugar was under the back tire. I heard her yelping and ran outside. I started crying, not a lot, but I did cry. I remember thinking I should have known better. It was my fault the dog was dead, I should have matched it up with one of the other kids. I shouldn't have made it my dog, I shouldn't have bonded with it, I shouldn't have fallen in love with it. I should have just believed it was passing through and would get mange. That's what I get, but I still felt sorry for the dog. Alcee said, "How was I supposed ta know the fuckin' dog was under my tire? I told ya to keep it put up! Shut up, ya rubber faced bitch and go dig a hole to bury it. You are the most dilatary son-of-a-bitch I've ever seen. You 'cain't' take care of a goddamned thing!" She meant 'dilatory,' but she always said 'dilatary.' I don't know if what happened to Sugar was intentional or not. Sometimes I believe it was, other times I believe it might have really been an accident because her brother gave us that dog. I will never know.

Anyway, you can see why '*Go Get In The Car*' didn't sound like much fun to us. Sometimes it meant we were going to sit in the car in a parking lot, while Gordon and/or Alcee went into a bar for a couple of drinks. That wasn't always totally bad, but it was always totally boring. But sometimes people would go in and buy pop and chips and bring it back out to us. They had to go ask Alcee or Gordon first or we couldn't accept it. Sometimes they said yes and sometimes they said no. Sometimes Alcee brought pop out to us. I know we sat in the car and waited for them for hours sometimes because the sun would be shining when they went in and it was dark when they came out. The little ones actually took naps in the car and woke up while we waited for them, or him. I hated sitting in the parking lots of bars. I remember sometimes it being so late when they came out that we had all fallen asleep. We went home and went straight to bed. I don't know what time it was. It was late.

I made sure Joey had nothing to dread when I told him to get in the car. Either he knew where we were going before we left, or it turned out to be a nice surprise for him. I loved watching him smile with anticipation when he didn't know where we were going, but he knew it would be something he liked. He would guess places he thought we were going, but I wouldn't confirm or deny. I loved seeing the excitement on his face when we pulled up to his favorite fast food restaurant or the movies as a surprise. One time I drove him and some of his friends to an amusement park over an hour away. Of course, all the parents knew we were going and helped keep the secret. It was a riot. I took a friend, Bea, with me and she couldn't believe how much fun, and how funny, those kids were. Those little boys guessed everything they could think of. They were so excited and chattered all the way there. I'll never forget the squeals and laughs when we pulled up to the gates of the park. It wasn't always a fun filled surprise trip, but I loved surprising him every once in a while. We also had boring trips to the grocery store, doctor's office or just running errands. But basically it was fun to go bye bye. He was singing along with the car radio before he was two years old. The point is, he had no fear or dread when he got in the car with me. My son has never been dumped in the country, he's never been taken somewhere and told to sit on the couch until I tell him he can move, he's never been made to sit in a car and wait for me and his pets have never been taken for a ride and slaughtered, neither in his presence, nor behind his back. When he was about five years old he had a goldfish that died. He was almost hysterical about his fish dying. While my husband took him to buy another goldfish, I buried the first one. I buried it in the back yard and marked it's grave with a rock. For years, Joey, and one of his little friends, periodically said prayers over the goldfish's grave. It was so sweet to watch those two little boys talk to that rock. They would go over and visit the fish and then go right back to playing baseball. I recently asked him if he remembers the goldfish, the rock is gone but he still remembers right where it was.

I didn't know why they kept getting dogs when it was inevitable what was going to happen to each and every one of them. I used to wonder why, but I couldn't figure it out. I used to think they got them because they thought they wanted them and then just got tired of them. Alcee and Gordon always said the dogs got mange because is kids didn't take care of them. There is no way ***all*** of those dogs had mange. Even if that were true, I think even back then mange was curable. I couldn't figure it out. Then at some point I decided that maybe they were just mean, but now I think it even goes beyond that. After my therapist explained what recreational abuse is, I thought about it again and I believe that's what the dogs were used for, too. I think it was another game of recreational abuse and the dogs were merely game pieces, just like a Monopoly game has game pieces, the dog, the car and the shoe. Only in this particular game of 'recreational abuse' Gordon and Alcee ***bought*** some of their game pieces and ***bred*** the others. The dogs, the car and us kids were the game pieces for ***this*** game, real cars, real dogs and baby factory babies. The little ones couldn't see what was going on from the car, but they knew. One of them told me after we grew up that it wasn't hard to figure out.

I would be in my thirties before I bonded with another dog, my son's beagle. He is white with light brown spots and he has been Joey's best friend for almost fifteen years. He is as sweet as Sugar was, his name is Buster. It took years for me to let him into my heart, but he's there. Even after he captured my heart, I never let anyone see how much I loved him. I wasn't mean or hateful to him, just indifferent when anyone was watching. When he was a pup and I was home alone with him, I pet him and played with him. I wouldn't do that when anyone was around because I didn't want anyone to know I liked him. I just gave the impression that I didn't care if I had a dog or not, I only got him for my son. He's just a dog. From the first night we brought him home, I had Joey feed him and take care of him. I wanted the dog to bond with him. I matched them up. I remember telling Joey not to let him on the furniture. The very first night at our house I put blankets down on the floor so Buster could sleep next to Joey's bed. I felt so sorry for the puppy. It was his first night away from his mother and he kept whimpering and whimpering. Finally the whimpering stopped. I went in Joey's room to check on them and see if they had both fallen asleep. What I saw was beautiful and funny. Picture this, Buster was in the bed on my six year old son's chest, my son's eyes were squinted shut so very tight and his nose was wrinkled up. He was pretending to be asleep. It was so precious. Now that was a Kodak moment. As soon as I saw those two in that bed, I knew the furniture rule was null and void. From that night on Buster has slept where ever he wants to sleep.

I know everyone thinks their pet, what ever it may be, is the best in the world. But Buster was surely heaven sent. Not only for Joey, but for me. I really believe that. He has the sweetest disposition, the cutest face, the saddest brown eyes, the cuddliest hair and even a good sense of humor. Do you think I'm being silly? It's all true. My dog has a sense of humor. I have to believe, okay maybe I just want to believe, he was heaven sent because I wasn't with Joey the night he picked Buster out of the litter he came from. He and his dad went out to buy a beagle. When my son carried him into the house that night, it was like a reincarnation of Sugar. I had never told him or my husband about Sugar, and they picked one out of the litter that looked just like her. Oh yeah, he was heaven sent. He's almost fifteen years old and I tear up every time I think about him not being here. That's pretty old for a dog. It will be very hard on me and my son when Buster passes on. I promise, as long as I have a breath left in me, it will be from natural causes. And when *he* is 'all the way dead' from natural causes, his remains will be handled with respect and love. My son will grieve and I will comfort him. And *I* will grieve for my son's grief, for Buster and for all the dogs I ever loved, or *wanted* to love, after I ……

'got used to it.'

CHAPTER EIGHT

Mommy, Would You Miss Me?

Alcee was constantly threatening to part company with us kids. As stupid as it sounds the thought of her being gone terrified me. One of her favorite threats was to call the orphanage and send us all off. I wouldn't see the babies because they kept them in a different room, remember that one? She said I didn't care because I was lazy and didn't want to take care of them anyway. Another one of her favorite threats was, "I'm gonna get on a bus after you little filthy bastards go ta sleep tonight, and when ya wake up tomorrow, I'll be so fuckin' far gone ya never will find me!" I used to try to stay awake all night so I could beg her to stay when she tried to leave. Sometimes I fell asleep and when I woke up I was so scared. I remember thinking, 'Oh no! I fell asleep! She's probably gone!' As soon as my eyes opened I started telling myself how worthless I was because I fell asleep. Then I jumped up and tried to find my mother, hoping she hadn't left us while we were sleeping. She said, "I don't care what happens to you bunch o' little worthless snot nosed bastards! They can give you to the fuckin' gypsies for all I care! The way youins all do me! I won't miss a goddamned single one of ya." It scared me so bad. I just knew that one day I was going to wake up and she would be gone. She sounded convincing. Sometimes she told me, "You and Dana can go live with my family and the rest o' the little son-of-a-bitches can live with Gordon's people. You'll never see me again! But you don't care!" I begged her over and over to stay. I said, "Mommy please don't go away! I'll help you more. I'll take care of the kids. I'll do the dishes. I'll do the laundry. I'll do *anything* you say, but please, please, please stay. I don't want you to go! Mommy please! I'll miss you. Don't go. I promise I'll be good!" She got a kick out me begging too. She and Gordon both loved it when I begged, I could see it in their eyes. It made Gordon chuckle and it made Alcee's face relax. They loved it. They looked satisfied, content.

The thing is, I always knew that she didn't care if I was there or not. Except for the work I could do, I had no value, and neither did the other kids. I believed she was doing us kids a favor by staying. It *was* a favor! Why else would she live such a miserable life and stay because of us? It was a *big* favor. I was no good, just like my real dad, I couldn't help it because it was in my blood. I was already so ugly when I was born that she had to hide me under the covers so the other mothers wouldn't make fun of her for having such an ugly baby. Then I made myself even uglier because I cried so much when I was a baby that I stretched my 'rubber face' out of shape. I didn't do my job most of the time because it seemed like there was always a baby crying. The house wasn't as clean as it should be because I was lazy. Sometimes the kids got hurt because I didn't watch them close enough. She said I embarrassed the hell out of her every time she turned around. I was afraid to fight and that made me cowardly and shamed the whole family. It's no wonder she wanted to smother me at birth, she should have. I was about as worthless as anyone could be. I felt sorry for her for having to be my mom, she deserved better than the likes of me. But at least I could work like a horse. Maybe if I did more to help her, she would stay for the other kids. God knew I was worthless and they needed more than just me. And if I was nicer to her, maybe she wouldn't feel so bad about me being ugly and stupid. She used to say, "You ain't got sense enough ta pour piss out of a boot with the directions on the heel." I would work harder and faster, so she wouldn't have so much to do. I would also be nicer and wait on her hand and foot. Anything she wanted. Anything to get her to stay. God, please don't let her go. She always said, "Other kids don't do their mommies like you do me! That's why they like 'em! If my kids was good ta me, I might like 'em, too! But no, you little worthless bastards are bound and determined ta make my life miserable!" I was bound and determined to show her how good I could be and how much I could do for her.

I even went to the laundry for her, even though it took me all day to shuttle the clothes back and forth. If we had enough money I would wash them *and* dry them at the laundry. If we didn't have enough money, she washed them at home on an old wringer washer, and I carried them to the laundry to dry them. Other times she loaded up a laundry basket and told me to go put those dirty clothes in the washer and bring back the empty basket. I did. She loaded the basket again and I took those and put them in the washer, put the first load in the dryer and took the empty basket back again. When the first load was dry I folded them, took them home and then went back. I shuttled the clothes between the washer, dryer and home, until they were all done. It was harder if she washed them at home because the clothes were heavier when they were wet. I couldn't carry as many and I had to make more trips. I started doing this when I was about six and did this the whole time we lived in the alley, about seven years. One time, while I was still pretty small, maybe six years old at most, I was washing the clothes and something was in the pocket of a pair of Gordon's pants. It was half in and half out of his pant pocket, so I picked it up and it looked like a balloon. I checked his pockets and found more. They looked like balloons. I had no idea what I was doing, I was little. I blew it up and it was huge. It was the biggest balloon I had ever seen. The old woman who ran the laundry came over and told me to give it to her. She asked if there were any more. I said yes and she took them all. I was going to give them to the little ones and she took them all! She put them in a little brown bag and told me to take them home. I didn't understand. She had always been nice to me and now she didn't want me to play with the balloons? I wasn't hurting anyone. Sometimes, if she wasn't too busy, she even helped me with my laundry. I thought I had taken advantage of her by playing. Here she was nice enough to help me sometimes and I was just playing around, like I didn't have work to do. I thought she was mad at me for taking advantage of her. That's what I get! I shouldn't have been playing around, when there was work to be done! I felt stupid and lazy. Now she probably wouldn't like me anymore, either.

When I took the next load home, Alcee was waiting for me and she was mad. The old woman at the laundry had called her and told her what I had done. I was so upset because I didn't think she would tell on me for playing a little bit. I had to wait for the clothes to dry anyway. I felt so betrayed. She had always been nice to me. That's what I get for accepting favors. I took advantage of her. As soon as I walked in the front door, Alcee screamed "Come 'ere!" and she grabbed my hair and jerked my head up. I dropped the laundry basket. She said, "Ya little stupid son-of-a-bitch! Everybody in that laundry is laughin' at you! Where did you get these? Do you know what they are? Do ya?" I said, "They were in Daddy's pocket. I thought they were for us kids." I was little, I didn't know. Alcee said, "It ain't good enough that you drive me crazy, is it? You gotta go to the fuckin' laundry and blow up rubbers! Where is yer fuckin' mind?" They were condoms! She kept hitting me and cussing me. I still didn't know what she meant by 'rubbers.' I said, "I don't want the balloons. I won't do it again." She jerked me around by my hair and pushed me to the floor. She raised her foot up and held it over my face like she was going to stomp on me. She said, "I could squash you like a fuckin' bug! Ya little fittified bastard! They ain't balloons! They're what yer goddamned daddy uses ta fuck his whores!" Then she swooped down, grabbed my haïr and jerked me back up on my feet. She picked me up by my hair with one hand and hit me in the face with her other hand. The whole time she hit me, screamed and cussed at me; I cried. I thought she was mad at me for playing around at the laundry. I had just promised her that I would be good if she would stay with us. Now she probably wished she *had* gotten on the bus. I was so sorry. I told myself what Alcee had already told me hundreds of times, that I *knew* better, I just didn't *do* better; that it would serve me right if she did leave. It would serve me right if she sent me to the orphanage. I messed up again! I couldn't be like other kids and be nice to my mother. I was rotten! Just like she said. I didn't blame her for not liking me. I just couldn't seem to mind her. I was in trouble all the time and it was because I was stupid and rotten. When Gordon got home he jumped on me too. He smacked me on the side of the head and said, "You just love to cause trouble don't 'cha? What did ya do that for? Huh?

I asked you a question! Answer me! What did ya do that for?" He kept smacking me in the face and on the side of my head as he screamed at me. I answered with my usual, pathetic little, "I don't know." By then I had already figured out that I got beat the same no matter what my answer was. "I don't know" was as good as any other. Years later, when I figured out that the 'rubbers' were condoms, I knew what they were so mad about. I brought it up to Alcee one time when I was a teenager. I said, "I was so little. How could I have known what they were? They looked like big balloons to me." She said, "That's when he was fuckin' around with ______. You went to school with her daughter and I thought they put ya up to it. I know'd he wasn't usin' 'em at home. It don't make no difference anyway. You didn't get anything you didn't deserve, Worthless. I'm sure ya did somethin' ta deserve gettin' the piss beat out of ya'." You know, I was totally innocent in blowing up the condoms. They didn't have to beat on me and scream all day and half the night. But now when I look back on the 'rubbers' incident, I can't help but smile because Gordon got caught. I didn't mean to do it, it was totally innocent on my part, but he got caught! I remember they had a big fight that night and he left. Alcee said he was going to be with one of his whores. I knew it was all my fault then, but it was years later before I realized what was really going on.

I was a nervous wreck all the time. I just knew every time I messed something up, that Alcee was going to leave in the middle of the night. I remember sneaking up and creeping around the house to see if she was still there. Whenever she caught me she said, "I know you ain't asleep yet. Go ta sleep, so I can get the fuck out of here. I'll be gone in the morning, Worthless! The orphanage is gettin' yer room ready! Ha ha ha." Sometimes she sang, "Please don't talk about me when I'm gone." The she laughed and said, "You little mother fuckers are gonna miss me. But I won't miss you, not a goddamned single one of ya!" I knew we would miss her and it bothered me that she wouldn't miss us. I just worked harder and harder to prove to her that she needed me. I knew she didn't want me, but if I could make her need me she might stay. I did anything and everything to please her. I even ironed. I had to stand on a chair, so I could reach the ironing board. Either it didn't adjust low enough, or I didn't have sense enough to adjust it, but I stood on a chair to reach it. I used a clothes sprinkler that was just a pop bottle of water with a little cork plug and holes in the end of a metal cone. You had to sprinkle the clothes and then iron them dry. What kind of a job could I have done? At the time, it seemed like I did a good job. But I can't imagine that a child that young could do a good job ironing. Alcee showed me how. She taught me to iron the button strips and collars of shirts first, then the shoulders, front and back in that order. And I can iron clothes like a professional now, so maybe I did okay. I tried to iron at night after I got the little ones in bed, but sometimes I cheated and ironed while they were up. One time the baby grabbed the cord and pulled the iron off the ironing board. I think it was Tim. He yanked the cord and the iron fell off the board and on his head. Besides having a knot on his head he also had a burn on his forehead. I got in trouble for that one. I wasn't standing at the ironing board when he did it, but I must have been ironing because it was set up and the iron was hot. I don't know where I was, but once again, I knew better and didn't do better. Alcee said, "Why weren't you watchin' 'im?" I whined, "I was tryin' to." She said, "Ya little lyin" bitch! He might die because you were too busy playin' instead o' doin' what yer supposed to be doin'! You let him do that on purpose, ya mean little bitch! You want him to die, don't 'cha? Well, if he does, I'm gonna kill you! You mean whiny little bastard." I remember asking myself, when I would ever learn to do *what* I was told, *when* I was told and *how* I was told to do it. I remember telling myself, "Mommy's right. I'm just mean as a snake and I can't even control it. I'm just rotten to the core, bad to the bone." I didn't know why she stayed with us. She was too good for us.

I remember one time when we went to pick Alcee up from work. Gordon told me to go in and tell her we were waiting for her in the parking lot. This lady she worked with came up to me and said,

"You must be Trena! Your mommy talks about you all the time. She said you are her right arm. She told me you iron her uniforms. You do a good job. If I bring mine over will you iron mine?" I said, "*My* mommy said that?" She said, "Oh, she talks about you all the time." She was so nice and smiled at me. After we got home I told my mother that the lady at the restaurant was nice. She said, "Well don't get the big head, idiot! She don't know the truth! What am I supposed ta tell people about you ungrateful bunch o' bastards? I have ta lie to people 'cause I'm too ashamed ta tell the truth! How worthless ya are! She's tellin' shit that she don't know nothin' about. Maybe she'd like ta take ya and keep ya. After a day or two she'd pay me ta take ya back! Ya think yer special? Well you ain't! You oughtta consider yourself lucky that I covered yer little worthless ass!" That certainly took the fun out of someone being nice to me. I was actually glad that the woman didn't know how bad I was. I thought it was nice of Alcee not to tell her how mean and rotten I really was. At least the whole world didn't have to know. I felt bad that she had to lie for me. She must have really been embarrassed and ashamed. I felt so sorry that she had *me* for a kid. God should have given me to a monster, that's what I deserved. I remember thinking, when the other mothers bragged on their kids it must have made Alcee feel bad. That's why she made up good stuff about me, because she was so embarrassed and ashamed. I felt sorry for my mother for having such a hideous kid, me.

I remember telling myself to stop playing around, work harder and do things *right.* I told myself that I had to stop thinking the world owed me a living. That's what Alcee used say. She said, "You think the world owes you a livin'? Well it don't. You ain't nothin' special! Yer a stack o' shit, just like the rest of these little bastards runnin' around here." I believed her. There was nothing special about me. There were horrible things about me, meanness, stupidity and worthlessness to name just a few, but I wouldn't call those things special. I told myself that I had to get over it, overcome it and learn to behave. But I just kept messing up.

One day, I was outside watching the kids and I guess temptation to play took over because I started playing on a tree branch. It was a small tree. I grabbed a branch, picked up my feet and started swinging on it. I was still watching the kids. I thought I could watch them and play at the same time. While I was swinging on the branch, I saw my mother looking out her bedroom window. She was standing back like she didn't want anyone to see her. It was like she was sneaking a look out the window. When I saw her, I thought I would be in trouble and I let go of the branch, but she didn't come running out. I acted like I didn't see her and walked away from the tree. I knew she would be mad if she knew I had seen her. After a minute or so I walked back over to the tree, and looked out of the corner of my eye to see if she was still there peeking out the window. She was. I felt like I had been caught doing something wrong, but she didn't act mad. I thought it must be okay if I played on the tree because I knew she saw me and didn't yell at me. Like the fittified idiot that Alcee had called me so many times, I grabbed the branch again and started swinging on it like a little monkey. I remember feeling like I was showing off. Well, I *was* showing off. I remember thinking 'Mommy's watching. She'll see how big I am! Look what I can do! I can swing like a monkey with one arm.' I was showing off, I must have thought it was cute or something. I was probably around eight years old and one would think I would have known better by then. I got so wrapped up in swinging on that tree branch that I didn't even see her coming. All of a sudden, she was there! She was right on top of me. She just appeared in what seemed like an instant. She started screaming, "Do you like that tree? Do ya?" I said, "No" and started backing away from the tree. She snapped a switch off the tree and started beating me with it. She grabbed one of my arms and kept hitting me on the legs with the switch. I couldn't get away, she had my arm. I tried to squat down so she couldn't hit my bare legs, but she kept hitting me where ever the switch landed. I know I got hit on my neck, arm and back a few times. She jerked me back up by my arm and beat my legs with it more. The whole time she kept screaming, "Do ya like that fuckin' tree? Do ya? Huh? How do ya like it now?" I kept saying "no" and crying. I remember telling myself that I shouldn't have been showing off. I shouldn't have been playing. I should have been doing my job and watching the kids. What if one of them got hurt while I was playing around on that tree? When would I learn? I guessed never. I told myself how stupid I was to think I could be cute swinging on that tree branch. I told myself that there was nothing cute about me. I asked myself, "Where is your mind?" I said, "That's what I get." After all, she gave me a chance by not jumping on me the first time she saw me on the tree. I blew it. After I was off the hook, I went back and got on the tree again.

Have you ever been beaten with a switch? It really hurts. It makes welts on your skin and it stings like you wouldn't believe. Sometimes it scratches your skin and burns for days, depending on how green or stiff the switch is. If it has already turned brown, it is more likely to scratch your skin. If it is still green, it's more flexible and makes welts. It makes a sound when it comes at you, a 'woosh' sound. It's awful. You hear the 'woosh' and feel the pain almost instantly. Then you hear the 'woosh' again while that hit is still stinging. I would never do that to anyone. It hurt so bad that even after I got bigger, no matter how hard I tried not to cry, I did anyway. That was usually if I was getting it again before the welts or scratches from a previous beating had healed. I couldn't help it. It was extremely painful. It felt like my skin was being split open. The next time I took a bath, all the welts or scratches burned like paper cuts with salt in them. When they started to heal, they itched. I used to scratch them and then sometimes they got scabs. My uncles used to call me 'walking planet' because I looked like I had craters on my legs. When ever I got beat with a switch, I could expect more trouble when Gordon got home. As soon as he saw me and my legs he said, "You been showin' yer ass?" I always whined my little pathetic, "I don't know." If I said "no" I got beat for lying, as well as, what ever I had done wrong. He said, "What did you get your legs striped for if you don't know?" Sometimes he 'beat my ass' and sometimes he just knocked me around a little bit by smacking me in the head and pushing me around the house.

To this day, I don't know why me playing on that tree set her off. Sometimes I think she just couldn't stand to see me showing off. You know how sometimes a kid thinks they are doing something big or cute? You can tell by watching them that they are just full of themselves, proud or something like that; I think it's a good thing. I loved it when my child showed off. It showed me that he was proud of himself and had some self esteem. I pumped him up even more when he showed off. I made a big deal out of it. I wanted him to know and feel like he was cute and special. I *still* want him to know and feel like he's cute and special because he is. Maybe Alcee didn't want me to feel that way. I can't think of any other reason that might have set her off that day. She said I was ugly, and stupid and it must have made her sick to watch me act like I wasn't.

It was like us kids had no value at all. We were a burden and we were lucky *anyone* let us breathe the same air that real people breathed. We were nothing but trouble. No one would miss us if we fell off the face of the earth. But on the other hand, Alcee and Gordon were ready to fight if someone looked at us cross eyed. Like one time this neighbor man got mad because us kids picked up apples that fell off his tree and into the alley. He didn't want us to pick them up, he said those were his apples. Sometimes when he wasn't home, I went up in his yard and picked them up there, too. He must have known about it because one night he came out and said, "If I catch you kids in my yard, I'll knock the tar outta ya's!" We went running in the house and told Alcee. Gordon was home and he heard us. He came outside and called the guy out of his house. He said, "My kids don't go in yer fuckin' yard, but if they do you ain't gonna touch 'em or yer ass belongs ta me!" The man snapped a switch off the very apple tree that we took apples from and said, "Really? Send one of 'em up here." Gordon said, "Trena, walk up in his yard." I was scared. I said, "No, I don't want to. He's gonna whip me." Gordon said, "Get yer ass up in his yard, right now!" Oh God! I was a nervous wreck. I didn't want to. Gordon took off his belt and screamed at me, "Get yer goddamned ass up in his yard or *I'll* whip yer ass! Get up there!" The man was standing there with his arms folded across his chest and had a switch in one of his hands. He was just daring me to set one foot in his yard. Gordon was shaking his belt at me and ordering me to go in his yard. I was shaking like a leaf. Who was I more scared of? Gordon. I kept inching toward his yard, while Gordon yelled at me to go up there. The man didn't move. I kept slowly inching closer and closer. When I got to the edge of his yard, I ran up there really fast and ran back out. The man lunged toward me and I heard the 'woosh' sound of the switch, but he missed me. Gordon went after him and they got into a fist fight. I don't know who called the police, but somebody must have because they came to our house. By the time they got there the fight was over and we were inside. Gordon went to the door and told them he didn't know what they were talking about. I don't know what happened after that. But stuff like that confused me because if we were so worthless why did they bother to defend us against anybody? I think we were like possessions, like kids' toys. It was like 'you can't play with it, it's mine.' I think it was like a kid protecting their plastic doll if someone else wanted to play with it. They could throw the doll down on the floor, put it under the bed or toss it in the bottom of the closet. But if someone else wanted to play with that doll the answer was 'No, it's mine!' It was so confusing. So there were times I felt protected by them, but I never felt protected *from* them.

No matter how bad things got, I still tried to do everything possible to get Alcee to like me. I told her she looked like a movie star. I rubbed her feet and legs at night. I dabbled the dirty diapers for her because she hated doing that. I hated it too, but I did it anyway. I had to dip the diapers in and out of the toilet until all the #2 was rinsed off of them and then wring them out and put them in the diaper pail. I did that for *her*. I told her she sang pretty, when she sang along with the radio. I went to the station and bought pop for her and I didn't drink out of it. When she sent me to the store, I sneaked candy bars in for her, so the kids wouldn't see them and cry for them, I didn't even ask her if I could have some of it. When she came home from work, I told her I missed her while she was gone. I told her I loved her every day. She never said that to any of her kids, not once. She didn't hesitate to tell us daily, how much she hated us and wouldn't miss 'a goddamned single one' of us if we weren't there. But she ***never*** said she loved us. One time I asked her about it. I was older, in my teens. I had lived with foster parents and then been sent back to her. But I had figured out that everybody didn't live the way we did and everybody didn't treat their kids like she treated us. She made fun of me for even asking. I said, "Mom, do you realize that you have never said 'I love you' to any of us kids?" She said. "Well, excuse me if I didn't tilt yer little heads back every morning and say 'I love you ya little mean bastard." She laughed at me and mocked me. She told me we should consider ourselves lucky that she didn't smother us at birth. She said that's what she should have done.

When I was in second grade one of my classmates died. I can't remember why he died, but it seems like it was from a ruptured spleen or appendix. The memory of why isn't that vivid, but what happened after he died is. The school arranged for our class to go to the funeral home and pay our respects. I was sick and didn't go to school that day. I remember being so worried that Nicky's mother would think I didn't like him. I didn't want her to think that because I did like him, he was nice. By the time I went back to school, the funeral was over and everything was supposed to be back to normal. Nicky's mother sent a thank you card to our class thanking us for our cards. That's how I knew the class had made cards and sent them to her. I hadn't made one because I wasn't there when they did that. That night I went passed their house on the way home from school. I went up to the door and knocked. When his mother answered the door I said, "I'm sorry I didn't go to see Nicky, I was sick." She teared up and said, "That's okay honey."

When I got home I told Alcee that Nicky's mother cried. She said, "She probably cried 'cause he didn't treat her the way you little bastards treat me! She's probably *sorry* her kid died." The way she said the word 'sorry' made me think she wouldn't be sorry if I died. I felt awful. I remember thinking that *nobody* would be sorry if I died, not even my mother. I think I felt scared, but I was never good at identifying feelings, so I'm not sure if it was fear or hurt. What ever it was didn't feel good. She was always saying she wouldn't miss us if she left us, or sent us off, but what if one of us died? I remember going back and forth in my mind, ask her, no don't ask. Yes, ask her, no don't ask! I should have left well enough alone, but no, I had to ask. I wanted her to say she would miss me. I was so afraid she would say that she wished I was dead. She had said it before when she was mad at me, but I still had a shred of hope that she didn't really mean it, that maybe she only said it before because she was mad at me. She wasn't mad at me right now and I wanted to know. I worked up my nerve and did it. I remember almost whispering the question and being afraid of the answer. I asked her, I mumbled the question, "Mommy, if *I* died, would you miss *me*? Would you cry?" She said, "What would I have ta cry about? I'd have one less mouth ta feed!" Then she started laughing and said, "No, I'm just kiddin'. I probably would cry 'cause I'd have ta come up with the money ta bury yer little worthless ass. Course, I could always just stick a ham bone up yer ass and let the dogs drag ya off." Then she laughed again. I got my answer and I felt like crying. She wouldn't miss me if I died. Nicky's mom missed him, but my mom wouldn't miss me. She would even be glad to have one less mouth to feed. She wouldn't even cry, unless she had to spend money to bury me? Her answer broke my heart and gave me nightmares. I dreamed that a pack of dogs was dragging me up the alley and I was naked. Everybody thought I was dead, but I wasn't. One time, I told her what I had dreamed and she said, "Some people's dreams come true" and laughed at me.

Some people might think what a cry baby I must have been. If they said something like that to their child, would the child know they were just kidding? On one hand, I do feel like a cry baby, on the other hand, I would ***never*** say something like that to a child, any child. But looking back, I remember it was the school year after I worked at the restaurant for Raymond and I think I was having emotional problems anyway. I was in the second grade. Maybe I was too little and weak and I just couldn't take it. I think I must have been as fragile as blown glass. It devastated me. I felt sad. I felt so alone, not just lonely, but alone.

I was convinced I wasn't worth loving, but if I tried harder maybe she could just like me. I just wanted a kind word every now and then. I wanted someone to say I couldn't help being the way I was and it would be okay. I wanted someone to say *I* would be okay. Instead, I was ridiculed, mocked and threatened when I cried. I was humiliated, intimidated and verbally and/or physically beaten almost every day for being mean and stupid. I was even pimped out for fifty cents a day at the age of seven. I know I wasn't an angel, I couldn't have been, but what could I have possibly done by that age to deserve that? I had only been alive for a few years, how could I have been bad enough to generate that much hate in such a short time? Alcee told me many times, "You smile just like your goddamned daddy. Every time I look at you, I see the biggest mistake I ever made." Was that it? She hated me because I looked like my dad? How was that my fault? It didn't make sense, Dana looked more like our real dad than I did and they didn't beat her and say she smiled like him. Other people told me I looked just like my mother, not my father. Maybe it didn't have to be *anybody's* fault, maybe that's just the way it was. I wanted someone to say it wasn't my fault that I looked like my dad. I wanted someone to say that it was even *okay* to look like my dad, if I did. I tried so hard to please her. I tried everything I could think of to make myself valuable, to get her to like me. I wanted to matter to somebody. I wanted to know that if I died someone would miss me and cry.

There's an old saying that Alcee used to say all the time, 'you play the hand you're dealt.' I tried to do the best I could with the hand I was dealt, but there's only so much you can do with a losing hand. No matter how good you are, if it's a losing hand you are going to lose. And if you are a little kid and your mother tells you she wouldn't miss if you died, you were dealt a losing hand. No matter how hard you try, you lose.

CHAPTER NINE

Getting Bigger and Stronger

We would continue to live in the alley until I was out of fifth grade. The older I got, the more I had to do. By the time I was in fourth and fifth grade there weren't enough hours in the day to get everything done. Probably because the older I got the more kids I had to take care of. I even started taking the kids to the doctor when they were sick. I had already been taking myself to the doctor for years. I either walked or took a cab, depending on what Alcee said to do. There was never any time to back up and regroup, there was no recovery time between the incidents of screaming and fighting. Actually, there was no 'in between' to the chaos at all, it was constant. It was like it never stopped for a minute. It was overwhelming.

I think I have so many memories of that place because more than half of the years I would spend in the same house with Gordon and Alcee were spent in the house in the alley. Most of the memories are bad ones. I know that there are a lot of people out there who had it worse than we did. It's not like we were locked in a shed and starved to death. They didn't put cigarettes out on our bodies, they didn't hold our hands over the flame of a stove or cut us up and dump us in a field. But they told us stories about those things and it scared the hell out of us. When Alcee read those stories to me from a newspaper, and said, "See you ain't mistreated! But ya will be if you keep on," it was scary. We had food to eat, and we had a roof over our head. It was a leaky roof, but a roof none the less. It was what went on under that roof that turned the baby factory babies into emotional midgets. I don't remember a single day that at least one of us wasn't beaten and called names. Somebody got it *everyday.* Like I said before, I thought everybody lived like we did. When you are little, you only know what you've been told and what you see in the world you are confined to. I didn't know it was that bad. Even today, I sometimes tell myself that it wasn't *that* bad. It's just very hard for a person to accept that they were so hated as a child. At least it is for me. I think I came to realize how bad it really was after I had my own child. I can't imagine doing the things to him, or saying the things to him, that were done and said to me and my brothers and sisters. I think back and remember how cute and sweet they were when they were babies. They were called the same names I was called and none of them were ugly or stupid. Dana was as mean as the devil, but she was cute. None of the others were as mean as she was, they were just kids. And they were all cute, too.

When I was in second grade my mother asked me if I still believed in Santa Clause. I remember being at the in between stage of being afraid not to believe and believing. I suspected there wasn't a Santa, but I was afraid to say it because if there was it might make him mad and he wouldn't bring me anything. She said, "Well, yer old enough ta know that there ain't no friggin' Santa Clause." She said I could stay up with her on Christmas Eve and help her 'trick the little ones' and put their stuff out so they would think Santa came. She said that would be part of my Christmas, being able to help her. I still got something for Christmas, but now that I didn't believe anymore, it wasn't the same. I remember Christmas morning watching the kids get so excited about Santa leaving them toys. I felt kind of sad. Alcee said I was being a big baby and having a pity party for myself. She said she told me because I was too big to believe anymore and other kids would make fun of me. She said, "I did you a fuckin' favor! But do you appreciate it? Fuck no you don't! Yer a greedy, ungrateful little bastard!" I remember when my little boy told me he knew about Santa. I cried. He was fine with it, but I cried because I knew the magic was gone for him. I would never have told him. He heard it at school. I remember thinking there goes the Easter Bunny and Tooth Fairy too. He smiles now because Santa and the Easter Bunny still come to our house. Wink, wink. Last Christmas he chuckled and said, "Mom, I'm over twenty years old." I said, "Hey, like I have any control over Santa. He does what he wants to do." I love it. Sometimes I tease him and say that I refuse to confirm that vicious rumor about Santa not being real. I would have never told him. Even in a good childhood the magic is gone too quickly.

The next year, third grade, I got a bicycle for Christmas. It was like gold to me. It was the nicest present I had ever gotten. That made up for the Christmas before, as far as I was concerned. It's the same bicycle that I was riding Georgie on when I fell and broke my nose. I loved my bicycle. I could ride it to the store if I knew I wouldn't have too much to carry. I could ride it up and down the alley while I watched the kids. I loved it, but not for long. That Spring I was outside riding it in the alley and two men pulled up and told me to get off my bike. I started screaming for Alcee and peddled to the front door as fast as I could. Alcee came out and told me to get off the bike. She started cussing the two men and told them the bike was a 'piece of shit' anyway. They repossessed my bicycle! She charged it at Christmas time and didn't pay for it. They came to my house, made me get off my bike and took it away! I was so upset I started crying. Alcee told me to 'shut the fuck up' before my face froze that way. I was crying and said, "Now I don't have a bike." She said, "Well ain't you pitiful? Maybe you'll get another one when ya learn to mind." I will never forget the name of that store, and I'll never spend a dime there. I know my mother should have paid for the bike. I know they had a right to repossess it. But I just can't get over them making me get off my bike and taking it away. I was heartbroken. I wish they had sneaked around and stolen it back, at least I wouldn't have known what happened. I would have thought it was my fault for not hiding it good enough or something. The bike was the only thing that was exclusively mine because I was the only one big enough to ride it. Everything else that was brought into that house for *any* of us kids was for *all* of us kids. I wouldn't have another bicycle until I was married and in my late twenties. It was after I had Joey. I got a bicycle and a baby carrier so I could take him on bike rides. Even though I'm good about paying my bills, I didn't charge the bike, I paid cash for it. My son always had a bicycle, too. He had several bikes between the time he was old enough to ride one and the time he was old enough to drive. None of them were repossessed and he always knew they were his for keeps.

Gordon used to make me sweep the yard while we lived there. It was a small yard, more like a little ring of dirt around the house. The landlords had built the little shack of a house in their back yard, at the corner of the two alleys that ran beside and behind their house. With all of us kids being locked outside most of the day during the summer, we pretty much killed any grass that tried to grow there. When cars went through either alley the tires kicked gravel into our yard, so our yard was just dirt and gravel. Gordon told me to take the broom out and sweep the yard. He told me to sweep the gravel back out to the alley and pick up any papers or trash that was in it. I did what I was told. I remember one time, he kept saying I didn't sweep the yard because he couldn't see the broom strokes in the dirt. I did sweep the yard. I swept the gravel out to the alley and picked up any paper or trash I found. It was so dusty, he had to know that I did what he told me to do. But he came outside after I was done and said, "Come 'ere. What did I tell you ta do?" I whined pathetically, as usual, "Sweep the yard, and I did." He said, "How's come I cain't see the broom marks? I don't think you did like I told ya to do." The dust looked like a dust bowl storm in the plains during a drought. He *had to know* I did what he told me to do. He and Alcee had even closed the windows so the dust wouldn't go into the house. I told him I would do it again and he said to come and get him when I was done so he could look at it. I swept the yard again and made sure I raised even more dust so I could prove it. It was dry and windy that day and every time I swept the broom through the dirt, the wind blew dirt over it and covered up the broom marks. I thought if I swept really hard it would raise enough dust to prove I did what I was told to do. I was choking in all the dust I raised. Every time I went in and told him I was done, he came out and said I didn't sweep the yard, but I did. He said, "It looks ta me like you just want an ass beatin' don't 'cha? How's come ya cain't mind? Huh? You little hard headed son-of-a-bitch. Come 'ere. Heh, heh, heh." He kept smacking me in the head and laughing. He wasn't screaming like he was mad. It was more like a taunt. He was drunk. It was one of those times that Alcee said he was just teasing me and I was being hateful and despisable. It wasn't funny, I thought he was really going to beat me. He was being threatening. Looking back now, I believe that he was just having some fun. It was obvious from all the dust that I had swept the yard. The wind kept covering the broom strokes and it was impossible for me to show him the marks in the dirt that he demanded as proof. I don't know how long it went on, but I know I swept the yard at least three times that day. He was just having fun with me. I think it was that 'recreational abuse' thing I learned about in therapy.

By the time I was in fourth and fifth grade, I was pretty brave. I was starting to get bigger and stronger instead of weaker and smaller. At least now I was headed in the right direction. One night while Gordon was eating supper he got choked. I think he almost choked to death. As awful as it makes me look, I have to tell you that I stood there and watched him. I didn't help him. I just stood there hoping he would die. He was choking so bad that he had food coming from his nose, as well as his mouth, and he couldn't breathe. I didn't care, *I wanted him to die.* His face turned purple and his eyes were bulged out. He looked scared to death and I didn't care, I just wanted him to die. He looked like my mother always looked when he choked her. I didn't even cry, I just stared at him and *hoped* he would die. He looked up at me and made eye contact with me. He looked desperate and panicked. He stuck his hand out like he was motioning for me to go get help. I just stared into his eyes and watched him choke. When he fell out of his chair, Alcee heard the noise and came into the room. She panicked and started helping him. He pulled out of it with her help and I paid dearly for not helping him. He beat me all over the house that night. He said, "Come 'ere you sick little son-of-a-bitch! I'll beat you to death! You fuckin' cold hearted bastard!" I lied to him and said, "I didn't help you because I was scared." He didn't believe me. I think he knew by the look I gave him when we made eye contact that I didn't help him because I wanted him to die. He said, "I fuckin' pay for the food you eat and the goddamned clothes on yer back and you do me that way? I'll fuckin' kill you!" He said he was gonna knock my teeth out. He kept getting me in a head lock and busting me in the mouth with his fist. I don't know how many cuts I had on my lips and in my mouth, but I was pretty bloody. I had blood all over my shirt and my mouth was full of blood. He said, "How 'bout if I send ya to prison and let yer goddamned daddy take care of ya. When's the last time that cock sucker bought ya a meal? You ain't even gonna smile like that son-of-a-bitch now, 'cause I'm gonna knock those fuckin' pearly white teeth out for ya!" I kept screaming for Alcee to help me, but she said, "You should've helped 'im after all he's done for you. I don't care if he fuckin' kills ya. It'll save me the trouble." I was around eleven or twelve years old. I was starting to get pretty tough and hard by then, I guess, because I didn't even cry. In fact, I distinctly remember feeling tough. My mouth was bleeding and my face felt like it was on fire, but I felt like I hadn't been touched. I didn't feel hurt or scared, I felt pissed off. I'm convinced that I wouldn't have helped him if he had been drawing his last breath. I looked him right in the eye and I believe he knew I wanted him to die. I'm not proud of what I did, or didn't do. In fact, I think how awful I must have been by that age to be able to stand by and watch anyone choke to death, even Gordon. I'm not proud of the way I was but I am realizing *why* I was like that.

It seemed like every year someone turned us in to the welfare department, or at least threatened to. Every time that happened Alcee tried to blame me first. I think it was her way of finding out whether or not I had talked to any of the teachers at school. When ever she knew, or suspected, there was an investigation in the works, she hired a babysitter for a while until 'things blew over.' She also stocked the house with food. I ate pretty good during those times, better than salad dressing and bread. One time when I was in fourth or fifth grade she said, "I'm gettin' a babysitter for you bunch o' bastards, 'cause I think somebody's been waggin' their goddamned lyin' tongue at school again." I said, "It wasn't me! And it wasn't the other kids, they won't talk to anybody. I think the teachers make stuff up because they don't like us! Maybe it was them!" I knew as soon as she started yelling about it that I better start vehemently denying any part of it. Dana and I were the only two in school, at the time, and the other kids didn't talk to neighbors or anybody else. She said, "It was probably your goddamned grandma that yer so fuckin' crazy about! The old bitch loves ta cause me trouble!" Alcee was standing in front of the bathroom mirror putting her make-up on while she ranted and raved about having to hire a sitter. She had to leave for work before the sitter could get there, but we would only be alone for a half hour or so. I was standing behind her, apparently with an attitude, making faces. She saw me in the mirror, and while my eyes were crossed, she hurled around and hit me on the side of my head and face. I didn't see it coming. It knocked me down. I guess I wasn't very bright. I should have thought about her seeing me in the mirror. She kicked me and jerked me up by my hair while she screamed, "Do you like ta make faces ya little fittified bitch? Make some more! Go ahead, make some more ya little ugly bastard!" Every time she said 'make some more' she hit me. She said, " If I find out you been waggin' yer goddamned lyin' tongue, I'll beat you to death!" I remember having a headache and my ear ringing all night. At least we had a babysitter, it was a little less work for me when we had one. But the little ones were used to me doing for them and they cried after me anyway. Most of the babysitters saw that as a blessing for themselves, and let me take care of them. I suppose it was better for the babies.

Looking back, I wonder how many red flags Alcee threw up on her own, without anyone calling the authorities on us. I remember Dana's second grade teacher telling me to have my mom call her. I told Alcee and she said to ask her what she wanted. The next day at school I did ask her. I said, "My mom wants to know why you want her to call you." She wouldn't tell me, but she sent a note home with Dana asking my mother to come to the school for a conference with her. Alcee accused me of not asking the teacher what she wanted. She said, “Why didn’t you ask her?” I said, "I did ask her, but she said she needed to talk to my mom not me." Alcee said, “Bull fuckin’ shit! Ya probably didn’t even ask her ya lyin’ little bastard! Yer just bound and determined ta make my life miserable ain’t ‘cha?” Now if I were a teacher, that would be a red flag for me. If I sent a message to a parent that I wanted to speak to them and they sent their older child to discuss the matter with me, I would consider that a problem. As years went by I would frequently be the one to deal with the kids’ teachers. Most of the teachers had a problem with it, but I was there and Alcee wasn’t so what could they do. One teacher told me I spoiled one of the kids too much and I should try to separate from her a little bit. I was about sixteen or seventeen. It was a regular parent teacher conference and I’m the one that went, not Alcee.

I remember having to go with my mother to have Tom circumcised. Back then they didn’t do that until the baby boys were so many days or weeks old. The mothers took them to the doctors office to have it done, at least that’s the way it was with my brothers. I don’t know the reason I had to go with Alcee to get Tom circumcised, but I did. I don’t know where the other kids were, Tim, Dena and Dana, but they weren’t with us. Thank God I didn’t have to take him by myself. We went to the doctor’s office and they strapped Tom on what looked like a plastic tray with a mold of a little body. He was screaming his head off. It scared me really bad to hear him scream like that. I started crying and the nurse asked Alcee if she could take me to the waiting room. I sat out in the waiting room, but I could still hear him screaming and it was awful. I felt so sorry for him. It was blood curdling. I thought they were killing him. I was so relieved when they brought him out and we left. Alcee said, “There ain’t nothin’ wrong with ‘im. It makes ‘em mad ta be tied down, it don’t hurt ‘em.” I didn’t believe her, I heard him screaming and it sounded to me like he was more than just angry. I don’t know what the purpose of my being there was, or if there even was one. Maybe whoever watched the other kids didn’t want to watch me.

Maybe it was so much per head and Alcee only had enough money to leave three of us. I don't know why I was there, but I wish I hadn't been. It seemed like after that I started going to the doctor by myself. I was seven when Tom was born. By the time I was eleven or twelve, I would frequently be the one who took the kids to the doctor if they were sick. We had a couple of different doctors that we went to. One of our doctor's office was already within walking distance of where we lived. Then the other doctor moved his office down the street from that doctor. So I could walk to either office. It was a long walk, but I could do it. Alcee had some sort of arrangement with them to let me bring the kids in when they were sick and they would see them. Sometimes we went to one, sometimes the other. I think she sent us to who ever we owed the least money to at the time one of us was sick. One of those doctors lost his license years later over drug related accusations.

One morning Alcee said, "You need to stay home from school today. Tony's sick and you have ta take him to the doctor." I walked to the doctor's office with him and carried him most of the way. It was winter time and he was only around two or three years old. I was eleven or twelve. It was too far for him to walk when he was well, let alone while he was sick. I carried him awhile, then stopped to rest. I did that until we got to the doctor's office, walk awhile, rest awhile. The nurse took us into an exam room and the doctor came in to check Tony. While he was checking Tony he said, "Your little brother's going to be fine. I'll get him fixed up, but I'm not so sure about you. I want you to breathe for me." He started checking me over and said he needed to talk to my mother. Later, he said I was breathing abnormally and that's what he picked up on. It turned out I had rheumatic fever. He sent me to a cardiologist and Alcee had to go with me. The cardiologist wouldn't see me unless a parent was with me. That was awful. She did not want to be there, neither did I. I had to take long acting penicillin shots every month. It was cheaper if I took a shot once a month instead of taking pills every day. Those shots were very painful. I couldn't hardly walk for two days after I got them. I always got them in my hip because they said the penicillin was to thick to put in my arm. I took them for a year or two, but it was kind of a joke because I was supposed to get a lot of rest too. That never happened. In fact, the doctor prescribed phenobarbital as a tranquilizer so I would rest. Like I said, that didn't happen. I still did the same amount of work that I did before I was diagnosed with rheumatic fever. Like Alcee said, "You think 'cause yer sick yer special? Well, you aint! Yer milkin' it ta get out of doin' what yer supposed to do! Don't even try it!" I wasn't milking it. I knew I wasn't special and I worked as hard as I did before. I didn't even ask for a break. I wouldn't have because I knew my only worth was the amount of work I could do. After a couple of years I said, "I'm not taking any more shots. I have a job and I'll buy my own pills." And I did.

I still had to **run** home from school so Alcee could get to work on time. Unless we were possibly being investigated, I took care of us at night. There was an alley I ran through on the way home from school, it was a short cut. I knew all the short cuts. Sometimes I saw an old woman standing out on the porch of a house that sat at the end of that alley. One day she yelled at me to stop. She knew my name. She said, "Hey, is your name Trena?" I told her it was and she said she was my great-grandmother. She was Grandma's mother. She said my cousin told her that it was me running through the alley past her house every day after school. She didn't know who I was until then. I had been running by her house for four or five years and she didn't know who I was, and I didn't know who she was. When I got home I told Alcee that an old woman said she was my great- grandmother. She said, "Don't ever talk to that old bitch! Don't even walk by that house again." I said I didn't talk to her, but then I said, "She asked me if you were my mom and said I look just like you." Alcee said, "I thought you didn't talk to her, ya little lyin' bastard! When you hear chains rattlin' under yer bed some night, don't yell for me to save ya. When Satan comes to get 'cha, I'll be glad to see ya go." I didn't care anymore. I still ran through the alley and if my great-grandmother was outside, I yelled, "Hi Grandma!" and kept running. It didn't matter if I lied or told the truth, I would be accused of lying either way.

Most of the kids in our neighborhood weren't allowed to play with us alley kids. To start with, their parents frequently read Gordon's name in the paper under arrests. They could hear the fighting and arguing coming from our house all the time, and I'm sure some of them had to see Alcee beat us with switches and belts out in the yard. Anyway, the alley was off limits for most of the kids in our neighborhood, except when they ran through to make fun us. One girl, Vicky, came up the alley every now and then and talked to me, she didn't make fun of us. One day she ran up the alley all excited and said, "Trena, there's a song on the radio and it has your name! There's a song named after you!" I was excited, too. The next time Alcee unlocked the door and let us in, I told her about it. I was still excited and said, "Mommy, there's a song named after me! Did you hear it on the radio?" She got instantly mad. She grabbed me and said, "You like to lie, goddamned you? Come 'ere, let me show what happens to little girls that lie. I'll beat you to death!" I said, "That's what Vicky said. I didn't hear it, but she said there's a song with my name in it. That's what she said." Alcee said, "I had the radio on all morning and I didn't hear any songs about ugly fittified idiots! You lie to me again and I'll cut yer fuckin' tongue out!" There really was a song with my name in it, but I never mentioned it again. The first time I heard it was when Vicky came up the alley with her transistor radio and we listened to it. I had told her my mother said I was lying and she wanted me to know that she was telling the truth about the song. I think maybe Alcee was afraid the song would make me feel special, that was definitely forbidden. Oh well. I don't think she had to worry about any of us feeling special, none of us ever did.

I had asked my mother for years to let me grow my hair long. The other girls in my family had long hair and I wanted my hair long too. I especially wanted it long after Raymond said I looked like a boy. But she kept making me get my hair cut short. She said I had a big horse face and if my hair was long, my face would look even longer than it really was. She said, “You ‘cain’t’ wear yer hair long, you idiot! As skinny as you are and as long as yer fuckin’ face is you’d look like a goddamned stick horse!” She liked to make fun of me in front of other people. One time at my grandma’s she started making fun of me for wanting my hair long. It started because she said I was walking like I was behind a plow. She said, “Straighten yer shoulders idiot! You walk like yer behind a goddamned plow!” Grandma, Georgie and my uncles started laughing. Then Alcee kept it going. She said to my grandma, “Can you believe the little fittified bastard wants long hair? As long as her fuckin’ face is, she asked me if she could let her hair grow!” Then they all started laughing again. That was my fault for letting her know what I wanted. At one point Grandma said, “Alcee, don’t do her that way,” but she was laughing when she said it. Then my mother said, “It’s the fuckin’ truth! She looks like a goddamned forty year old farm woman! All she needs is a fuckin’ plow.” They all kept laughing and I started imitating an old farm woman behind a plow. It made them laugh more, but at least *I* was making them laugh at me instead of someone else making them laugh at me. I was getting tougher every day. Bigger and stronger.

I had learned that if you let them know what you wanted or needed, you could be sure you wouldn’t get it. The best thing to do was ***not*** tell them what you needed or wanted and you might get it by mistake. The odds have to be on your side sometimes. The best thing to do was act like you didn’t want anything. If they didn’t know you wanted it, they might accidentally get it for you by chance sometime. Like one time I told Alcee what my favorite color was and she said it wasn’t. She actually told me what *she* decided my favorite color was. It was like she assigned me a favorite color. From that time on, I never got anything that was the favorite color that I picked. One year for Christmas she gave us sweatshirts and she gave my favorite color to Dana. That wasn’t even Dana’s favorite color. For years I said my favorite color was the one she assigned to me. If I hadn’t told her what my favorite color was, she might have accidentally given me the one I wanted.

My mistake. I knew better, I just didn't do better. If we said what we wanted or needed, it went on a 'don't give that to him or her' list. She told me I couldn't wear a certain other color because I looked ridiculous in it. I have a blouse that color now, but I didn't dare wear that color at all until my late thirties.

It was the same principal if you hurt somewhere. If I fell and skinned my knee, they could see that I had a sore. They would grab my knee and laugh as they asked, "Does that hurt?" If I had a sunburn, they would slap me on the back. Gordon did it more often than Alcee. She like to come up behind me and hit me in the back as she said, "How was your trip? Glad to see your back!" She acted like it was joke, but it hurt. Sometimes she knocked the wind out of me. If I had a headache, I could count on them screaming in my face or smacking me in the head. It was just fun for them, I guess. One time I hurt my finger and Gordon said, "Come 'ere and let me see yer hand." I knew what he was going to do and he did it. He grabbed my hand and squeezed it and asked, "Does that hurt?" in a snide, taunting voice. I went to my knees and said, "yes it hurts," but I didn't cry. Oh yes, God help us if we asked for anything we needed or wanted or told them where we hurt. Both of them called us 'greedy little bastards' and put it on the ***never*** list, or went for the soft spot. If you didn't tell them you were hurt, they wouldn't know to go for the soft spot. Duh. You stood a better chance of getting what you wanted if you just went with the roll of the dice. We took what was given to us and were happy with it. That's just the way it was and that was okay. It had to be. We learned to be glad for anything thrown our way. We accepted it as enough, because we didn't want to be greedy. I still don't tell people what I want or where it hurts. Can't be too careful. I have been told that I am great at comforting people in their times of need. I think it's because I learned to read people at such a young age. I'm very good at sensing what others need and meeting their needs, but I don't want anyone to know what I need. I don't *really* need anything anyway. That's probably why I'm still in therapy. I think I'm supposed to need something or somebody to be normal.

By the time I was in fourth and fifth grade I was one tough little girl and that makes me feel sad. The only picture I have of myself as a child is my second grade picture and it was taken while I was still somewhat soft. I wasn't a raving beauty of a child, but I wasn't ugly. I was good too, not lazy, mean and hateful, like they told me I was. I wish I could travel back in time and talk to that little girl (me) before she got so tough. I would pick her up and hold her so close to me and I'd tell her it was okay to be scared. I would tell her she was going to make it even farther than she believed she could. I would tell her to believe Wendell, the guy at the station, when he tells her she's cute because she is. I would tell her that she was doing a fine job and that she is not lazy. I would tell her not to worry when she gets tough because she would, eventually, come back around after she escaped the madness of her childhood. I would hold her and let her cry until her hurt was all cried out. And, as I put her back down, I would tell her that she would be okay, that she would make that uphill climb. Because soon she would be getting bigger and stronger.

CHAPTER TEN

No Cabs, No Cops

Shortly after I graduated fifth grade we moved from the alley. By then Denise was over a year old and I took care of all seven of us. Alcee and Gordon told us we were moving to a three bedroom house 'way out' in the country. Well, call me psychic, but I knew it wasn't going to be a good thing. I knew I wouldn't be able to sneak around and see my grandmother and that bothered me. I knew I wouldn't be able to pop bottle hunt and go to the store everyday, that worried me. Some days we ate off the pop bottle money. There were a lot of days that I cashed them in and bought food for supper. I remember cashing them in one day and buying pancake mix, milk and syrup. That's what we had for supper. I was very worried about moving to the country and my worries would prove to be legitimate.

They weren't kidding when they said 'way out' in the country, it was out in the middle of nowhere. Our nearest neighbor was over a quarter mile away, and the perverted teenaged boy who lived there watched our house with binoculars all the time. The driveway alone was almost a half mile long, it wound back and forth with curves. The house did have three bedrooms, that's about the only benefit of being there. The roof leaked, there was a coal furnace in the basement, which would be my job to learn to bank and keep the fire going. The stairs had rotted off the front of the house, so if you tried to go out the front door you had to jump about four feet to the ground. The school we went to had out houses, one for the girls and one for the boys. The sixth and seventh grade class rooms were in the same room, separated only by a sliding curtain. Each class could hear the other class, it sounded like a blab school. It was so far out in the country that taxi's wouldn't come out there. It was hard to even get cops to come out there. Gordon was in a very safe position with that one. Alcee didn't drive yet, so we were at

Gordon's mercy to be able to go into town, and that was not a good position to be in. It didn't take her long to realize how stuck and isolated we were. She learned to drive, and obtained a license within months of us moving there. There were no private phone lines, only party lines, so it was hard to get the line clear to use the phone if you needed to. The only thing behind our house was a forest and the sides of our house were surrounded by tens of acres of brush. It was so infested with poisonous snakes that no one would clear the brush, not even the guy with a bull dozer the landlord hired. Most of the people who lived out there seemed to be right out of Deliverance, or some other horror movie. That's where we lived when I thought Alcee was beating Tim to death for playing with fire. It was after her hospitalization for a nervous breakdown, which I will talk about in this chapter. But in spite of how awful it was, Alcee would be forced to form an alliance with me during the three years we lived there. I was getting older, and I was figuring out some things that were going on. She would soon need *me* to help cover *her* ass.

By the time we moved there Dana and Tim had both outgrown me physically. I still got blamed for everything that happened because I was the oldest. No matter who did what, I got in trouble for it because I was the one 'in charge.' One time while I was 'in charge' Tim got mad about something, I don't remember what, and he picked up a little nicknack that I had given to Alcee for mother's day. He actually said, "I'm gonna break this so you'll get beat with the belt." And he did. He banged it on the edge of a table and broke it. Sure enough, when Gordon and Alcee got home, it was my fault for not watching him. I even told them what he said, but it didn't matter. Gordon called every body into the living room and ordered the kids to line up on the couch to watch. Then he made me stand in the middle of the living room and bend over while he 'whipped my ass' with a belt. He said, "I guess when ya learn to make these kids mind, ya won't have to get yer ass whipped ever' time I turn around. Yer a dumb little fucker, ain't 'cha?" After all, how much fun could it be beating someone, if you didn't humiliate them too? I told Tim I would get him the next time I had to take care of them. The next time we were there alone, I went after him. He out ran me and climbed a tree so I couldn't reach him. I was so mad, I was going to punch his lights out. I couldn't climb the tree like he did, but I got high enough to shake the branch he crawled out on. I shook him out of the tree. I was getting fed up. I didn't know how much longer I could stand the insanity. Anyway, he got away and stayed hidden until the wardens got home. I never got even, but that's okay. God knows he had enough to deal with.

I was starting to develop physically. I was self conscious and ashamed of it. Gordon kept grabbing me and saying, "Get yer boobies! Let me see those boobies!" He grabbed at me and pinched me and laughed at me. I was so embarrassed. Alcee said, "He's just teasin' you! He don't mean nothin' by it. You are without a doubt the most despisable, hateful little mother-fucker that ever walked this earth!" Gordon did that all the time, every day. He pinched them so hard they were sore, but that didn't stop him. I remember worrying that he would make one them not grow, by pinching and twisting them so hard, and I would look even more like a freak than I already did. Whenever I pulled away from him and said, "Stop it," he got mad and hit me for being so 'fuckin' hateful.' One time I said, "Stop it! You make them sore! Leave me alone!" That caused him and Alcee both to jump all over me. He said, "You little hateful bitch! Ya ain't got nothin' to make sore! You ain't got nothin' anybody wants!" Then Alcee said, "As much as he does fer all you little bastards and you 'cain't' even take a joke! How 'bout if he stops feedin' ya too? Huh? How 'bout that?" I didn't even have a bra yet, I needed one, but I didn't have one. It was so awful. One day he told me to go out and clean up the yard. I went in my bedroom to put on an old shirt and he barged in on me. I had one shirt off, but I didn't have the other one on yet. I held the shirt that I was going to put on up in front of me. He said, "What did I tell you to do?" I said, "I'm changing clothes and I'm going to clean up the yard." He said, "No ya ain't! You don't need a shirt! You ain't got nothin' anybody wants to look at. Get your ass out there like I told you." I tried to put the shirt on and he grabbed it away from me. I screamed, "Stop it!" He grabbed me and jerked me toward him and said, "Come 'ere and let me see. Ha ha ha. Your boobies ain't even that big yet. Ha ha ha." He kept laughing at me while he grabbed at them and made fun of me. Then he said, "Ya little lazy cunt! You think yer a woman now? You ain't! Yer 'tomater' don't even spurt yet, does it? Get yer ass out there and clean up the yard! That fuckin' yard better be clean! Come and get me when yer done so I can look at it." I was so humiliated. I hate that word, the c___ word, I could hardly write it as a quote. It was one of Gordon's favorites. I had to walk outside without a shirt and work in the yard. I just knew the little pervert with the binoculars was watching. I don't *know* that he was, but it sure was one of my fears that day.

The same thing happened when I started having periods. I begged Alcee not to tell him. I said, "You know how he is. He'll tease me about it and it's not funny. It's embarrassing." She said, "Why in the fuck don't you whine about somethin'? That's all you do! Shut up! I ain't gonna say nothin' to 'im." That very night when Gordon got home, he found me and made fun of me. I tried all night to avoid him just in case she had told him. I crept around the house and watched where he went so I could hide in another room. But it didn't work. He caught me in the doorway of our girls' bedroom and said, "Yer mommy said yer 'tomater's' spurtin' now." Then he started laughing. I felt like I could die of embarrassment. Then he started grabbing my breast again and making fun of me. He said, "If it's spurtin' you probably got peach fuzz on it too. Heh, heh, heh." It was so awful. He wouldn't let me through the doorway and I couldn't back up because he kept grabbing me and pulling me back towards him. He said, "What's yer face so red for? Heh, heh, heh." He just wouldn't shut up and leave me alone. He kept laughing and pinching my breasts and saying those vulgar, disgusting things to me. He said, "You let any boys get in that pussy now and you'll get caught like yer mommy did." I was so full of emotions, or something, but I don't know what. I don't know what I felt. I just know that it was horrible. I said, "I thought I was so ugly no boys would have me anyway." That made him mad. He started hitting me in the head and said, "Don't sass me, you little hateful bitch! They could always put a fuckin' sack over your head." It was so awful. That is one of the things that makes me realize *it was that bad.* Alcee would say I'm making a mountain out of a mole hill. She's also the same person who told her seven year old child she wouldn't miss her if she died.

Gordon still yelled and screamed at me if the kids made noise. I remember Denise crying one summer night, actually it was early evening, and I couldn't get her to stop. I could tell she was hurt somewhere by her cry, it was a hurtful cry. I was trying to figure out what was wrong and Gordon started screaming, "The next time that baby cries, I'm gonna whip yer ass. I'll give you both somethin' ta cry about and you can cry together!" I got her out of the house so he wouldn't hear her cry as loud. It turned out she was being stung by, what I think was, a wasp. It had gotten under her little shirt and was stinging her over and over. I couldn't believe it. I thought they lost their stinger the first time they stung someone, it didn't. It looked like a wasp. She was stung eleven times. No wonder she was screaming her head off. I didn't know what to do, I was afraid she would die. I got Alcee and we mixed baking soda and water to make a paste. We put that on Denise's stings. It turned out that there was a wasp nest inside the house. They didn't even take her to the doctor. Alcee said, "You let her get hurt. You can fuckin' rock her to sleep!" I was going to anyway, I was the only one she would let touch her. I was really afraid she would die. She got really sick. I held her most of the night. She was so little and pitiful. She was a fun baby. She was as cute as she could be and laughed a lot. She was just plain cute. She was an easy baby to take care of.

The fighting between Alcee and Gordon was the same as it had always been. The only difference was that I couldn't get the police to come out there, even if I could get the party line cleared to use the phone, and we didn't have any locks on the doors. We used to stick a butter knife in the door trim as a makeshift lock. We had to lay it flat on the door and slide the knife blade under the trim on the door jamb. The problem was, if Gordon hit the door hard enough, the knife fell out and the door was unlocked. One time he and Alcee were fighting and he tore her clothes off her. He yelled for us kids to come and watch. I kept trying to get the kids together in one room and he kept bellowing, "Kids! Come and look at yer fuckin' mommy! She's naked! Get in here right now! All you little fuckers get in here!" He made us come in there and look at our naked mother. And she wouldn't shut up and stop fighting either. She was hitting him, he was hitting her, and they were both screaming as loud as they could. She said, "You cock sucker, me and the kids all want you out of here. Don't we?" Then she looked at us to answer her. He said, "No they don't, you whore! Do you?" Then he looked at us to answer him. It was pure chaotic insanity. It never stopped. And we were so stuck.

They called me a coward because I didn't like to fight. They even told me that if they ever heard of me running from a fight, they would 'whip my ass.' I hated to fight with anyone. Not that I was that good and pure, but I didn't like to fight. I was also afraid to fight, so call me a coward. Dana, on the other hand, loved to fight. She picked fights and when I didn't help her I got in trouble. She picked fights with big girls and sometimes big boys. She got into a fight with a girl in her grade at school. That girl had an older sister, older than me, and a lot bigger. Dana beat the girl up and her mother called Alcee. They went around and around on the phone, screaming and cussing at each other for I don't know how long. The mother told Alcee she was going to 'kick her ass.' A few minutes after they hung up we heard a car horn, over and over. Gordon and Alcee looked out and said the woman was at the end of our driveway. Gordon said to Alcee, "That crazy bitch is callin' you out. Let's go." Gordon told all of us to get in the car so we did. We drove down to the road, remember our driveway was about a half mile long. I was already shaking. My mother was going to go out in the road to fight this woman! We got down to the road and Gordon told us to get out of the car. The woman brought her two daughters.

This was not going to be a good thing, I knew that, and I was scared. Alcee went out in the road and argued with the woman. They kept going in a circle like they were both waiting for the other to make the first move. Then the girl that Dana had fought with, dared her out in the road. She went willingly and started beating the daylights out of that girl. Then my worst nightmare, the older, bigger girl called me out. Gordon said, "Get yer ass out there and beat the fuck out o' that bitch!" I said, "I don't want to fight." He got enraged. He grabbed me and pushed me into the road. He said, "You're gonna whip her goddamned ass or I'm gonna whip yours." She grabbed me and it didn't take long for her to pin me. She was big and heavy. She had me pinned and was laying on top of me, I couldn't breathe. By then her mother and my mother were fighting all over the road, hitting and cussing each other. Dana and the other girl were still going at it, too. Gordon stood over me and the bigger girl who had me pinned, and screamed, "You get up and kick her ass or I'll beat you to death! You goddamned cowardly little bastard!" The girl was laughing at me. She was smirking and I was getting as mad as I was scared. I couldn't budge her, but her breast was hanging in my face, so I bit it. She screamed and jumped off of me, but she was pretty mad and I could tell this was not the end of it. She came at me like a bull. It really scared me. She was wearing a skirt because their church didn't believe in girls wearing pants. I tore the button off her skirt and then tore the skirt off of her. It worked, she ran to her car screaming. She could have killed me, I'm sure of it. That one was over, but it wasn't the last time I would be forced to fight.

Dana picked so many fights that we got thrown off the school bus, not because of her fights, but because of Alcee being her coach. Dana kept picking fights with people on the bus, including the same two girls that we had been forced to fight, and two other girls who were bigger and older than me. Then she went home and told Alcee and Gordon that I let people pick on her and get away with it. She said, "Trena just sits there and won't help me when they pick on me." Alcee said, "You're gonna start treatin' her like she's your sister, goddamn you! You ain't too good to help her! She'd do anything for you and I'm tired of you treatin' her like she's a fuckin' dog! You ain't no better than she is, you both came from the same stack of shit! At least she ain't lazy! She ain't a goddamned coward either, by God!" It went on and on and on. I was afraid of those girls. They were older, bigger and meaner. I didn't want to fight, for whatever reason, I just didn't want to. Alcee got tired of waiting for me to defend Dana, so she armed her and told her how to use her weapon. She gave both of us, I never used mine, a knee sock with a bar of soap in it. Really! She put a bar of soap in a knee sock and tied the sock just above the bar of soap in the toe. Then she showed us how to use them. It was awful. Dana went crazy with hers on the bus on the way home that day. She stood up in the aisle of the school bus and swung it around like a lasso. She was hitting anyone or anything in her path. She put some heavy duty knots on a lot of heads that day. We got thrown off the bus over that. Of course, Gordon and Alcee said it was my fault, not Dana's. They said if I had been taking care of her and defending her like I should have, they wouldn't have had to give her the soap in a sock.

One day Dana was crying at recess. I asked her what was wrong and she said her teacher was mean to her. I knew I better at least try to find out what happened. I went to her classroom and asked her teacher what happened. I said, "Dana is crying and if I don't find out what happened my mom will be mad at me." She said, "It's none of your business. If your mom wants to call me she can." I said, "Well if I tell my mom *that*, you and I will both be in trouble." She slapped me in the face and pushed me down in a chair. She said, "You just wait right there, young lady!" and she left the room. I sat there for a minute, in shock. I didn't expect to be treated like that at school, too. I wasn't being disrespectful to her. I was being polite, but serious. At least I thought I was. I didn't sit there, I got up and went to my classroom. That's the only room that had a phone. I called Alcee at work and told her Dana was crying and her teacher hit me when I asked her why. It got so ugly. Dana's teacher had touched some of Alcee and Gordon's toys! She better look out now. There was a conference with Alcee, Gordon, Dana's teacher, the principal, Dana and me. I thought Alcee and the teacher were going to come to blows. I thought Gordon and the principal, who was also my teacher, were going to come to blows. It was loud and ugly. I told the teacher that if she thought I was being rude, I was sorry. Gordon told me to "shut up." Anyway, it did come to an end. That night at home, Alcee and Gordon kept mocking me for saying I was sorry. They kept calling me a coward and saying, in a mocking voice, "I'm a little cowardly kiss-ass. I'm sorry."

Alcee and Gordon were always telling me that I thought I was better than them. Before we moved to the country one of my old teachers had stressed using proper word endings. Every time I used a proper ending Alcee said, "Well, ain't we little Miss Proper! You might as well get off your fuckin' high horse 'cause you ain't no better than the rest of us." Then she mocked me. When ever Gordon heard me 'talk fancy' he mocked me too. As bad as the school in the country was, I still tried to do my best. I stayed up at night to do homework after I got the kids in bed. I thought if I worked really hard at school, someday I could go to college. I figured that would be my ticket out of the hell hole. I remember one night when I was up doing homework, Gordon came through the kitchen and said, "Get yer fuckin' ass in bed." I said, "I'm doing homework." He said, "What did I tell you to do?" I said, "If I don't get good grades, I can't go to college." He said, "There ain't gonna be no college. They don't let dummies in. Get yer ass in bed!" My grades were never very good, anyway. By the time I got my chores done and got the kids to bed, I was usually too tired to learn. And when Alcee and Gordon were fighting, it was impossible to concentrate. Even when I *was* at school, my mind was a million miles away. My comprehension level was very low and I just wasn't anywhere near the top of my class. I got some B's, mostly C's, but sometimes I would get a D. I wasn't exactly a genius. He was right, college was not going to happen. I started feeling more hopeless than I ever had.

I was feeling hopeless and frustrated, but I was getting braver. I don't know if it was due to teenage hormones, or if I had just taken about as much as I could take. One day Alcee was on a screaming binge. She threw things, she cussed all of us kids, she ranted and raved like a maniac. Then she started singling us out and being abusive, verbally and physically. She had a list of derogatory remarks for each one of us, except Dana. She went on and on about Tim being ugly, clumsy and stupid. She ranted about Tom being a dummy and how other kids made fun of him because he looked like a goofy kid that was on TV. She said Tony was an obnoxious little mother-fucker and she didn't care if the bigger boys beat the shit out of him. She said it would save her the trouble. She said Dena was a little lazy, fat ass bitch just like one of her aunts on Gordon's side. She screamed because Denise was under her feet all the time and said she would like to drop kick her like a football. She said I was the biggest mistake she ever made and every time I smiled, I looked just like my goddamned no good daddy. I said, "Mom, just leave us alone." She turned to me and said, "Well, well, well! Is the little cowardly bastard gettin' some backbone or what?" I could tell by her eyes that she was going to hit me, anyway, so I said, "I can handle being a bastard, it's not my fault. But what does that make you, Mom?" She was going to beat me up anyway, so I might as well say what was on my mind. I thought she was going to kill me. She got me in a headlock and kept busting me in the mouth, like Gordon had frequently done before. I didn't care, I made my point. I kept trying to cover my mouth, but she kept pulling my hair and twisting my head, it hurt my neck. I just gave up and let her bust my mouth a few times. I didn't cry either, I didn't even want to. I didn't say near as much as I could have. I just didn't care anymore. It was worth it.

After Alcee learned to drive, a few months after we moved to the country, I got a job. She took me to work at night and picked me up when I got off. I was twelve when I got a job as a car hop at a drive-in restaurant. It's the one where the lady told me to give back the one dollar tip that a teenaged boy gave me. Anyway, it was winter time and that was a cold job. Georgie worked there, too.

Grandma had moved right behind the drive-in, so it was easy for her to get to and from work. Sometimes I could go to Grandma's after work because Alcee was too tired to pick me up, until they started fighting again. That complicated me getting to school the next day, but by then it was obvious I wasn't going to graduate anyway, so it was no big deal. It was so cold and wet some nights that the skin between mine and Georgie's toes cracked and bled. We didn't have any boots, so we wore tennis shoes. Going to Grandma's after work also complicated the money issue. When I stayed at Grandma's she wanted part of my tip money, but I was supposed to give it all to Alcee. Grandma said, "She ain't gonna know how much you made in tips. Give Grandma some of it and tell her what ever you got left is all you made. Grandma won't say nothin,' Trennie. I know how she is." So that's what I did. I gave Grandma some of it and told Alcee that what I had left was all I made the night before. It didn't take her long to figure out that I seemed to have made more in tips when she picked me up directly from work than when I went to Grandma's. She accused me of 'givin' that old bitch' money, but Grandma and I both denied it. Georgie only lasted a week or so as a car hop. Grandma said it was too hard on her because she had had rheumatic fever a few years before that. Yeah? Me too. I kept working there for a few months until I found an indoor job at a chain hamburger restaurant. Then I got Georgie on and we worked together again. We used to hire in together and quit together. I usually didn't want to quit, but if she did I had to. If I didn't, everybody said I was stabbing her in the back. She liked working where ever I did because I would work for her on what should have been my days off. I usually worked seven days a week, she worked three.

Sometimes I think I was getting braver because I was helping Alcee keep secrets from Gordon. She said he didn't give her enough money to run the house, so she needed my money. She said, "The cock sucker makes enough, he just don't bring it home. It won't hurt you to help me." Gordon frequently asked me where my money was and what I was doing with it. Alcee said if I told him about giving her money, she would kill me. She said to tell him that I was buying my medicine and putting most of it in the bank. That was one secret. She also wanted me to get the mail and hide it so Gordon wouldn't see it until she went through it. One day she said, "Go get the mail before that mother-fucker gets home and sees it." I said, "What about the snakes?" There were poisonous snakes all over the place where we lived. They even got in the basement and on the back porch. You couldn't walk down our driveway without seeing some. She said, "Go-get-the-fuckin'-mail!" I got the mail before he got home so she could hide it. When she wasn't home, it was my job to get the mail in and hide it in a drawer so Gordon wouldn't see it. That was another secret. She made me lie to him all the time about a lot of things. I started feeling like we had an alliance. I don't think she felt that way, but I did. She had a way of making me feel like she was doing me a favor by 'letting me' give her my money and 'letting me' lie to Gordon for her.

When I was thirteen my grandmother told me my real dad was in town. She said he had been paroled and was staying with his sister. I was so excited thinking about finding him. I didn't know he had a sister. Even if he didn't want me to live with him, I wanted to meet him. But before I could sneak around and find him, he got into trouble again. He had only been paroled two months earlier and he was on his way back to prison. One morning Alcee shoved a newspaper in front of me and said, "There ya go! There's yer goddamned daddy that ya wanted to know so much about. Remember, curiosity killed the cat!" There was a picture on the front page of the paper of a man on a stretcher surrounded by police. He had on handcuffs and it looked like he was biting his wrist. He looked like he was in pain. He was wincing and I wondered why he was biting himself. I asked, "What's wrong with him? Did he die?" She said, "No such luck! The son-of-a-bitch got shot by the cops. I told ya he ain't no goddamned good! The stupid mother-fucker was tryin' to take somethin' that didn't belong to 'im. They shot the son-of-a-bitch and they're carryin' his ass off to jail where he fuckin' belongs. Ain't ya proud to belong to that? You wanted to know about 'im! Well, there he is! Hold yer head up high, that's yer goddamned daddy!" Even if everything she said was true, I was still worried. I felt like crying, but I didn't. I knew I would get in a lot of trouble if I cried over him. The thing is, I wanted to find him, meet him, talk to him, and now he was going to be gone again. I think I kind of felt abandoned. Even though he had never been around, I was hoping to make contact with him, and now that hope was gone. I didn't realize that he would be in the hospital for months, recovering from the injuries of being shot. Months later his name was in the paper again. This time for jumping bond. Apparently, after he was released from the hospital and put in jail, he posted bond and left the state. I figured I would never find him, so I might as well get over it.

Every Christmas we could count on Gordon to, at the very least, turn the Christmas tree over and sometimes throw it out in the yard. One year he came home late Christmas eve night, drunk of course, and started stomping the toys Alcee and I had put out for the kids. He yelled, "Wake up you little bastards! There ain't no Santa clause and you ain't gettin' a goddamned 'thang' for Christmas." I called his parents house to see if they could talk to him, and his sister answered the phone. She could hear him in the background, she said she would come out and try to calm him down. He had already busted some of the kids things that Santa had left for them. I kept mouthing off to him so he would chase me. Alcee was fighting with him too. I tried to get the kids to go back to bed, but they were getting older and it wasn't easy to do anymore. While Alcee fought with him in the kitchen, I hid as many things as I could that weren't broken. When his sister came into the house, she jumped on him like a tiger. She started screaming at him and pushing him. He ran into his bedroom and told her to go away because he didn't want to hurt her. He said, "It ain't none o' yer fuckin' business anyway!" She pushed him down on his bed, jumped on his chest and pinned him by sitting on him and putting her knees on his upper arms. She screamed, "You cock sucker! These kids are gonna have Christmas! Do you understand me?" She picked up a bedside lamp, held it up like she was going to hit him with it and said, "I ought to kill you right now! I love you, you're my brother, but I will fuckin' kill you if you don't leave these kids and their Christmas alone. Now, I'm gonna get off of you and you better not start any shit with any of these kids. Do you understand me?" She got off of him and he just layed there. She stood there watching him for a few seconds. Then she said, to me, "I'm gonna go now, Trena, but if he even looks at one of you cross eyed, you call me." Then she said to him, "I'll tell you what, get your damn clothes on and you can just leave with me. Then I don't have to worry about you bothering these kids." He said, "No, I won't bother 'em. I'm just gonna sleep it off, now. I won't bother 'em." She left and he stayed in bed. I couldn't believe his sister went after him like that. I had always liked her, she was always nice to me, but she was a hero to me now. What Gordon hadn't busted, Alcee and I put back out for the kids. It was like that every Christmas. He came home drunk and started a fight.

Dana just kept getting meaner and meaner to the rest of us. One time I was in the kitchen doing dishes, and she picked up a plate and stared at me with a nasty little grin. I said, "What do you want? If you're not gonna help me, get out of here." I had complained that I had done the dishes for weeks and asked Alcee if she would make Dana and Dena do them. She said, "You're gonna do the fuckin' dishes, I want 'em done right! It ain't gonna hurt ya." When ever she found a dirty dish in the cabinet, she took out every dish from every cabinet, including pots and pans, and made me wash every single one of them. Anyway, Dana yelled loud enough for Alcee to hear her, "No! Don't throw it!" Then she slammed the plate on the floor and broke it. She set me up. Before I could say anything, she started screaming, "I'm tellin' Mom!" By the time she said that, Alcee was in the kitchen smacking me around. Dana said, "She picked that plate up and acted like she was gonna throw it at me and I told her not to, but she did it anyway! She's mad 'cause I wouldn't help her with the dishes." Alcee said, "I heard what went on. I'm gonna kill the little dispisable son-of-a-bitch if she keeps on." There was no way to win, I just shut up and took it. By that time I didn't care if they killed me. I was already starting to think that death was probably the only way to peace. I was going backward instead of forward. I was starting to get weak again, I think I was probably depressed. I don't know what I was or what I felt, but I know I wasn't happy or unhappy, just blank or something. Maybe I was indifferent, I don't know.

One Sunday morning in the dead of winter, Alcee got up and was very quiet. Gordon hadn't come home the night before, I don't know if that's significant or not, but he didn't. She was so quiet it was creepy. I tried to talk to her but she wouldn't answer me. She just kept staring at me with a wild eyed look. Suddenly, she started breaking everything she could pick up. She threw dishes, lamps, flower pots, bottles, knickknacks, chairs, anything that wasn't nailed down. She ripped the curtains off the windows and turned chairs upside down. It was the worst rage I had ever seen out of her. The look in her eyes scared me, her eyes shifted back and forth really fast and they were opened so very wide. It scared me. She started staggering around the front room and fell onto the couch. It looked like she passed out or died. I looked around at the destruction and it was awful. It was a huge mess. There was dirt and glass all over the place. It looked like a bomb had gone off.

The little ones were crying and pulling at her, I kept shaking her to try and wake her up. She didn't move. Her body was so limp. I knew to look for dilated pupils when the kids got hurt because that was a sign of a concussion. I tried to open her eyes to look at them, and at first she didn't look back. It was like she was sleeping and couldn't wake up. I thought she was dying or in a coma. I told the kids that she was taking a nap and she would get up later. I told them everything was okay. Then after a while, I don't remember how long, I pried her eyes open again to check her pupils, and she looked back at me with that wild look she had earlier. It was so frightening, I was thirteen years old and I didn't know what to do. One would think I would know what to do by that age, but I didn't. She instantly jumped up and started screaming. She screamed,

"You bunch o' son-of-a-bitches! Who did this? How many of ya did it take to do this?" She started kicking the debris and hitting us. She screamed, "That's it! I'm gettin' on a fuckin' bus and leavin' ever' fuckin' one o' ya here!" I said, "Mom, you did it. Don't you remember? I'll clean it up, but you did it. Don't you remember?" She went berserk. She came after me with everything she had. She kept hitting me with her fist while she screamed, "Don't try to make me think I'm crazy! Who did it? I'm sendin' every fuckin' one o' you to the fuckin' police and they can do what ever they want with ya! I hope they put every one o' you in the fuckin' orphanage and beat ya three times a day! Don't tell me I did this, you little cock-sucker!" I didn't know what to do. I just let her beat on me and tried to clean things up. I didn't get much done because within minutes she said, "Every fuckin' one o' ya get yer ass in the car." We did.

It was a scary ride to town. She was all over the road and her head kept swaying back and forth. It was like she couldn't control her neck muscles, her head would fall back on the head rest and then fall forward towards her chest. Her eyes looked heavy and droopy. They would get droopier and droopier until they closed. I screamed and she opened them again. This happened several times while we drove into town. She kept going back forth. Her eyes looked wild and she sat up in the car seat, then she slumped and got droopy eyed again. I thought we would die if I didn't get her to pull the car over. I tried to get her to pull over, but she wouldn't. As we got closer to town I kept trying to talk to her. I asked her where we were going and when we were going back home. I just tried to get her talk so I would know she was awake. She wouldn't talk. When we got to town I said, "Let's go by Grandma's house and I'll go in and talk to her." They were not speaking to each other again. Alcee gave me that wild look again and I knew I had said the wrong thing. I said, "I don't really want to talk to her, I just have to pee. I know she'll let us kids use the restroom. I won't let the kids talk to her. We'll just use the rest room and come right back out." She still had that wild look. I don't know how long we drove around town, maybe an hour or so. The kids were so scared that they weren't making much noise, but now a couple of them really did have to use the restroom. I kept watching for cops in hopes they would stop us. She was all over the road. Finally, she started down the street Grandma lived on. She pulled up in front of her house and collapsed over the steering wheel. She had passed out again, or what ever it was that happened when she fell onto the couch earlier. I put the car in park, took the keys and went up to the door. I told Grandma what was happening. She said, "The goddamned bitch ain't comin' in here! Not the way she's talked 'ta' me." I told her Alcee was passed out and I couldn't very well drive the car. She sent her husband out to the car to look at Alcee. He went back in and they called an ambulance. When the ambulance came, they took Alcee out of the car, she was still out, and put her on a stretcher. I told them my grandmother lived there, so the kids and me would stay there with her. They were talking about calling the police to come and get us. They left and I asked Grandma if we could stay there. She said, "You and Dana can, but I'll be goddamned if any of Gordon's kids are stayin' here!" I told her I didn't know what to do because I had to stay with them. She let us in and then called Gordon's parents to come and get his kids. The three youngest kids were crying and hanging on to me. They didn't want to go, they wanted me. Gordon's parents took them and left, Dana and I stayed with Grandma Frankie. I was upset about the little ones crying and I felt guilty.

One of my uncles drove me back out to the house to get clothes for Dana and me. I also got some clothes for the others and had my uncle take them to Gordon's parents house. Apparently, when Gordon got home and saw the mess, he figured out something was wrong. He called his parents and they told him they had his kids, and Dana and I were at Grandma Frankie's. I had to work that night at the drive-in, but Grandma still lived right behind it so it was easy for me to get there. When I got home from work that night Gordon came to the door and said he needed to talk to me. Grandma said I didn't have to talk to him, but I wanted to. I wanted to know if he had been to the hospital and seen my mother. I went out and sat in the car with him to talk. He had a hang over from the night before, and he was in his remorseful, pathetic mode. He said, "Yer mom had a nervous breakdown and I'm gonna need yer help for thangs to get back to normal." I asked him if Alcee woke up and if she knew where she was. He said she did. He said he needed me to go home so all the kids could go home. He said, "Them little kids are cryin' for you and they won't let anybody else touch 'em. They keep cryin' for you. They don't understand what's goin' on. They don't have their mommy or their sissy now." I asked him how long Alcee would be in the hospital. He said at least a week, maybe longer, the doctors didn't know for sure. It would be longer. I said, "I'm afraid to go with you. How do I know you aren't tricking me? What if you come in drunk and scare the kids? What if you don't come home and I can't get to the store?" He said, "I promise, I'll be sober and I won't bother any of you kids. I'll go to the store or take you to the store, whatever you want me to do." I said, "I don't believe you, you lie to us all the time. I have to ask Grandma." He said, "You don't have ta' ask her a fuckin' thang. I'm yer daddy and yer mommy's in the hospital. Yer goin' home!" I told him I'd go get Dana. When I got back in the house, I told Grandma what he wanted me to do. She said, "You don't have to go anywhere, by God! I'll tell the hog headed son-of-a-bitch myself. He ain't takin' you nowhere!" Pretty soon Gordon was at the door telling me and Dana to 'come on.' He and Grandma started arguing. She said Dana and I weren't his kids, our mother was in the hospital and she didn't have to let him have us. He said, "The babies won't go to sleep if you're not there. They ain't ate all day, they just keep cryin' for you." I told Grandma I'd go, the babies needed me. I was kind of mad at her anyway for not letting them stay with me at her house. They were used to me taking care of them. Dana and I got in the car with Gordon and went to his parents house to pick up the others. His mother was not in favor of me taking care of the kids by myself, but as usual, Gordon won. We stopped by the store, I sat in the car with the kids while Gordon went in to get some groceries. We went home. The mess was still there. I picked up the dangerous stuff, like broken glass and knives. I got the little ones to eat and put them to bed.

The next day I stayed home from school and cleaned the place up. I kept the babies, the four youngest ones, with me. Dena was the most disturbed by everything that happened that weekend, and I probably should have kept her with me, too. But I'm pretty sure I sent her to school with Dana. Dena was so quiet when she was scared that I wouldn't remember if she was there or not. She was a quiet, easy child to take care of. She wasn't very demanding. I guess she figured out at an early age, the more you asked for, the less you got.

While Alcee was in the hospital, Gordon brought home groceries after work every night and then went to the hospital to see her. I did all the laundry, cleaning and cooking. She was in the hospital for, the best I can remember, about two weeks. I really didn't do any more work with her gone than I did when she was there. The only thing is, I couldn't go to school the whole time she was gone. And as bad as she was, sometimes, the little ones were asking, "When's Mommy comin' home?" Even I was afraid that she might never come back. I didn't know what to do. I didn't know what to tell the kids. Before she came home, Gordon took me to the hospital to see her. She told me that she was going to need my help with the kids and the house. Where had everyone been for the last thirteen years? It was physically impossible for me to do any more than what I had done in the past! I said, "I'll do what ever you need me to do. But I want to know if Gordon is still going to be there." She said, "He's gonna change. He's gonna stop drinkin' and come home after work. Things are gonna be a lot better, but you have ta' stop bein' so hateful and actin' like you hate him. He's gonna be there, whether you like it or not, so get over it." Uh-huh. She finally came home with tranquilizers, I went back to school, and for a few weeks Gordon came home after work. But he wasn't any nicer sober than he was drunk. In fact, he was like a bear with a thorn in it's paw. He smacked us in the head just for walking by him. Every time he passed one of us kids in the house he hit us. Then everything went back to what had always been 'normal' for our house. He started drinking again, I really don't believe he ever stopped. The fighting was the same as always and we were back to square one. Alcee and Gordon were either fighting each other or having fun berating, ridiculing and/or beating us kids.

At least Alcee and Grandma had made up while she was in the hospital. I had to quit my job while she was in the hospital because I had to be home with the kids. They took me back, though, as soon as she came home and I was free to work again. I got to see Grandma more, but she was getting ready to move again and I was worried about where she would move. As it turned out, she was still within walking distance of the drive-in. But soon after she moved I got the job at the hamburger stand, it was inside and paid more money. It was a longer walk, five or six more blocks, but I could do it. Gordon started complaining about me staying at Grandma's so often, he didn't want me there at all.

While I still worked at the hamburger stand, Grandma and one of my uncles told me that my dad was back in town but he was in jail. They said they found him in another state and brought him back to stand trial. Oh yeah, the same uncle that ratted me out time after time. But this was a big deal and I just had to take a chance. He said he talked to my dad from the alley behind the jail. He said my dad asked him if he would take me up there to see him. My uncle said he would take me there! I was finally going to meet him! It had to be a secret from Alcee and Gordon, he and Grandma both said that. Since he and Grandma weren't fighting, I didn't think he would tell on me. The plan was for me to take my supper break at the restaurant during visiting hours at the jail one night. I did, and my uncle took me there to see my dad. I was so nervous and excited. The deputies, or who ever, took me and my uncle up some stairs and told us to stand in a little square entryway. There was a double layered steel door with a little crisscross steel opening near the top. We couldn't see through it, but we could hear through it. It was kind of like the window in a confessional booth at a Catholic church, but not as big. We were standing there and it was kind of quiet. Then I heard a male voice say, "Hey! Ya know who I am?" I said, "I think so. Are you my dad? Am I your kid?" He said, "Yeah, yer mine." I was so glad he said that, I was afraid he'd say I wasn't his. I didn't know what to say, the silence was deafening. My uncle started talking to him and I just listened. It was almost time to go when he said, "Hey, ya gonna come back next week and see me?" I said I would.

The next week I went back alone. He asked me what I did, where I worked, where I went to school. He asked me if Gordon was good to us. I said, "No. When will you get out of jail? I need to talk to you away from here, out of jail." He said, "Well, that son-of-a-bitch. I always heard that he wuz good ta you kids. I didn't know he wuz mean to ya." He said, "I want ya to go see my lawyer fer me. I told her I wuz sendin' ya to talk to 'er." He gave me her name and I called her, she wanted to see me and I met with her several times. She and her husband would eventually become my foster parents. But in the meantime, I visited my dad at the jail when ever I could sneak away from work on my supper break. Later, I would figure out that he was using me to try and get a lighter sentence, but I'll talk about that later. I knew it was a matter of time before I got caught, especially with my uncle setting it up to begin with. I talked to my manager at work, and he was very understanding about my situation. I told him I was afraid my mother would find out I had been going to the jail by questioning him about what I did on my break. He told me, first of all, that he wouldn't tell her and secondly, he said not to punch out when I went to the jail to talk to my dad. He said that way my lunch breaks wouldn't show up on my time card at the same times jail visiting hours were. Well, although my uncle would later swear that he 'didn't say anything to anybody' about me visiting my dad at the jail, I eventually got caught. One night Alcee showed up at my job and said, "Go get yer time card, I wanna see it." First I said I was working and too busy. But she said, "Go get yer fuckin' time card now, or I'll drag you across this counter by yer friggin' stringy hair." I went to the back and got my time card, took it to the front so she could look at it. The times I went on break didn't match visiting hours at the jail. But she was mad because I hadn't only clocked out for supper breaks, I had been clocking out when ever I took a ten minute break, too. Sometimes I was tired, especially if I worked a double shift, and I took a ten minute break now and then. She said, "You been clockin' out for ten minute breaks? You fuckin' idiot! Ya don't clock out fer ten minute breaks! They been takin' advantage o' you! Do you know how much money they beat you out of? Yer so goddamned stupid!" Oh well, at least I hadn't been caught yet, but within a week I would be. I came out of the jail one night after talking to my dad, and she was sitting across the street watching. I was caught now. She called the jail and told them not to let me in to visit my dad anymore. I was a minor and she could, and did, do that. So I couldn't see him or talk to him anymore. I called his attorney and asked her to explain to him why I stopped coming to see him. I didn't want him to think I just dropped him.

Shortly after that, Gordon came home late and drunk one night, as usual, and he and Alcee started fighting. I got up and did my job, keeping the kids out of the front part of the house and threatening to call the police. Calling the police was a joke and Gordon knew that. The whole time we lived out there, I could never get the police to come out and break up their fights. When I threatened to call the police he laughed at me and started his disgusting tirade against me. He said, "What the fuck you gonna do when I throw yer sorry ugly ass out o' here, ya little sneakin' bitch. Yer goin' to the pen ta live with yer daddy!" I was on the verge of tears, I don't know why I felt like crying because I was used to this. He said, "Oh, you gonna stretch yer ugly face fer me? What's a matter? Ya knocked up? Ya knocked up yet, huh? I thank ya are. I thank yer daddy knocked ya up! I know ya been sneakin' around seein' 'im. How many boys been in yer pussy by now? Wuz there others er just yer daddy?" He just kept laughing and saying, "I thought you wuz gonna call the cops. Go ahead, heh, heh, heh."

I had made a deal with Alcee for me to have enough of my money to buy lunch at school. I was in eighth grade then, so I went to Jr.

High instead of the 'out house' school in the country. I wanted to cash my check and keep some money out of it. She said, "Sign yer check and bring it to me. I'll cash the fuckin' thing and give you lunch money. I need the fuckin' money and it won't hurt you ta help me!" Sometimes she did, but I didn't use it to buy lunch. I went to a dress shop on my supper break at the restaurant and put an outfit in lay-a-way. I paid on it every week until I got it paid off. I knew I would have to explain how I got it, but I would cross that bridge when I came to it. I figured I would just tell Alcee that it would look good to Gordon when he asked what I did with my money, I could tell him I was buying my own medicine and my own clothes. The night I got my outfit out of lay-a-way I had to work until eleven. It was a school night, but that didn't matter. I was still on medication for the after effects of rheumatic fever, that didn't matter either. I always worked until closing, which was eleven on week nights, midnight on Friday and Saturday. By the time we did the clean up and Alcee drove me home it was around midnight. I was excited about my outfit, but it needed to be hemmed. As soon as we got home I got out the sewing box so I could hem it and wear it to school the next day. Gordon was drunk and still awake and he started picking on me. He said, "What do ya think yer doin'?" I said, "I want to hem this dress so I can wear it to school tomorrow. It will only take me about ten minutes." He said, "Where did it come from?" I said, "I bought it with my own money. I'm gonna hem it so I can wear it tomorrow." He said, "I'll be goddamned!" By then he had awakened all the kids and they were scared. Some of them were crying. He grabbed the dress and said, "Don't tell me what yer gonna do! I tell you, you don't tell me!" I tried to grab the dress back and said, "Stop it! Leave me alone." He said, "You little mother fucker I'll kill you! I'll tell you what yer gonna do! Yer gonna quit yer goddamned job and wear what I tell ya to wear."

I grabbed the dress back and held on to it and the sewing box. He was hitting me in the face and head while he yelled at me. Some of the kids were still crying and I could tell they were scared. Alcee just stood there. He said, "I'll tell ya what we're gonna do! We're gonna send you to the pen and let yer goddamned daddy take care of ya, you sneakin' little bitch. Maybe you two can share a cell!" I don't know where I got the courage, or stupidity, but I pushed the sewing box in his chest, brought my knee up between his legs and kneed him. I must have hit him hard because he couldn't even talk, he tried to, but he couldn't. His face looked weird, too, and he was frozen. He didn't move, maybe he couldn't, I don't know. While he was incapacitated I got right in his face and screamed, "If you ***ever*** touch me or any of these kids again, I will kill you! Don't even think about it ***ever*** again! You have to sleep sometime and I promise you will not wake up some morning if you ever touch us again!" While I was screaming at him, I pushed him several times. When I stopped screaming I pushed him so hard, he fell to the floor, and I walked away and left him laying there. Eventually, Alcee helped him up and they went to bed. I hemmed my dress and wore it to school the next day. A few days later, Gordon said I had 'disrespected' him and he was not going to speak to me until I apologized. I wish that declaration had lasted forever, but it didn't. I was scared all the time, waiting for Gordon to sneak up on me and get even, but I tried not to show any fear.

Shortly after the night I fought back, against Gordon, I found out we were moving back into town. Thank God! I didn't care if we moved back into the alley, as long as we lived back in town! It was even better news when I found out that we were moving about four houses down the street from Grandma. I remember thinking, this is good! And it would be for a while because Alcee and Grandma weren't fighting, so I would be allowed to speak to her. The news got even better, Gordon was going to work out of town and only come home on the weekends. He could make even more money on some big out of town jobs. He did make a lot of money, he was a skilled tradesman and only worked on huge commercial projects. Anyway, we moved back into town and he was gone more than he was home. It was easier for me to get back and forth to work, I could walk it. And on top of all that, Alcee wasn't going to work because Gordon would be making so much money she didn't need to. That meant I could go to school, even if the kids were sick, because Alcee would be home all day.

It sounded like things were looking up, but it wouldn't be as rosy as it first sounded like it would be. I felt like I was starting to go in the right direction again, getting stronger. But within the next couple years, I would go backwards again and give up all hope of making anything out of my life. Within the next few years, I would turn into someone who teetered back and forth between hopelessness and rage. I *think* that's what I felt, but I don't *know* because I could never identify my emotions. I was going to get stuck on an emotional teeter totter, and I would be on it alone. My body would sit on one end of the teeter totter, and my grab bag of unidentifiable emotions would sit on the other end. And when one of us fell off, the other end would crash and turn into a jumbled mess.

CHAPTER ELEVEN

Helpless, Hopeless and Defeated

I was happy to be moving back into town for a lot of reasons, but one of them was so I could change schools. The only dance I was ever allowed to attend in all my years of school was my eighth grade dance. It was before we moved back into town, while we still lived out in the sticks. It was a semi-formal, which at the time meant a short dress as opposed to a long one. While I was at the dance I had a good time, but it would turn into an embarrassment afterwards. I bought my own dress, shoes and purse. I was really excited about going. Gordon found out I was buying an outfit for the dance (gee, I wonder who told him) and he started harassing me about it. He said, "You ain't got no business at a fuckin' dance. Let alone spendin' a bunch o' money fer somethin' that ain't gonna make you look any better anyway." But I bought the stuff for the dance anyway.

I should have been suspicious when Alcee acted so supportive of my wanting to go. She even told me that a boy, who's mother she worked with, wanted to go to the dance at my school, but he didn't have anyone to get him in. She said his mother asked if he could go with me. He went to a different school than I did, so I had never even met him. She said I would be doing him a favor and I couldn't get a date anyway. She said, "Ya know you ain't gonna get a date and if you walk in by yerself everybody's gonna make fun of ya." She said he was cute, actually too cute for me, but he really wanted to go to that dance. I figured she was right, I couldn't get a date on my own, so I might as well go with him. I remember wondering why she was being so nice about the dance. I should have known something was up. They counted on me being stupid and maybe I was. There were so many things I should have seen coming, but for whatever reason I let them sneak up on me and hit me in the face. I thought I was on my toes all the time, on alert, in survivor mode or whatever it took to be ready for anything, but apparently I wasn't as 'on alert' as I tried to be because they still slammed me almost daily. I just couldn't seem to keep up with what was coming at me all the time.

The night of the dance, Alcee drove me into town and waited in the school parking lot for the boy's mother to show up with him. He showed up alone, riding a motor scooter, dressed in a paisley shirt, plaid jacket and striped pants. At first, I thought he looked like a clown because of the way he was dressed, but he was cute. When we went inside a bunch of girls flocked around him, I think because he was from a different school and because he really was cute. The way he was dressed turned out to be fine for the times, I guess, because everyone thought he looked cool, so as it turned out he was dressed okay. He was also very polite and spent most of the evening talking to me and staying close. He did dance with other girls, he had to if he wanted to fast dance because I didn't know how, but he still treated me as his date. I remember that I really enjoyed the girls oohing and ahing over *my* boyfriend. He was a friendly, nice boy and I really enjoyed that evening. I remember feeling special that night, but Alcee would soon set me straight on how special I *wasn't*. The next week she said she had to work on what would have been her day off for the boy's mother. She said, "I hope you had a good time at the fuckin' dance! I had to tell her I'd work my fuckin' day off for her so her kid would take you." I said, "What do you mean? You said he wanted to go and he didn't know anyone to get him in." She said, "Yeah, I know that's what I *told* ya. What was I gonna do, tell ya that yer too fuckin' ugly to get a date on yer own? I had to pay his mother to make him take ya!" I asked, "You really paid her to make him take me?" I was so embarrassed, I felt like crying but I didn't. She could tell I felt like crying and she said, "Boo hoo hoo! Why don't you stretch that fuckin' face? I cain't be nice ta you! You gotta fuckin' stretch yer rubber face over every little thing! Well, I have ta' get ta' work and pay off yer date!" I felt so embarrassed, or something, and I wondered if anybody else knew that my mother paid someone to get me a date. I didn't know it that day, but thank God I would soon be moving and switching schools. That was the only school dance I ever went to. I never even wanted to go to another one. Alcee told me more than once, "Yer so fuckin' ugly I'd have to tie a pork chop around yer neck ta get the dogs to play with ya." I guess working for that boy's mother was the pork chop. Even today I wonder how he felt about going to that dance with me. He was a very nice boy and he acted like he had a good time, but he must have been miserable. I feel sorry for him.

At least the move back into town got me away from that school. I also got to work more hours because I could walk to and from work. Gordon was gone through the week and only came home on the weekends, so I tried to work as much as I could on the weekends. Sometimes I would go in early to help open, work a double shift and close that night. Alcee needed the money. I worried about the kids when I was at work, especially on the weekends when Gordon was home. He still liked the same games, milk a mouse, look where a horse bit me and taking us mushroom hunting. He made us kids go with him to hunt mushrooms so we could move the leaves for him. He said, "There might be snakes under them leaves and I cain't afford ta' git bit and miss work" We had to take a stick and move the leaves, while he used another stick to scare us. Just as we moved the leaves to see if there were any mushrooms under them, he took a stick and rustled the leaves behind us while he yelled, "Oh, goddamn! Snake!" He and Alcee still fought when they were both home. He still drove drunk and his dad still got him out of it when he got into trouble. One time he totaled his car while driving drunk and his dad showed up and talked to the cop on the scene. The cop went over and let the air out of one of the tires and said, "Looks like you had a blow out." Uh-huh. The only thing that had really changed was our address.

Alcee started babysitting, that's right, *babysitting* for other people's kids. She had a real gold mine going there. She mostly had infants and toddlers, non-verbal aged kids. You guessed it, she wasn't very good to them, in fact, she was mean to them. She wasn't as bad to them as she was to her own because she couldn't put marks on them, but she screamed at them and jerked them around as if they were hers. Yet, the parents just loved her. She was mean to those kids all day, and then an hour or so before the parents were due to pick them up she made over them, or had me to, so they were smiling when the parents showed up to get them. One of her most cunning tricks was to watch for the parents to pull up in front of the house, then she showed the child a candy bar, ice cream or popsicle to get them excited about it. Then, depending on what it was, she laid the treat on the counter or put it in her pocket and carried the child out to the living room to answer the door. The kids were always glad to see their parents, but they kept reaching for Alcee because she had the treat. She was really slick. What a lie!

One little boy who she took care of was a little more than a year old and his mother was trying to potty train him. Alcee jumped right on that. She told the mother she would be glad to help train him during the day. And she did, the same way she did her own when they were little. She tied him to a potty chair for hours at a time! Sometimes he fell asleep tied to that potty chair, and when we finally got him off of it his little butt was like a ring mold of the seat. As soon as we put a diaper on him he went to the restroom in it and that infuriated Alcee. She used to shake him, just like she had done her own in the past, and call him a 'little bat mouth bastard.' I knew the little boy's older brother, I went to school with him and they just lived a few doors up the street from us. He was really close to his little brother because he was like a second generation sibling. He was fourteen years older than the baby and there were five of them all together. Anyway, his home life was similar to mine and we sometimes confided in each other. I told him to get his brother out of there. He swore he wouldn't tell anyone that I told him what was going on, and I don't know if he did or not, but I know his mother questioned mine and she stopped bringing the little one there for babysitting.

It was sickening and scary to watch Alcee abuse the babysitting kids. The parents would go on and on about how great she was and how much their kids loved her, but they only saw what Alcee *wanted* them to see. She frequently took pictures of the kids playing and laughing, then showed them to the parents when she got the prints back. She said, "I thought ya might want a print of this picture, the kids looked so cute that day." So, what the parents saw was their children reaching for Alcee when they arrived to pick them up, pictures of their kids laughing and playing during the day and Alcee carrying them around when they came in to pick them up at the end of the day. What they didn't see was Alcee giving them some toys and setting a scene, taking a few pictures and then grabbing all the toys away and screaming at them when they cried for them. She actually enjoyed it. I saw her take the pictures of the kids playing and then get right in their little faces and say, "You like this don't 'cha? Is it fun? Ain't you cute?" Then she grabbed the toy, stuck her face right in their face and screamed, "Ya can't have it though 'cause yer a little ugly bastard!" Then when they cried, she called them names and threw them in a playpen, literally. She did the big bird swoop thing, that she had done to my little brothers and sisters years before, and tossed them in an empty playpen. The more they cried, the more she screamed at them. Those parents didn't have a clue, Alcee was too slick for them. I remember wanting to tell them, but I knew better than to even think about it. I do remember a few people who only brought their kids for a short time. I don't think they knew *what* was going on, but I wonder if they knew *something* was because they just stopped bringing them with no explanation as to why. When my son was born I vowed to do everything possible to avoid babysitters. I started thinking back about the way Alcee treated the kids that she was paid to be good to and I shuddered to think my baby would be subjected to any such thing.

Anyway, when I went to the doctor for my monthly check up of my rheumatic fever, he said I didn't appear to be getting any better and told me he was going to put me on a half day schedule for school.

My first thought was that I would never get out of high school if I only went half days. Then I thought, 'Who are you kidding? You're never gonna graduate anyway.' I remember thinking I was going to be like one of my great aunts who I frequently saw walking around town. She had gotten married, had two kids, got a divorce and worked two jobs to support herself and the kids. I figured that was the best I could hope for. What I really *wanted* was to go to college and what I *dreamed* about was going to law school, but I had accepted the fact that it was not going to happen. Me going to school was like beating a dead horse. My attendance was not good because I still had to stay home a lot to help take care of the babysitting kids Alcee had. Speaking of Alcee, she was happy to hear about the half day schedule, she said, "If the doctor puts you on a half day o' school you can get more hours at work, I can use the money and I'll make sure ya get some of it back." I thought 'what ever' and started working more hours through the week. I left school at eleven thirty, and I could get to work before the noon lunch rush and work until closing. By doing that, and working double shifts on the weekends, I got in over fifty hours per week. Plus, I had the twenty hours of school per week, except when I had to stay home to help Alcee. It's funny how she needed me to help her during the hours I should have been at school, but she could make it on her own while I worked over fifty hours per week at the restaurant. The kids missed me, and I missed them, but they were getting older and Gordon wasn't there through the week, so I worked as much I could and tried not to worry about them. Alcee was still mean to all of us, but with Gordon gone it only made it half as bad and, as shameful as it is to say, she took a lot of it out on the babysitting kids and that meant less for my little brothers and sisters to have to put up with. I know that sounds awful. I feel ashamed to say that, but I remember thinking it.

I did start getting some of my money back after Alcee cashed my check. I didn't need lunch money, but I still got some of it back. Sometimes Alcee brought the kids up to where I worked and had me to talk the manager into giving me sandwiches for their supper.

It was a cash only, pay as you go, chain restaurant, but the manager gave me credit. I could let the kids order what ever they wanted and pay him back on pay day. That's why Alcee gave me some of my money back after she cashed my check. I used to lie about how much I had to pay back when I got paid. That's how I 'knocked down' and 'dark holed' money for the other stuff I bought. Anyway, I saved my money and bought stuff for the little ones. I bought a bike for the boys, they had to share it because I could only afford one, but later that year they got paper routes and saved for the kind of bicycles they really wanted. They saved points at the paper office, or something like that, and when they got enough points they could spend them on a bike. Tim and Tom saved up and got their own bikes. Tony wasn't big enough for a paper route so I bought him one like the other boys had. It was so much fun to watch the three of them riding up and down the street on their new, in style bikes that were paid for. They were so happy and proud. They actually strutted, and I loved seeing them that full of confidence and pride. Denise was too little for a bike so I bought her a tricycle and she loved it. I felt good about helping them get what other kids in the neighborhood had, especially with the little ones, it kind of made up for me being gone so much. Looking back, I think I kind of neglected Dana and Dena and focused more on the four youngest ones. I don't have an excuse or an explanation for doing that, but I think I must have done it because I don't remember buying for them like I did the younger ones. Dena was always very quiet and sometimes it was like she wasn't even there. I'm not using that as an excuse, but she didn't make enough noise for you to even know she was in the house.

It seemed like Alcee was still on my back all the time. No matter how much I worked or how much money I gave her, she still made fun of me. It wasn't like she was just criticizing me, she had to ridicule me. I remember being tired all the time and it seemed like the kids and my co-workers were the only people I had a kind word for. Alcee was always telling me, "You better get that chip off yer shoulder before I knock it off. You despisable son-of-a-bitch."

When ever I said I was tired or didn't feel good she said, "You act like yer forty years old instead of thirteen! Tired? What the fuck you got to be tired about? Yer problem is you think the world owes you a livin' and it don't! You ain't never had to work three fuckin' jobs and come home to a cryin' baby! You don't know what tired is. Yer lazy! Not tired! There's a difference ya know." I just stopped complaining and did what I had to do, but I think I was a little hateful, maybe even 'despisable' like Alcee said. I was old enough then to realize that there were only so many hours in a day. I didn't know how I could possibly do more than what I was doing. I was getting, and staying, depressed.

With Alcee and Grandma being back on speaking terms and living just a few doors apart, it seemed like Grandma and Georgie joined in with her to make fun of me more and more. Alcee liked to mock the way I embarrassed her when I was in a school program years earlier, and Georgie loved watching her do it. I figure the only reason I was allowed to be in it was because there was an investigation going on at the time and it looked good for me to be involved at school. I don't know that, but I suspect that. Anyway, Alcee said, "There the little fuckin' idiot was up there with the whole goddamned class and she was rockin' frontwards and backwards and blowin' her goddamned bangs off of 'er forehead. She looked like Popeye up there bouncin' up and down fer everybody to see. One woman asked which one was mine and I told her I didn't have one up there with that class. I had to tell her I wuz just there fer Dana. I wuz never so embarrassed in my life!" Then Georgie said, "Show me how she did again." And Alcee did just that and they laughed and laughed.

Alcee said she marked me by naming me after a character in a movie who was in an insane asylum. Grandma backed her up on that one and told me about 'marking babies.' She told me about her cousin who went to the zoo while she was pregnant. She said, "I told her, I said 'don't go to the friggin' zoo while your a carryin' that youngin. You're gonna mark that baby.' But she didn't listen to me.

I had the awfullest feelin' about her goin' to the zoo that day, but she wouldn't pay no attention to me. Well, she went to the zoo and got bit by a monkey and when that baby was born you should o' seen it. It looked just like a goddamned monkey! Still does! And I told your mother not to name you after that woman in that movie. I said 'Alcee that youngin'll be nutty as a goddamned bug if you do.' And just look at 'cha, I was right!" Then they all laughed. So did I. It was easier. It was just the right thing to do. When Alcee wasn't around Grandma would say, "You don't care about Grandma teasin' you do ya? You know I'm jus' kiddin' ya don't 'cha?" I did the right thing and said, "Oh no, I don't care. It's funny." It was easier. It was the right thing to do, *and say*. What I really wanted to say was, "Grandma, I love to hear your laugh, but not when you're laughing at me. Not when you laugh while Mom makes fun of me." But it would have only created more problems. I did love to hear Grandma laugh, it was a beautiful laugh. When she really got tickled about something, she tilted her head back and it sounded like her laugh was coming all the way from her toes. I loved her voice.

It was the era of Shindig and Hullabaloo and the dancers on those shows wore white go-go boots. Georgie, one of my cousins and I said we would kill for a pair of those boots, they were really popular at that time. They kept telling me to ask for a pair for Christmas, but I said no. I knew the best way not to get something was to ask for it, but they kept nagging me to ask. We all talked about how neat it would be if we all three had a pair. We talked about getting matching outfits and wearing them with the boots to school on the same day. It sounded like fun, but I wasn't going to ask. They kept pushing me to ask, my cousin said, "Ask your mom and I'll tell her that me and Georgie are gettin' a pair and she'll get 'em for you for Christmas." I actually started thinking that maybe Alcee would, if I asked. After all, she knew I couldn't and wouldn't buy them for myself, because I gave her almost all of my money. I remember saying to Alcee, "Georgie and Sue are gettin' white go-go boots for Christmas and they want me to ask for a pair too. I told them I didn't expect you to get them for me, but I said I would ask." Another time that I *knew* better and just didn't *do* better. I shouldn't have listened to the other two girls, I should have just gone with what I knew.

Christmas morning came and the other two girls got theirs, but I didn't get mine. My cousin was wearing hers and Georgie was showing me hers, and I said, "You are so lucky! I didn't get any." I reached for one of Georgie's and she had a fit. She pulled it back and said, "Don't touch 'em! You'll get 'em dirty. Here, I'll hold one and you can look at it, but don't touch it." I said, "I'm not gonna eat your boots, I just wanted to look at 'em." I was kind of hateful when I said it. Alcee heard me and said, "Oh you poor little thing! I tried my best ta' find ya a pair! I looked everywhere tryin' to find some fer you, but they don't make 'em that big, Slew Foot Sue!" She was always saying my feet were too big. Everybody started laughing, even Grandma, so I just made a joke out of the situation. I said, "You could have brought home the boxes, maybe I could have squeezed my feet into them." Then I grabbed a couple of boxes that were laying around, it was Christmas and there were empty boxes all over the house, and I put my feet in the boxes and slid around the house making them all laugh even more. I didn't ask for a whole lot when I was a kid, in fact, I tried not to ask for anything. I really was disappointed when the other girls got their boots and I didn't get a pair. I felt sucker punched, like when Gordon made me walk up to his chair and then punched me in the belly and knocked the wind out of me. I actually thought, if the other two were in on it I might get the boots, but I was wrong. Maybe I was being selfish, petty, spoiled or just a big cry baby, but I was expecting the boots. I figured with as much of my money that I gave to Alcee, she would surely come through, not because *I* wanted them, but because the other two wanted me to have them. I have to ask myself where my head was. I know, wah wah wah, so I didn't get the boots. I had worse things than that to deal with and it sounds trivial now, but it didn't *feel* trivial then. By the way, Georgie never wore her boots because she didn't want to get them dirty. As far as I know, they rotted in the box they came in. The next summer Alcee bought Dena a pair of white go-go boots that she hadn't even asked for, and a few months later Dana got a pair for Christmas. I never did get a pair, but that's what I got for asking.

A couple of older girls I worked with moved into our neighborhood, about four blocks away, and I befriended them, or they befriended me. I was such a loner that I don't know how we became friends. My two friends were white and they both dated black guys, with which each of them had a child. It would turn out to be a short friendship when Alcee and Gordon found out they were involved in interracial relationships. Sometimes I stopped by their house on the way to or from work, but one day I took Denise for a walk and went by there just to visit. I rarely went anywhere without taking at least one of the kids with me. One time, when we still lived in the alley, I got invited to a birthday party and my mother made me take Dana, even though she wasn't invited. The birthday girl's mother made me go back home because she hadn't invited any little ones to the party. Alcee said if Dana wasn't welcome, I wasn't going either. Anyway, when I stopped by to chat, my friends said they had some errands to do and asked me if I would watch one of the kids. I said I would. One of them took her child with them, the other one left her child with me. He was around two or three years old and it was a nice summer day, so I took him and Denise walking. Gordon drove by and saw us walking down the street and he brought the car to a screeching halt. He said, "What the fuck do you think yer doin'? Walkin' down the street with a goddamned nigger baby! Take it back where it belongs and git yer ass home!" He was still in the car, hanging out the window saying this stuff while I was walking with the two little ones! I told him I was babysitting the little boy and that I couldn't go home until his mother got back. He said, "Where ever in the fuck it lives, take it there and git yer ass off the street. Git yer ass home as soon as the nigger lover gits back." He took Denise with him.

I was dreading going home and with good reason. As soon as I hit the door Gordon was on his feet and in my face. He said, "You like niggers? Goddamned you, I'll kill you if I ever know o' you goin' around them nigger lovin' bitches again." I said, "I only watched him for about an hour while his mom went to the store." He said, "You dumb fucker! Do you know how I felt when I seen you walkin' down the street with that goddamned nigger baby? Huh? Huh? What if people wuz ta think it was yers? Did ya think o' that?" I said, "I just watched him for a little while. I work with his mom and she's my friend." He said, "I better never know o' you bein' around them nigger lovin' whores again. What's a matter ain't you got enough ta do around here? You gotta go out and find nigger babies to take care of? If you got time to help them whores, maybe you ain't got enough ta do around here." He kept yelling and screaming and calling me and my friends names. Alcee was right there helping him. She kept grabbing my 'stringy hair' and jerking my head around, while she hit me in the face. She said, "I'll see you dead before I see you with a goddamned nigger." It was the sixties in a college town. It was the era of the civil rights movement, Bobby Kennedy, hippies, peace, love and liberal thinking. *It was the sixties!* And there was a big movement to breed out the difference between whites and blacks. People were either strongly for that theory or adamantly against it. Guess which slant Alcee and Gordon had on it? It was awful. Even though the girls I worked with didn't hear it, I felt bad about all the name calling.

I was starting to feel angry a lot of the time. I actually didn't realize it, but I must have been feeling that way because I think one would have to be angry, at the very least, to do what I did. I am pretty ashamed of it to this day. I don't know what got into me, but something did. One day at school some girls came up to me and told me to stay away from the boy who lived up the street from me. They said their friend had a crush on him and I was in the way. Now I mean really, I worked all the time, the guy had a drug problem and I didn't want to get into that mess because I was afraid if I started using drugs the little ones would follow my example. He was cute, I was ugly, we were friends and that's all we were. He wouldn't have had me on a silver platter. I told them to buzz off, but they literally carried me into the girls restroom and got pushy. One of them had a knife strapped to her thigh, which she showed me, but she didn't take it out and point it at me. These girls were rough and tough little hoods. I guess I should have been rough and tough by then too, but I really wasn't and I still didn't like to fight. There were three of them, and one of me so I just agreed with them and told them I wouldn't talk to the guy anymore. That night I told Georgie about it, she had stayed home from school that day, but she was going back the next day, and we decided to walk into school together the next morning. We did. And the girl with the crush followed us down a hallway and kept mouthing off. She kept talking about what she would do to me if I didn't stay away from her potential boyfriend. Georgie and I went into the girls restroom and the other girl and one of her friends followed us. As soon as they got in the restroom and opened their mouths, I grabbed the one that was causing all the trouble. I don't know where it came from, but I was full of rage. I whirled around and grabbed her hair, then I slammed her head against the sanitary napkin machine which was mounted on the wall. I pinned her on the floor and sat on her and just started beating her in her face. I hit her over and over and over. I don't know what happened to me, it was like I snapped. Her friend jumped on my back and Georgie plucked her off of me and smacked her around enough to make her back off. I talked to that girl the whole time I was beating her up. I said, "If you ever send your friends around to scare me again, I'll track you down and kill you." I kept saying, "I will kill you. I will kill you." Some boys ran into the restroom and said some teachers were coming down the hall. Someone pulled me off of her and I took off with Georgie. I remember sitting in class waiting for the police to show up, but they never came. I kept waiting for the principal to call me to the office, but he never did. Some kids told me they took the other girl to the hospital and she had broken bones in her face. I kept waiting for her mother to call Alcee, but she never did. I don't know why no one came after me, but they didn't. Georgie told everyone that night how I 'kicked that girl's ass' so bad they had to take her to the hospital. Everyone laughed and talked about how the girl had it coming for messing with any of us. I felt bad at the time it happened and I feel bad about it today. I didn't even like to fight. I don't know why I did that. I really don't. After the fight, she didn't bother me anymore and neither did her friends. Two of her friends were sisters and they stared me down a few times, but they never came after me again. I was glad because they had a reputation of being the toughest girls at that school. I found out later that their dad had served time in prison for dealing drugs. In fact, he and my dad knew each other from prison.

I was having a problem at work because a girl who worked there knew how old I really was, or *wasn't.* I had lied about my age to get on there and I wasn't old enough to get a work permit. I was afraid if she kept asking questions, I would lose my job. I worked a lot more hours than she did, she was in high school and I was still in Jr. high school, she couldn't figure out how I got in so much time. Our timecards were in a rack and there was no way to hide it from her. My boss thought I was in high school and she was about to blow it for me. I got a promotion and she couldn't understand why I got it instead of her. She knew I couldn't have been as old as I said I was because she never saw me at the high school. She wasn't really a mean girl, just nosy. One day she came right out and asked me why she never saw me at the high school. I told her I had flunked several grades and was held back so many times that I was still in Jr. high. She said she didn't believe me because I was smarter than that. Really? She thought I was smart? Or was she tricking me? I figured she must be tricking me because *nobody* thought *I* was smart. I told Alcee I had to get a work permit or I might lose my job. I wasn't legally old enough to work at all, let alone work that many hours. She got out a document that I thought was my birth certificate, but it was really an application for a birth certificate that should have been filed with the state at the time of my birth. She and Grandma had stolen it from the hospital when I was born. Who knows why, I have heard several versions of the 'why' so I really don't know. One version was that they were going to smother me and throw me away and they didn't want any records of my birth, so they stole all the documents they could get their hands on from nurses' station when I was born. Just one of the myths, legends or facts of my childhood. I don't know which one, myth, legend or fact. Anyway, Alcee changed my year of birth on the document, as well as the spelling of my name, and told me that would work. It did. I went to the school administration office and they issued me a work permit with no problem. They didn't even look up my records to verify what grade I was in! It was too easy. But the girl at work then became concerned about how I got one. She just knew I wasn't that old, but she couldn't prove it and she finally gave up. I don't think the manager really cared anyway. He was just happy to have someone show up as much as I did. I was a hard worker and never called in sick. I was always willing to work a double if someone else didn't show up or called in. He would have been crazy not to look the other way.

After living back in town for a couple of years, things weren't as good as I thought they would be by then. Instead of me getting anywhere in my life, I seemed to be going backwards and getting weaker again. I think I was depressed most of the time and I know I was tired most of the time. My dad was *still* in jail awaiting trial and I was *still* hoping he would get out and let me move in with him. I had it all figured out in my mind. I would go to school *and* work to support myself. I wasn't asking him to support me, just give me a place to sleep and study. I told myself that I could do all the house work and cooking. I could still buy stuff for my brothers and sisters and make sure they had what they needed. I knew I would feel bad about leaving them, but I would see them almost everyday and try to be there for them. I thought that if I got out and got set up to graduate and go to college, I could save them one at a time. I had tried to go visit my dad at the jail again but one of the deputies called my mother and told her what I was up to. She started taking me to different counselors trying to get them to declare me nuts and/or incorrigible because I wanted to see my 'jailbird' dad, but when ever they asked *her* to come back alone she dropped them and found someone else to drag me to. She finally got a pediatrician to say the only reason I wanted to get to know my dad was because I had a 'Bonnie and Clyde' complex. She liked that one. He wasn't trained in psychology or psychiatry, but she thought he was right on point with that theory. He said I probably fantasized about robbing banks and committing felonies with my dad. In all fairness to that nit wit, I didn't talk to him about anything because both times he saw me Alcee was in the room. She did all the talking and I just sat there like an obstinate teenager. Maybe that was the best he could do, but I still think he was a nit wit. And even if he had talked to me alone, I don't think I would have trusted him enough to tell him anything. I had decided a long time before then to just bide my time and wait for a chance to get out of the situation I was born in. But I didn't know how much longer I could take it. I was sick of hearing that I was too ugly to get a boyfriend, too clumsy to dance, too stupid to 'pour piss out of a boot with the directions on the heel' and that I was the biggest mistake my mother ever made. I was sick of having to let my doctor, who was treating me for rheumatic fever, think I was just a stubborn teenager who didn't have sense enough to take it easy. He probably thought I stayed up too late at night playing records and dancing, or doing what ever other teens did, and I wanted to tell him that I worked at least fifty hours per week and see if he could ***make*** them ***let*** me stop it. I could feel myself coming to the end of my rope and there was a hangman's noose on the end of it.

One of my teachers came into the restaurant one afternoon during school hours and questioned why I was there working instead of in school. I told him I was too sick to go to school *all* day, so I got out early. I knew he was going to make an issue of it, at least I hoped he would. Grandma came up with the idea that I should start dropping hints in front of some other teachers about how I liked to come to school, but I had to stay home and help my mother. By the way, Grandma had already moved again by that time. The truant officers were starting to knock on our door and one of them even threatened Alcee with court action if I kept missing school. Like I said earlier, she didn't like them and they didn't like her. That's when Grandma and I came up with a plan to get Alcee to sign legal papers giving Grandma guardianship. We told her that I would still live at home with her, but I could change schools and go to the one in Grandma's district. I told her I hated the school I was going to and that the truant officer that was causing the most trouble would be out of the picture. Alcee fell for it, she signed the papers and I tried to move in with Grandma. But it wasn't that easy, it was a long struggle because Alcee said the papers only covered ***where I went to school***, not ***where I lived***. Grandma believed her, and I guess I did too, because I ended up staying at Alcee and Gordon's house for awhile longer.

Finally, my dad was going to court! Maybe he would get out of jail just in the nick of time to save me! His lawyer wanted me to come and talk to her and I did. My dad was going to take a plea bargain, instead of going to trial and she wanted to explain it to me. She said if I went to court for the sentencing hearing and talked to the judge, maybe he would go easy on my dad, but she really thought my dad would have to go back to jail. Okay, I didn't really know my dad, but he had been a source of hope since I was just a little girl. Unrealistic hope, but I didn't know that then, and it was *still* hope. I went to court that day and they brought my dad in with handcuffs on his wrists and shackles on his ankles. The judge asked him if he understood the charges and what his plea meant, and so on and so forth. My dad said he understood, his lawyer told the judge I wanted to say something and the judge allowed me to speak. I told the judge that I had never known my dad. I told him how I met him for the first time in jail over a year earlier and that my mother wouldn't let me visit him anymore. I told him my step-father was not a nice guy and how I really needed my dad to get me out of where I was so I could graduate high school. I kind of begged, not like I used to beg Alcee and Gordon when I was little, but I did beg. I said, "I really need my dad now. Please give him a break and I will live with him and make sure he stays out of trouble. I'll make sure he doesn't do anything wrong. I know he will stay legal for me.

He was never allowed to see me when I was growing up and now he has something to stay out of trouble for, me. He wants me to live with him, too. Please give him a break, for me." The judge said no. He was very nice and sympathetic to me, but there was no way he was going to let my dad out of jail. He sent him back to prison. Looking back, I think the judge did give him a break because he could have gotten over ten years and the judge only gave him two with several years of probation. They took my dad away and his lawyer tried to console me. I was heartbroken. I started crying, no I was sobbing, and I couldn't pull myself together. There he goes again, now it would be two years before I could hope for *that* route of escape again. That sounded like an eternity to me. A few days later the court news was printed in the newspaper and Alcee laughed about it. She said, "I guess I don't have ta' worry about ya sneakin' around to see that mother fucker anymore. It's a long walk ta the state pen. 'Course he'll never really be dead or gone as long as yer alive 'cause you look just like 'im. The cock sucker!" The end of my rope was looking better all the time.

There was a new manager where I worked and he wasn't as easy to get along with as the one before. The nosy, or concerned, girl I worked with had this new manager questioning my age, why I worked so much and how I got a work permit. I quit there and went to work at a little neighborhood grocery store, the blind man's store. I didn't work there very long, Alcee saw to that. The man paid me in cash, yeah cash, and she didn't like that. She didn't know how much I got paid every week. She kept track of my hours and knew how much I made per hour, but she didn't know to the penny how much I got paid every week because there was no check to cash. I started knocking down and dark holing more money. I lied about how much I got paid every week and she knew it, but she couldn't prove it. She wanted me to quit and go back to work at the restaurant, but I didn't want to. So she wrote a five or six page letter to the store owner and his wife that was full of ethnic slurs and derogatory statements. She called them every name she could think of and told them that they were a bad influence on me because I had become rebellious and belligerent since going to work for them. All that because I didn't want to go back to the restaurant to work! Of course, I didn't know about the letter until my boss received it in the mail. I guess Alcee wanted it to be a surprise, and it was. I went in to work one afternoon and the woman showed me the letter they received in the mail that day. I was so embarrassed. I felt so sorry for them. She said horrible things to those people, who had been good to me. The woman was kind of a 'stubbed toe' and wasn't very friendly, but the old blind man was nice and generous. Every day when I got to work he told me to help myself to the deli case and fix myself a sandwich. It was the same thing everyday. I didn't want to take advantage and assume it would be okay, even though he said it would be, so everyday I came in the door and started to work right away. And every day he said, "You get yourself something to eat and then you work." Now, Alcee had called them every ethnic slur she could think of and told them they were a bad influence on me. The old woman said, "We don't want any trouble with your mother. I think we're gonna have to let you go." The old man said, "She can't help what her mother does and if she wants to stay I think we ought to let her." They had been good to me, they were old and he was blind. I agreed with the old woman, I didn't want them to have any trouble with my mother either. This is the man my grandmother wanted me to rob. I left there and went to work at another hamburger stand, got Georgie on and started working for her on my days off again. Alcee took almost all of my money and Gordon demanded to see my 'imaginary bank book,' that I could never produce, as proof that I was saving it. He said, "If you ever expect to get married ya better at least have some money 'cause you ain't gonna snag nothin' with yer looks."

Shortly after my dad went back to prison, the same summer, Alcee and Gordon said we were moving back out to the country. Not nearly as far out as we had lived before, but it sure wasn't within walking distance to town. I said, "I'm staying at Grandma's. I work in town, I go to school in town and I'm not moving back out to the sticks." Alcee said, "Yeah ya are! You little ungrateful son-of-a-bitch! You - are - movin' - where - I - say - you - are - movin'! Yer gonna keep on 'til I have yer fuckin' head examined again! Oh yeah, yer goin' where I say yer goin'!" Then Gordon got his two cents worth in. He said, "What's a matter? Ye cain't sneak around and see daddy? Is 'at what yer nose is hard about? Yer fuckin' nose ain't too hard fer me to bust! I'll knock yer fuckin' teeth out if you thank yer gonna tell me what yer gonna do! I tell you, you don't tell me!" Alcee said, "I'm tired o' you actin' like yer too good fer the rest of us! You ain't! You just might as well get over it!" I never thought I was better than anyone, how could I have thought that. I knew I was worthless, probably the ***most*** worthless, ugly, stupid, clumsy, hateful, despisable bitch that ever walked the face of the earth. Did she think I hadn't been listening or what? I had heard her all my life, why would I think I was *better* than anybody? I wasn't even *as good* as anybody else, let alone better. She even told me that I should latch on to the boy up the street, who had a drug problem. She said, "There ain't nothin' wrong with him. Not a thang! If I wuz you I'd think twice about bein' so goddamned picky! You'll fly around all the flowers and land a turd! That's what you'll do! 'Cause you got it in yer head that yer so goddamned much better than everybody else."

That's the summer I found out that Alcee knew Raymond was a child molester, *before* she sent me up there to work for him when I was seven. That was a real hard hit to take. I couldn't get it off my mind. It just haunted me all summer. How could she have done that? I looked at my seven year old brother and thought about how much he still looked like a baby. I wondered if I was like that at seven. Was I that little and frail? Was I that innocent? Was I that vulnerable? Could I let that happen to him? How could she do that? I thought about how I could kill someone with my bare hands, if they touched one of my brothers or sisters like that. I tried to get it off my mind, but it wouldn't go away. All those years, I was so afraid Alcee would find out and now I knew that she had to have known all along. The teeter totter of jumbled emotions was not only going up and down, it was swaying too. I felt like I was on a teeter totter that had turned into a merry-go-round and it was spinning too fast. I felt sick to my stomach, my eyes hurt, I couldn't jump off because I didn't have the guts, I was a coward and I felt helpless, hopeless and defeated.

This was a bad summer, very depressing. What else could go wrong? My dad went back to prison, Grandma moved, I found out that Alcee knew about Raymond all those years, it was more obvious every day that I would never be able to graduate high school, let alone go to college, I didn't even dream about law school anymore, my political idol Bobby Kennedy was assassinated, I started a new job, Alcee and Gordon were moving away from town and I had finally had all I could deal with. I felt weaker than I had felt when I was seven or eight years old. And I believed that I was the most miserable, lousy, worthless piece of shit anywhere on this earth. I told myself, "You're not gonna make it. Give it up. You're like a baby fighting sleep, it's inevitable. You can't keep doing this, just like the sleepy baby, it's going to happen, you're going to fall asleep."

The week we were moving into the new place, I bought Alcee a new refrigerator, she wanted it and I had credit at the store where I had bought the boys' bike earlier. I made a deal with the owner and they delivered it to her house the same day. The deal I made with Alcee was that I could stay at Grandma's, so I could get to and from work easier. I would have to work as many hours as I could get to pay off the refrigerator. But she didn't keep her end of the bargain and then blamed it on Gordon. She said I had to start staying at the new place Friday night, that's when Gordon would be home and he wanted me home. She said, "Don't make us come after ye or you'll be sorrier than you are now!" Now she wanted me to let Gordon think she spent the money he gave her to buy the refrigerator. Okay, so here we go with the imaginary bank book again. She would kill me if I told him I bought the refrigerator, he would kill me if I didn't come up with the bank book he wanted to see so badly. So in spite of our deal, Friday was to be my first night at the new place, I decided that it would also be my only night there. It was time for the sleepy baby to go to sleep, she had kept her eyes open as long as she could. It was time for *her* to rest now.

That Friday morning on the way to work, I stopped at my pharmacy and got my phenobarbitol refilled, I had a few pills left, but I had a plan that would require more than a few. I went to work and acted as if nothing was wrong. Actually, I remember feeling pretty good that day, like a weight had been lifted off my shoulders. After work I went back to the pharmacy and told the druggist someone had stolen my pills out of my purse. He refilled it again! I don't know if he called the doctor for authorization or if he did it on his own, but he gave me another refill. I now had more than sixty tablets of phenobarbitol. I figured that should do it. I had tried this one other time, a couple of years earlier, but no one even knew about it. I didn't even get sick because I took something harmless, I don't even know what it was, but instead of dying I woke up the next morning and went to work. But this time I was bound and determined to do it right. I had seen the movie Valley of the Dolls and I was sure barbiturates would work. That night I went home and played with the kids for hours. I wanted our last night together to be happy for them. I remember being so calm and relieved. Alcee had her new refrigerator, the kids had a happy evening and it was time for me to go. After I got the kids in bed, I took all sixty plus tablets, went to bed and felt fine about it. But I obviously screwed that up, too, or I wouldn't be writing this would I?

I slept for over sixteen hours, more than rare for me, that had *never* happened before. Alcee and Gordon were both home, but I guess they didn't notice, not even when my boss called to see why I didn't show up for work. Later Alcee said she couldn't get me awake, but she just thought I was extra tired. Really? Uh-huh. When I finally woke up I couldn't see. I remember thinking, "You stupid little fucker! You're still alive but you're blind! Way to go!" I laid in bed for a while trying to figure out what to do. I tried to get up but I couldn't stand. I rolled out of bed, and crawled on my hands and knees into the living room. I knew where the phone was and I crawled around the corner and along the wall to get to it. I counted the holes on the dial and dialed Grandma's number. She answered and I tried to tell her what was going on. I asked her if she would send one of my uncles to pick me up. She said there was no one there at the time to drive. I asked her if she would call Lori, my dad’s attorney. Grandma said Lori had been by there earlier to leave a note for me. She said she didn't have my grandmother's phone number, so she went there to ask Grandma how to get in touch with me and leave her home phone number. Anyway, Grandma called her and told her I had tried to commit suicide. I laid on the floor holding the phone and when it rang I answered it right away. The whole time this was going on I could hear Alcee and Gordon giggling, but I didn’t know if they knew what was going on or if something else was funny. Grandma called me back and said Lori told her to have me crawl outside and lay in the yard, someone would come and get me. I crawled outside like she told me. Gordon and Alcee had to see me, I could hear them chuckling and whispering, but they didn't try to stop me. After I got outside, I could see a little bit, my vision was blurry, but I could see. Soon after I crawled into the yard, Lori showed up and helped me into her car. That's when Alcee and Gordon came out of the house like a couple of gorillas. Gordon said, "Hey! Who in the fuck do ya thank you are! You ain't takin' her no goddamned place! If the little bitch wants to die she can die!" What were they thinking? Did they think I took a bottle of aspirin and it made me sleep for sixteen hours? Did they really not care if I lived or died? Did they think it was funny? Did they think I was just fooling around or what? Alcee said, "Get yer ass outta that fuckin' car you little fittifed mother fucker!" Lori locked the car doors and said, "If you want to follow me that's fine, but I'm taking her to the hospital." As we drove away Gordon said, "No ya ain’t! Come back here you son-of-a-bitch!" But we went on to the hospital.

Shortly after we got there Gordon and Alcee came in screaming.

They said they wouldn't sign authorization papers for any treatment, the insurance wouldn't pay for it, they wouldn't pay for it and the doctor's had better not treat me or they would sue them. It was a good thing I had a lawyer with me. She demanded the hospital treat me, although the doctors said there was nothing they could do for me because the drugs had been in my system too long. I don't know if they were trying to scare me or not, but one of them said, "Do you know you can go to jail for attempted suicide?" I remember smiling at him, if I hadn't been so sick I would have laughed, like that would be the worst thing to ever happened to me? Another one said, "It's in her bloodstream, either she makes it or she doesn't. There's nothing we can do for her and it sounds like a family matter anyway." While Lori was picking me up and taking me to the hospital, her husband, Keith, was picking up my grandmother. When she showed up at the hospital it got even louder and uglier. Grandma showed the guardianship papers to Lori, who said they stipulated full guardianship! That meant I could go with Grandma and there was nothing Alcee and Gordon could do about it. Alcee said, "I hope the little sneakin' bitch *does* die." Gordon said, "She ain't leavin' here with nobody but me and 'er mother. Just let the little bitch lay there and die, that's what she wants." Lori had a nurse to call security. When they got there she showed them the guardianship papers and told them I was to be released to my grandmother. They still hadn't admitted me because no one would sign, so there was no release to be done. The doctors said the only thing worth trying was to keep me awake, get as much black coffee in me as they could, try to get me on my feet and make me walk. The screaming and fighting kept going on. Finally Grandma screamed at Gordon, "I'm takin her to my house you hog headed son-of-a-bitch and if you come after her I'll shoot yer fuckin' head off!" Alcee and Gordon still insisted that I leave with them, but Lori explained the guardianship papers to the security guard and he kept them back while Lori and Grandma took off with me.

When I got to Grandma's my uncles took turns holding me up, one on each side, trying to get me to walk. I was so weak I couldn't do it, I couldn't even hold my head up. They kept holding my head up, so I could try to drink coffee, and dragging me back and forth across the dining room trying to get me to stand. It was a long day and a long night. It was dark by the time I could even sit up. I remember hearing Grandma say several times, "Get her up and walk her, boys. Hold her head up. Make her move her legs, get some more coffee. C'mon Trennie, drink this coffee for Grandma." Sometime that night, after I started to become coherent again, Grandma said, "I'm not gonna let yer mom and Gordon get you again. Somethin' has got to be done! Yer gonna stay right here with me." Later I heard her tell my uncles, "It ain't no wonder she'd rather die than live with that bunch o' little bastards hangin' on her all the goddamned time. That youngin' can't take anymore, she looks like a goddamned whipoorwill." I was still pretty thin and scrawny.

The next day I was sick, sore, embarrassed, disappointed, scared and still depressed. I knew this wouldn't be the end of it. Alcee would be even more dangerous now than she normally was because Grandma and I had tricked her. She would *have* to get even. I wondered what Lori and Keith would think of me and I wondered what Lori was trying to contact me about, when she left the note with her home phone number. I really wanted to talk to them, but Grandma said they were on their way out of town, when she called them for help the morning before. I felt temporarily safe from physical harm because I knew it would take some time for Alcee to come up with a plan, but I remember still feeling so scared. That night upon returning to town, Lori and Keith came by to see how I was doing. They were very nice and I found out why Lori was trying to contact me. She said, "I know you don't have any way to visit your dad, now that he's been sent away. I would be willing to take you there for a visit in exchange for you cleaning my house." This was good. I was out of Alcee and Gordon's house, I was living at Grandma's, Lori would take me to the prison to see my dad and my boss said I still had my job.

This really was good. Then why did I feel as scared as I had ever felt? I think it was because I still *knew* better and this time I was going to *do* better. There was no way I was going to give up my jumbled mess of emotions, I couldn't identify most of them, but I knew that's what would keep me on my toes and keep me from getting sucker punched again. My life would get less brutal at times over the next couple of years, but I would still be on a teeter totter. There would be extreme highs and extreme lows. And when I finally thought I had it all together, Alcee would hurl me back into the bowels of helplessness, hoplessness and defeat.

CHAPTER TWELVE

The Gun

So now I was living at Grandma's, working as much as I ever did, and missing as much school as I ever did. I gave Grandma most of my money, but I was able to keep enough to send some to my dad every week so he could get what he needed or wanted from the prison commissary. I wrote to him as much as I could, at least once a week, and he wrote back to me. He even sent me a paint by number that he had done there, and a purse. He said the inmates made the purses there and he bought one for me. Grandma was good about either giving me money to eat on during my supper breaks at work, or having someone bring me something to eat, and she always made sure there was plenty of food in the house. There were about five teenagers living with her and we all had a job to do, writing bad checks. As I mentioned earlier, Grandma kept a log of where we wrote the checks, whether or not we had picked them up and who wrote the last one. She said they didn't prosecute minors for writing bad checks like they did adults. We moved several times within the first six months of me living there and Alcee frequently called to let us know that she knew where we were living and to say that "it ain't over 'till the fat lady sings."

Grandma was a little different than the stereotypical grandma. She was pretty young to be a grandmother, she was superstitious, she loved to party, drink and gamble, and she had some idiosyncrasies. For example, if someone licked a serving spoon she had a fit and threw it away. She said, "That ain't a friggin' spoon to eat off of and nobody wants to use it after you've had yer goddamned mouth on it." Now, that didn't make sense to me because we didn't throw away the regular spoons after we had eaten off of them, but whatever. We also had to wash dishes in a dishpan, ***never*** in the sink. If you put her dishes in a sink, she threw them away and bought all new ones. She said, "You don't know what's been in that fuckin' sink! Throw the goddamned things away! I ain't a gonna have 'em now!" But that was okay, Grandma was just Grandma. She was fun to be around, most of the time, and she laughed easily. I was so grateful for being rescued from Alcee and Gordon that I would have done *almost* anything for her. I helped keep the house clean, Georgie usually did the light weight stuff like dusting, when she felt like it, and I did the heavier stuff like mopping and waxing the floors. One thing about Grandma's house was that it was immaculate all the time.

Sometimes she said things and I had no idea where they came from. For instance, one night I went to bingo with her, she frequently made one of us go because she liked to play at least fifty cards and she needed us to help 'watch her cards,' she turned to me and out of the blue she said, "I 'm gonna tell you somethin' Trennie, all the little bastards are at yer mother's house, not mine!" I said, "What's the matter, Grandma? Did I do something to make you mad?" She said one of my uncles told her I called him a bastard. It was a lie, but that's what she was mad about. I said, "Grandma I didn't say any such thing." She said, "Well I'm just tellin' ya, that's where all the bastards are!" That same night when we got home, actually early the next morning, she said, "C'mon Trennie, come and lay down with Grandma. I ain't gonna let nothin' happen to you. Yer my first grandchild and there'll always be somethin' special about you to me. Why, I helped name you." Really? She had told me before that she begged Alcee not to name me after the insane woman in a movie. But she explained herself. She said, "After Alcee decided to name you Trena, I picked out yer other name 'cause it sounded good together." Uh-huh, okay. I figure I'll never know the truth about how I got my name, any more than I will know the truth about anything else that happened in my childhood. I just don't understand why I could never get the same story from two different people. Even over something as simple as how I got my name couldn't be agreed upon by two different people in my family, each one had their own version and, as far as they were concerned, theirs was the only version. I don't know if they didn't remember or if they just didn't want me to know. Anyway, I said, "Grandma, you're drunk." That wasn't the smartest thing I ever did. Of course, I wasn't known for being smart anyway. She said, "No by God I ain't! I wanna tell you somethin' Trennie, I'll remember ever' fuckin' thing I said and did tonight when I get up. Don't tell me I'm drunk! By God, I been too goddamned good to you fer you to talk to me that a way!" As I said earlier, Grandma was very confusing to me.

I had told Lori I would clean her house in exchange for a trip to see my dad at the prison. She finally called and set it up with me. She and Keith were going out of town for the weekend and she was bringing me a key so I could go clean while they were gone. I liked that because I didn't like people hovering over me while I worked. That weekend I spent all my spare time cleaning their house. It was a big house and it was definitely much in need of cleaning. I worked very hard to make sure everything was as immaculate as Grandma's house always was. I scrubbed everything in sight. I even washed curtains and sheers, waxed the floors and polished the fixtures in the bathroom and kitchen. That Sunday night when they got home Lori called me and went on and on about how clean the house was. She said it hadn't been that clean since they moved into it years before. She was very complimentary and offered to pay me money *and* take me to see my dad. I wouldn't take any money, though. A deal was a deal and I just wanted to go see my dad. To this day I know she meant every word she said about how clean her house was, she wasn't just being nice. I knew how to work hard at everything I did and I always gave it my best. Especially, if I was going to be compensated in any way for what I did. I always wanted to make sure I gave more than I received. I didn't want anyone to think I took advantage of them or that I was lazy.

Lori arranged for her and Keith to take me to the prison to see my dad within the next couple of weeks. That would be the first of several visits to the prison that she arranged for me. They picked me up early Saturday morning and we headed out on our trip. I remember it being so pleasant, almost fun, just to be riding peacefully in the car with two people being nice to me. It was a nice trip and neither of them made me feel like I owed them for taking me. We stayed in a motel that night and I was kind of uncomfortable about that, but it turned out okay. They got one room with two beds and I fell asleep easily watching TV. I remember thinking, "this must be what a vacation is like." We went over to the prison Sunday. Lori went in with me to see my dad, and that was okay with me because she was still his lawyer and I was kind of scared. When we went in we had to walk through a metal detector, which I set off about three times before they figured out that it was a snap on my garter belt that held up my nylons, then we walked into a little area that was similar to a cage and the steel barred doors slammed shut with a loud clank. After that we walked through another steel barred door that slammed 'clank!' behind us. Then we were led down a hallway and through a solid steel door. It was unnerving to me having all those doors slam shut and lock behind us. The guards gave us rules to follow and then let us go through the last door to the visiting room. It had a bunch of long wooden tables, maybe ten or twelve, that were extra wide and had wooden dividers down the middle of them. On the dividers was stamped in big bold letters, **KEEP HANDS BACK**. We sat down at one of the tables and waited. Then I saw my dad through a huge plate glass window, he was coming down a corridor towards the door at the other end of where we came in. I remember thinking about all the doors I had to come through and I wondered how many he had to come through to get to the visiting room. When he came in the room a guard asked him where his relatives were and my dad pointed to me and Lori. The guard escorted him over to our table and told him he could sit down.

I sat and talked to him for about an hour, or however long visiting hours were, I really don't remember. He thanked me for sending him money every week. He said he worked in the kitchen and they only paid him three cents per day, he said he couldn't even buy shaving cream on that amount. He told me about 'the rock,' which he said was on the roof, and said that's where the guards took prisoners when they got mad at them. He told me horror stories about it. It sounded awful. Lori asked him if he was staying out of trouble in there. He said he was, but he didn't know for how much longer because some guys wanted to kill him. That scared me. I told him if those guys tried to kill him to tell a guard and he laughed. He said, "Yer funny." I told him what grade I was in at school and he laughed again and asked, "You smart? You know stuff in school? Are ye good at it?" I lied to him and told him I did okay at school, but the truth was, I didn't even do average work anymore. He didn't act like it mattered either way to him, but I lied anyway. When we got ready to leave, my dad walked to one end of the visitation room where the inmates were allowed to kiss their relatives good bye, and he said, "Give yer ol' pop a kiss." I leaned forward a little to kiss him goodbye and he grabbed my head and kissed me back for way too long of time. It embarrassed me and I knew this wasn't right, but at first I thought he was just clowning around or teasing me. As I pulled away from him, Lori said, "Let her go. Don't do that, turn lose of her. I'll write, okay?" She didn't say it in a very nice voice either, she had a short, abrupt tone about her. The guards took my dad one direction and we went the other. When we got out to the car, Lori said, "I don't want to say anything derogatory about your dad, but you need to know that the way he kissed you is *not* the way a father kisses his daughter." I said, "I think he was just teasing me, don't you?" Lori said, "I think, before he gets out, we need to talk about that." And we both dropped the subject for then. I don't know if she wrote to him or talked to him about his behavior, but he later told me that Lori 'jumped his ass' about it.

The drive home was as pleasant as the drive over there had been the day before. Lori and Keith talked to me like I was a real person. I didn't get yelled at once, in fact, they were complimentary about me. When we stopped to eat they worried that I wouldn't get what I really wanted and kept insisting that I didn't eat enough. Once Lori looked at Keith and said, "What *do* teenagers eat?" He laughed and said, "I don't know. I guess the same things we ate when we were teenagers." Every time we stopped for any reason they offered me candy bars, pop, ice cream, chips, anything I wanted. I didn't want to take advantage, so I declined most of their offers. They laughed and talked to each other as much as they talked to me, and that was a lot. They told me I could clean their house again for the same deal, they would take me to the prison to see my dad again. I couldn't believe that these people had spent most of the last two days with me and they were willing to do it again! Were they serious? Were they just saying that to be nice and I would never hear from them again? They had spent two days with me and they were willing to spend more time in my unsightly, ignorant, miserable presence? Was I awake? Did they want something from me? Were they tricking me, and if so, what was the trick? Maybe they really were that nice, but if they were, why would they want to be so nice to me? I remember thinking, "They don't know about me. That's probably why they're being so nice. Wait until they find out how no good I am and see how nice they are." I told them I would love to make the same deal. Then I silently hoped that they never found out about me. I thought if they didn't talk to any of my relatives, maybe they would *never* find out about how stupid, worthless, despisable and lazy I was. What if they found out that I hardly ever went to school and that I was never going to have an education? They talked about school a lot, they would know I was trash when they found out I had missed so much school! I thought as long as I work extra hard to clean their house and mind my manners in front of them, they might not have to ever know. I hoped they would never know because I really liked them and I liked being around them. I decided to make sure I cleaned the house better than what the trip would be worth, so I wouldn't be taking advantage of them. That way, when they found out about me I wouldn't owe them anything. At least they wouldn't feel like I cheated them. I would rather over pay them so I wouldn't have to feel guilty when they found out about me. I knew where my value was, as minimal as it was, it was in manual labor. My only value was measured by how well my work was done and how fast I got it done. I would over earn the cost of the trip, so I could allow myself to accept it.

Alcee decided to have some fun with Grandma since they were not speaking again, so she called the utility companies and gave them all of her aliases. As I said earlier, when any of the utility companies turned off the lights, gas or water, Grandma would just have them turned back on in a different name. It was pretty easy to do that back then. So Alcee waited until winter came and then gave them all the list of names which she knew Grandma had used, and they came out and shut off the utilities. We got the gas turned back on and then the electric company came out and shut off the electricity. We got the electricity turned back on and the water company came out and shut off the water. This went on for months. Even after we got them turned back on in a different name, Alcee called the companies and told them the same people were living there and pulled a fast one on them again. Sometimes we moved so we could use a different name *and* have a different address. Grandma was getting pretty enraged about it, and I felt guilty about it. Alcee called me and said, "As soon as you decide ta ' mind and get yer ass back here yer grandma 'ill be able to keep her utilities on." Grandma said, "Let the fuckin' bitch sit down there and die fer all I care. Ya reap what 'cha sow and that bitch 'ill get hers!" So we just kept moving around and pulling fast ones on the utility companies.

Alcee had decided, since I thought I was 'better than the rest of them' and moved into Grandma's, that she wouldn't let me see the kids or even talk to them on the phone. I worried about them a lot and did everything I could to try and see them or talk to them. But there was no way she would let me see them. I called her house, hoping one of the kids would answer the phone, and sometimes they did, but she always grabbed the phone within seconds of them answering and said, "If ya wanna see 'em move yer ass back in here where ye belong. Ya don't wanna live with 'em? Then ya don't wanna see 'em or talk to 'em!" I tried to find out how they were by talking to people who knew them, but I was getting very little information about them. I tried going to their schools during recess time so I could catch them on the playground and see how they were, but Alcee found out, Dana told her, and told the school authorities not to let me around them. One of my uncles told me that Dena was having serious problems. He said that she got physically sick almost every morning while she was getting ready for school. The school authorities had insisted that she see a doctor and Alcee took her to one, but the doctor couldn't find anything physically wrong with her. He said the school then told them to take her to a counselor and they did. The counselor said that she was grieving because her older sister, Trena, had left home and that Dena saw her as the most stable thing in her life. The counselor supposedly said that Dena's world had been turned upside down. I felt awful. I didn't know what to do. I remember so many thoughts rushing through my head. If I moved back I would be blowing possibly the best chance I would ever have to break away, but it wasn't worth sacraficing one of the kids, was it? Oh God! I don't know if I ***can*** make myself go back there! I'll never have a chance to get back out. I told myself that if I didn't stay out and make it myself, I would never be able to help the kids later. Then I screamed at myself, not literally but in my head, "That's just an excuse! You're being selfish! You're not gonna make anything out of yourself anyway. How many times have you been told, 'you can't make a silk purse out of a sow's ear?' You are a sow's ear! You will never be a silk purse! Where is your fuckin' head? Get over it, you idiot!" I have to wonder, do you know how sad it is for a fifteen year old girl to be the most stable thing in her household? I do, I know it's very sad. I felt like I was between a rock and a hard place, but before I had to decide, something else would happen and the decision would be out of my hands.

Shortly after I heard about Dena, while I was still torturing myself trying to decide what to do, Alcee called and made an offer for me to see the kids. I really wanted to see them, but I was so suspicious and uneasy about it. I just knew Alcee was up to something, and I was right. She offered to pick me up at school at eleven thirty, I was still on a half day schedule, and take me to her house. She said, "I'll pick ya up and bring ya down here, so you' ll be here when the kids get off the school bus." I said, "Why so early, they don't get home until almost three o'clock?" She said, "Cause I'll be in town around that time and I ain't drivin' back ta pick you up when I could pick ya up then." I said, "I'm afraid, what if you're trickin' me? How do I know you'll bring me back to town?" She said, "Why wouldn't I? Look, I don't give a fuck if ya see 'em 'er not. Either ya wanna see 'em or ya don't, make up yer mind." I made her promise to take me back into town that night for sure. I also made her promise that she would take me back to town even before the kids got home, if I wanted to leave for any reason. She said, "I'd sure like ta know who's fillin' yer head full o' so much shit! What ever in the fuck ya want! I'll pick ya up around noon and I'll take ya back to town as soon as you say you wanna go. How's that, Queenie?" Well, I should have backed off right then, but it was *another* time that I *knew* better and just didn't *do* better. In my mind I was thinking, or hoping, that maybe this could turn into a long term visitation arrangement with the kids. That way maybe I could be there a little bit for the kids, especially Dena, but not have to move back there. I was hoping, and I knew better than to hope but I did it anyway, that Alcee was on the level and there wouldn't be a lot of trouble. I wasn't totally stupid, just ninety-nine percent, the other one percent told me there would be a catch somewhere, I just didn't know how rough the catch would be.

I arranged to get a day off from work within a few days of Alcee's offer, I didn't want her to change her mind about me seeing the kids. I figured what ever the price was for me to see them, I would pay it. There was a price for everything with Alcee, nothing was free. On Thursday, she picked me up from school around noon, actually she was late but I don't remember how late, and we went to her house. It was a cold winter day and it was raining with sleet mixed in. She was quiet, yet belligerant, on the way. She wasn't saying anything, but her body language and stares gave me an eerie feeling that she was up to something. I figured I had taken her best shot many times over throughout the years, and seeing the kids was worth taking one more. I should have jumped out of the car and walked back to town, but like the idiot Alcee had always told me I was, I didn't. We got to her house and went inside. It was only about twelve thirty or one o'clock, somewhere around that time. It would be over two hours before the kids got home. She had a babysittng child with her. She was still babysitting and this child was one she had watched at the old place. I remember thinking, "So this kid's mother still doesn't have a clue."

I sat in the kitchen and tried to be as quiet as I could. I didn't want to make any noise because that might set her off. She came into the kitchen, sat down at the table and just stared at me. It was so quiet and I knew something was up, so I tried to make conversation to keep her mind off of what ever she was thinking. I said, "How do the kids like their new school? Do they like riding the school bus?" She just stared at me for a few seconds, got up from the table, got out a bottle of whiskey and poured herself a drink. I started feeling scared then, I never knew from one day to the next if she would be drinking or preaching the gospel, but today she was going to be drinking whiskey. And when she drank whiskey she got very mean. She finally answered my question, she said, "If ya wanna know how they like their fuckin' school, ask 'em yerself. You don't give a fuck about 'em anyway or you'd be livin' here!" I said, "Mom, just take me back to town. I want to go now, I'll see the kids later." She said, "No ya won't! You'll see 'em today! Sit yer ass down and shut the fuck up!" I said, "You promised to take me back when I wanted to go. I want to go now." She poured herself some more whiskey and laughed at me. She said, "Yeah, and you believed me! You ain't as smart as ya thought 'cha was are ya? ***If*** I decide to take you back to town, it'll be when ***I*** get ready ta do it! Not when you tell me to, but ***when I tell you*** I'm goin' to!" She started her ranting and raving ritual about how ungrateful I was, how I thought the world owed me a living, how I thought I was better than her and the rest of the kids. She went on and on and on, while she drank her whiskey. The longer she ranted and raved, the louder she got. I finally said, "Okay, I'll walk back to town, so you don't have to drive me." She said, "No, no, no, the kids 'll be disappointed if they don't get ta see their big sister, Queenie! I'll leave ya alone." I sat back down and she got quiet for just a few minutes. But it was for a very few minutes. She looked at me and said, "I cain't believe you and that ol' bitch thought ya could out do me. You just think yer real smart don't 'cha? Well yer gonna find out that ya ain't near as smart as ya thought 'cha was!" She kept taunting me and laughing at me. She had done it before, I was used to it. At that point the only thing I was worried about was if or when I would make it back to town.

I stood up to leave, I was going to walk back to town. I didn't care how bad the weather was, I wanted out of there. I thought I could get so far, at least out of Alcee's sight, and then find a phone to call Grandma and have her send one of my uncles to pick me up. I got to the door and Alcee followed me out. She said, "Don't take off on foot, I'll get my keys and drive ya back." I stayed back away from the door, but I did wait to see if she came back out. She came out the door, threw some glasses, which I had bought for her, on the concrete and they busted all over the walk. She said, "You bought them fuckin' things and I don't wanna goddamned thing you ever gave me. You can shove 'em up yer ass! And don't ever give me anything else 'cause I don't want nothin' from you! Not a fuckin' thang! Take what ever you've got and give it ta that ol' bitch ya wanna stay with!" I said, "Okay, I won't buy you anything else." I started walking backwards away from her. Then she got calm again and said, "No, I'm not shittin' ya, I'll drive ya back into town as soon as the kids get off the bus." I did not want to go back into that house. She kept telling me to go back in, I just stood out in the driveway trying to decide whether to go back in or start walking to town. She got mad when I didn't go right back in, but she didn't scream. She kept walking towards me and I kept backing up. She said, "What the fuck's a matter with you? Yer actin' like yer crazy! Are ya on drugs or what?" I just stood there and stopped backing up as she came closer to me. When she got close to me, she calmly said, "I hope you know that I've fixed it so when I die you cain't come to my funeral." I said, "Oh, I'll be there because I'll probably have to pay for it." Then I made a run for it. I took off up the road as fast as I could. I really thought I could pop off like that and get away. (I told you I was stupid.) I really thought I could out run her, especially since she was drunk, but I was wrong again. She chased me up the road and as she got closer behind me she grabbed my hair and yanked me backwards. I fell, and when I did she started kicking me. I tried to get up, but the road was wet and slick and I kept sliding. She grabbed my hair and started dragging me down the road like a caveman dragged his woman in ancient times. The pavement was burning my skin and tearing my clothes. Actually, the friction was rubbing holes in my clothes. She dragged me all the way back to her house and up through her gravel driveway. Then she sat on me and kept beating my face with her fists for what seemed like forever. She had rings on both hands and the sets in the rings dug into the flesh on my face every time she hit me. I was covered with concrete burns, there were chunks of flesh dug out of my face, some of my hair had come out from her dragging me by it, my nose was bleeding, my mouth was bleeding and it was sleeting on us. The whole time she beat me, she screamed all of her usual degrading remarks. I tried to get up, but there was no way I could budge her. She kept screaming and beating me in the face with her fists. I finally felt myself go limp and just laid there. She was still in a rage and I knew this would go on until she was out of her rage. It would go on until she was too physically tired to keep it up. I just gave up and tried not to move a muscle. I tried not to be there.

While she was still sitting on me screaming and beating my face, the babysitting kid's mother pulled up. She got out of her car and ran over to us. She looked down at me, grabbed Alcee's wrist and said, "My God Alcee, what have you done? Look at her, let her up. My God, Alcee, you're killing her." Alcee jumped up and jerked her arm back from the woman as she screamed, "That ain't nothin' compared ta what I'm gonna do to the little bitch. Oh, I'm gonna kill her alright!" The woman ran into the house, grabbed her child and ran to her car, but she couldn't leave until the school bus came because she had another child that rode the same bus the kids rode.

Alcee grabbed my hair and started dragging me again, the rest of the way up her driveway and to the door. While she was dragging me the school bus pulled up and Dena was the first one off. I could see her a little bit because my head was pulled up with Alcee dragging me by my hair. Dena looked terrified, she was so scared. I knew she was because I had always been the one to take care of her when she got like that, and I knew how scared she was by the look on her face. Alcee dragged me inside the door and across the room. She pulled me up by my hair and then shoved me back down on a couch. She kept screaming, "I'm gonna kill you! I'm gonna kill you!" By then all the kids were inside, and they all looked terrified, except for Dana, she was actually smiling, like it was funny. The woman put her kids in her car and stood next to it. Alcee left the room and I whispered to Dena, "Go to the neighbors and call the police." When she tried to get out, Alcee reappeared in an instant and she had her gun in her hand. That scared Dena and she backed away from the door. She stood there, not knowing what to do. She started to cry a little bit, like she did at night when she was little. The woman outside had yelled at a neighbor to help. That neighbor came over to see what was going on and left right away. I would find out later that she called the police. Alcee came over to the couch and stuck the gun in my face. She kept trying to stick the barrel up my nostrils, but it was too big. She was screaming, "I'm gonna blow yer fuckin' brains out! How 'bout that, huh? I'm gonna blow yer fuckin' brains out!" I was in a lot of pain and my eyes were starting to swell shut, but I could still see a little, I had blood all over me and I could taste and feel that my mouth was full of blood. I tried not to move at all, not even breathe heavy.

I saw Dena backing out of the room, and I was glad because I knew she couldn’t stand to see what was going on. That was the first time she had seen me since the psychologist had told them she was grieving over me leaving. She had to be watching one of her worst nightmares. In later years, she would tell me that it was. Soon after she backed out of the room, she came back in and said to Alcee, "Somebody's on the phone for you." Alcee was still shoving the gun in my face, my nose was cut where she tried, several times, to shove the barrel into it, I was in so much pain and she just kept hitting me. She turned to Dena and said, "I didn't hear the fuckin' phone ring! Tell 'em I'll call 'em back!" It was scaring me the way she kept shoving the gun in my face and waving it around. The neighbor, who had left earlier, came in and stood next to Dena. She started getting the kids out of the house, while Alcee was in my face with the gun. She was still screaming and she had cocked the gun, it was ready to fire. I thought that was the day I would die. I had wanted to die earlier and screwed it up with a botched suicide attempt, I guess I didn't have anything to complain about. Like Alcee said, "You worthless back stabbin' mother fucker, I'm gonna put ***you*** out of ***everybody else's*** misery!" Finally, the kids had gotten out one by one, without Alcee even knowing it. The neighbor went to a different door and yelled, "Alcee I called an ambulance. The police are on the phone, talk to them." Then she took off. When Dena had told her someone was on the phone, it was the police. She had called them from another room and they told her to put her mommy on the phone. They were still on the other end of the line waiting, and probably listening, to what was going on. She picked up the phone and screamed, "Somebody better get here fast or I'm gonna shoot my fuckin' daughter." She was still screaming, hitting me and trying to stick the gun up my nose. She put it to my head and said, "You still wanna die? Let me help ya with that!" Then she screamed into the phone again, "Somebody better stop me! I'm gonna kill my own daughter!" Then she slammed the phone down.

I think I was a little scared, but not terrifed, I honestly don't know what I was. The kids were out of the house, so I knew they were safe. Maybe temporarily safe, but at least for the moment, they were out of the line of fire. I remember saying in a soft voice, so as not to antagonize her, "Let me go. Just let me go and I won't say a word to anybody." She shoved the gun in my mouth and screamed, "Shut yer fuckin' mouth or I'll blow yer fuckin' head off!" I sat as motionless as I could and it was getting harder and harder to see. One eye was swollen shut and the other one was swollen, but not as bad. When she wasn't screaming, I could hear her breathing, her breaths were heavy, deep fast ones. It sounded like she would hyperventilate, but I don't think she did. The sounds of her breathing and the gun in my face should have made me tremble I guess, but maybe I dissociated or something, I don't know. At some point in all the chaos and fear, I just turned limp and calm. Especially with the kids out of the house, I figured I would just play whatever hand I was dealt, what ever happened would happen. Looking back now, I know I should have been terrified throughout the whole ordeal, but I wasn't. I don't remember exactly when, but at some point it just didn't matter. I didn't even hurt any more. Finally, I heard some cars pull up in the gravel, it was the police. They were from two different departments, one county level and one state level. The county deputy looked in the window, jerked the door open, came into the house and walked straight over to Alcee and took the gun out of her hand. He knew her and said, "Alcee, did you do this?" She started ranting about how no good I was and how I asked for it. She said, "You don't know the little son-of-a-bitch! She drove me to it!" The state cop walked in right behind him and came over to me. He said, "It's okay now. Can you tell me what happened? Has this happened before?" I didn't respond to any of his questions, I just sat there. He said, "We need to get her to a hospital." The other cop said, "There's an ambulance enroute." The state cop said, "Cancel it, I'm not gonna wait. I'm taking her now." He was very nice and his voice was calm as he said, "C'mon Honey, let's get you to the hospital." He picked me up, carried me to his car and laid me in the back seat. He tried to talk to me a couple of times, but I didn't respond. He kept saying, "It's okay." It wasn't that I didn't want to be responsive to his questions, I just didn't think anything good would come of me talking. I don't remember feeling like I was afraid to talk, it just didn't matter or something. I wasn't trying to be hateful, by not talking to him, I just didn't feel like it.

I remember the state cop carrying me into the hospital emergency room, but I don't remember how I left there. I know, or at least I believe, I didn't talk to anyone there either. I wanted to go home and go to bed. I didn't want to talk about it, I didn't want to think about it, I didn't want to remember it. I think the hospital staff called my grandmother, but she couldn't get there so she sent someone else. I can't remember for sure who she sent, but I think she called Lori again because I remember her being there after I walked into Grandma's house. I don't know if she was already there, or if she came in after I got there. I had a concussion, so maybe that's why my memory of a few hours is a little fuzzy. There is about a three hour block of time, after I was carried out of the house by the state cop, of which I only remember bits and pieces. I do remember someone helping me walk into Grandma's. She was standing in the dining room watching the front door, and when I walked in, she grabbed the back of a chair and her knees buckled. She said, "Oh, my God. What did she do ta you?" and she got teary eyed. I thought she was going to cry. I felt sorry for her, so I tried to cheer her up. I didn't want anyone crying over me, it was embarrassing. I told her I was okay. I said, "Don't worry Grandma, I can do this standing on my head." She did chuckle, but she was still choked up. I remember Grandma and Lori talking about my injuries and the incident itself, but I don't remember details of the whole conversation, just bits and pieces. I just wanted to sleep, but they kept waking me up. Looking back now, I know they probably were supposed to keep waking me up because I had a concussion. I don't know when Lori left or when they let me go to sleep for the night, but I remember waking up the next morning.

Grandma got teary eyed every time she looked at me that morning. She said, "Somethin' has got to be done with that crazy bitch! She liked ta killed that youngin' yesterday." Lori came in that morning and said I needed to go with her to three different agencies to give statements about the events of the day before. Apparently, Grandma had told her that Alcee got away with anything and everything because she knew someone in every police department in the county. Lori wanted to take me to the county police department, the county District Attorney's office and the state police office. She said that with three different agencies involved, it would be harder for Alcee to persuade the officials to look the other way or lose evidence to be used for prosecution. I hadn't thought about it, but she said the police didn't even take Alcee to jail after they got me out of there the day before. I don't know if that was supposed to surprise me or not, but it didn't. It never occured to me that they *would* arrest her. Why would it? I just figured they would 'let the air out of *her* tire and call it a blow out,' so to speak.

Anyway, Lori took me to three different offices where they took pictures of my injuries and the clothes I had worn the day before. She and Grandma had put the clothes in a bag the night before and Lori had them with us. It really embarrassed me because they wanted to keep the clothes, that I had worn the day before when I was dragged and beaten, as physical evidence, including the underwear and bra I was wearing when I was dragged. They had holes worn in them too from when I was dragged by my hair on the pavement. Think about it. I was fifteen years old, and I didn't want anyone to even *see* my underwear or bra, and these people said they were *keeping* them! I argued about it a little, not too much because I didn't want to make anyone mad, but Lori finally said, "They are keeping all of the clothes you were wearing yesterday. Now hush." She didn't say it in a mean way, but I could tell my protest was futile. I dropped it, but I didn't like it. It was a rough day for me. Besides people keeping my clothes, including my underwear and bra, they were taking pictures of every bruise and scrape on my body that they knew about. Some of them were on parts of my body that I didn't want anyone to see. I was only partially dressed for some of the photos, it was humiliating and embarrassing, but I kept quiet and cooperated. I just wanted to go home and go back to bed. I was sore, depressed and exhausted. When we finally got back to Grandma's she said Alcee had been by her house. Apparently, she sat out in front of the house and honked her car horn, until one of my uncles went out to her car. Then she asked if she was welcome to come in. When he went in and asked Grandma she said, "Hell no, the bitch ain't comin' in here. If she don't get out o' here, I'm callin' the police." Lori suggested that I go to her and Keith's house, so Alcee wouldn't be able to find me if she came looking for me. She said the police were probably going to arrest Alcee that night. So I went home with Lori and spent the night there. Later I found out that they did go to arrest Alcee that night, but she told them she couldn't leave right then because Gordon wasn't home yet and (are you ready for this one?) *she didn't have a babysitter*! The cop knew her, so he told her just to come on in whenever Gordon got home that night. She arranged for a bail bondsmen and he met her at the jail. They booked her, bailed her and released her within thirty minutes. Later, she would laugh in my face about it. Is it any wonder that I didn't expect her to be arrested?

Lori and Keith talked to me a lot that Friday night. They also asked a lot of questions, and for what ever reason, I gave them a few answers. Most of my answers weren't totally truthful, but I did talk to them a little. One thing Lori brought up was the fact that, whenever they tried to contact me, I was at work. She asked how many hours I worked per week, and I told her a lot. She asked how I worked 'a lot' and made it to school every morning. I told her I didn't go every morning because Grandma was sick 'a lot' and I had to stay home to take care of her. I told her I only went to school a half day anyway. I said, "In a few months I'll be sixteen and Grandma said I can just quit." Lori said, "I don't want to embarrass you, but I saw your name posted on a bad check list at the grocery store. Did you know one of your checks bounced?" I said, "Yeah, actually I have several checks that bounced. I wrote them to get Grandma's medicine, she was sick." That's what I mean about not being totally truthful. They knew I had bad cheks around town, or they wouldn't be asking, but I didn't want to tell them I wrote them so Grandma could play the slot machines, bingo and get drunk. They asked me what I did with all my money, since I worked so many hours. They wondered if I saved it or if I spent it. *Sure they did*! I knew they were pumping me for information about my environment. I told them I helped my grandmother, because she was too sick to work and she was nice enough to let me stay there, and I sent some to my dad every week. I told them I just blew the rest on whatever.

Other than them pumping me for information, it was a pleasant night. I was in a lot of pain and I was pretty sore. They were very kind and offered me food and drink all night as we watched TV. It was really sweet. They had me to sit in between them on the couch while we watched TV. Lori said, "You've been through a lot the last couple of days. Sit between Keith and me and you'll feel safe and secure." She laughed and said, "We'll save you from any monsters that try to get you," and they both made funny growling sounds like lions or tigers make. They were being funny, they were playing. I felt uncomfortable, like a big baby. I said I could sit on the floor, or in the chair, but they said no. Keith said, "Let us take care of you tonight, you've had a rough day." And he said it so sweet, he was a very sweet and loving man. I sat between them and they each put one of their arms around me. I thought I was going to cry! (Maybe even die) Here I sat on a Friday night, on a sofa between two very nice people with their arms around me, watching TV. I felt like I was in a cocoon, it was nice, but it wasn't for someone like me. I remember thinking, "What is this? You should be at work, not sitting on your lazy ass feeling sorry for yourself, and above all, not letting other people feel sorry you!" I was screaming at myself for being such an idiot, such a cry baby. I felt a lump in my stomach, then it started moving up to my chest and then into my throat. I couldn't help it, I was going to cry if I didn't make them stop 'babying' me. I said, "That hurts. Your arms are hurting my neck and shoulders. I'm sorry, I don't want to sound mean, but you're hurting me." My voice was quivering because I was about to cry. They both jumped like they were startled and apologized profusely. Then I felt bad because I had made them feel bad, and they were just trying to be nice. They weren't really hurting my neck and shoulders, I just didn't know how to let them baby me. And what if I had started crying just because they were holding me? Would they think I was crazy, as well as being trash? Then they each tried to hold my hands, Keith had one of my hands and Lori had the other. I thought I was going to cry again. If they touched me, I was going to cry! I just wanted to scream, "Stop it! Don't treat me like I'm like a regular person, I'm not! Do you know what I am? Don't touch me or you'll make me cry! I'm not like other people, I don't need that baby stuff!" I kept pulling away from them by acting like my head or arm itched, eventually I had my hands back, and I didn't cry. Actually, I think they were amazed that I hadn't cried throughout the whole ordeal of the past two days.

That night Lori fixed up a make shift bed on the couch for me. When we were all going to bed, she and Keith came over to the couch and she started tucking me in! There I went again, I thought I was going to cry. I could hardly talk because of the lump in my throat, but I managed to say, "I can tuck myself in." She said, "Not here you can't." I said, "No really, you don't have to do that." They both laughed, not a mean laugh, a nice laugh, and Lori said, "It's a rule." Then Keith smiled at me, kissed me on the forehead and said, in such a sweet sympathetic voice, "You poor baby." I felt like I was going to explode! My God! Which planet were these people from? I couldn't wait for them to shut off the light and go away. I thought, "They are gonna keep this up until they make me cry!" ***Finally***, they did shut off the light and go away. It was just in the nick of time too, and I prayed, "God, please don't let them come back for *anything*." Because I didn't want them to know that I could no longer control ***all*** of my tears, I could control ***most*** of them, but not every single one of them. I didn't want *anyone* to know that a few of them had escaped, and that they were trickling down my bruised, scabby cheeks. Why didn't I want them to know? Because *I* could tuck *myself* in, that's why!

CHAPTER THIRTEEN

Waiting For The Other Shoe To Drop

Lori and Keith called me frequently and sometimes came into where I worked to eat. I had never seen them in there before I made friends with them, and I wondered if they were just kind of checking on me. But I decided I was being self centered to even think such a thing. I remember saying to myself, "So you think you're special enough for them to waste their time checking on you? Think again, you idiot!" They invited me out to dinner a couple of times within a week of the gun incident. I figured they knew I was working harder to clean their house than what the value of the trips to the prison were. I thought they wanted to take me out to dinner to even up the score. I told them they didn't have to do that. I remember thinking, "It's only me, it's not like they really owed somebody. I should be working harder for them than the cost of the trip. If nothing else, just for them putting up with me on the way to and from the prison." I really enjoyed being around them. They were funny, pleasant and peaceful. Grandma, on the other hand, was starting to complain about the time I spent with Lori and Keith. She was starting to not like them at all. She told me they were using me and said some pretty vulgar things about them, Lori in particular.

I thought it was nice of them to ask me to dinner, but I felt like I owed them. I wanted to pay them back, so I invited them to dinner. First they kept saying no because they couldn't allow me to pay, but I talked them into it, and they finally agreed to let me take them to an inexpensive fast food place. I knew they didn't really like that kind of food, that they were just making it easy for me. I knew that's what they were doing, but it was the best they would let me do for them. I asked Grandma if I could have enough money to take them out, and kind of repay them, for all they had done for me. She said, "Well, I'll tell ya somethin' Trennie, I don't think it's a good idea for you to be hangin' around them too much. I don't like the way Lori does 'er mouth." I said, "I just want to take them out for a hamburger and fries, they've been real nice to me, Grandma. I just want to pay them back, I don't want to owe them." She got mad and said, "I'm gonna tell you somethin' by God! They're both lawyers and they got more goddamned money than all of us put together, and you wanna take what we got to feed them supper! One time! One goddamned time and don't you ever ask again!" I said I wouldn't ask again, if I could go this one time because I had already set it up with them.

The night we were supposed to go out to eat, Lori and Keith were picking me up at six o'clock. I had to ask Grandma for money because I signed my checks and turned them over to her like I had done for Alcee. She hadn't given me any money back, yet, and I thought she forgot. I said, "Grandma, they'll be here in a little bit, are you gonna give me some money?" She was instantly mad and said, "Bull frig! I can't believe you're gonna really take what we got ta go feed them! By God no! I ain't givin' ya no goddamned money for them! I told you to stop hangin' around with 'em anyway. You just tell 'em you ain't got no fuckin' money to go and stay right here." I said, "Grandma, they are on the way to pick me up and they think I'm buying, what am I gonna tell them? You said I could go and you would give me five dollars of my money back. Now, what am I gonna tell them? I only need a few dollars, I'm not hungry so I probably won't eat." She said, "Don't you talk ta me like that, Trennie! I'll tell ya exactly what ta tell 'em! Tell 'em you ain't goin'! Goddamn you! You say ya wanna help me and then pull a goddamned stunt like this! You're already sendin' five dollars a week ta yer daddy! It don't do me no good fer you to help me one day and then have yer goddamned hand stuck out every other day wantin' money! You're a fuckin' Indian giver! That's what cha' are! A fuckin' Indian giver!" It had only been a week or so since the gun incident at Alcee's, and I thought Grandma was mad because I had a short paycheck during that time period. But now I think she would have been mad about me asking for money even if I hadn't had a short paycheck.

Lori came to the door while Grandma was yelling at me, and to this day I don't know how much she heard if anything. Georgie opened the door and let her in. She smiled at me and said, "Ready?" That's when Grandma said, "I wanna talk ta you, Lori. It ain't nothin' personal, but I don't think I'm gonna let Trennie go tonight. She's gettin' a little too big fer her britches and I think she oughtta just stay right here tonight. She's been gettin' awful sassy lately and I'm gonna have ta put my foot down with her." Lori looked at me and said, "Is that true, you sassed your Grandma? Did you tell her you're sorry? I'm surprised to hear that." Then she looked at Grandma and said, "Let us take her to dinner and I'll try to talk to her about that. If you don't want her to go I understand, sometimes you do just have to put your foot down." Grandma said, "Well, maybe you can talk some sense in to her. She ain't really bad, she just likes ta get mouthy every now and then. But I can't have it! I been too good to her ta be a puttin' up with that." Lori said, "Of course not, I don't blame you. You have been good to her." So we left and I was worried because we were going out to eat, I had said I would buy and I didn't have any money. I was so embarrassed, not just because I didn't have any money, but Grandma was starting to tell them what I really was. She was making me sound like a worthless, ungrateful piece of trash. I wished that Grandma had just said no from the beginning, instead of waiting until time for us to go and then not giving me the money. I was embarrassed and humiliated, but I had to tell them I didn't have any money. What if we went in and ordered food and then they found out? I'm sure they had enough on them to pay for some burgers, but what if they didn't? That wasn't the point anyway, I was going to take them to dinner and now I was reneging.

When we got to the car and pulled away Lori asked, "Do you and your Grandma argue a lot?" I said, "No, almost never, she's good to me and I'm just rotten to the core. I don't know why I aggravate her, I just do. I guess I'm just mean." I thought, "Well, they probably won't take me to the prison anymore because I was so mean to Grandma. They probably think I'm ungrateful and no good." We pulled into the fast food restaurant and I said, "I don't know how to tell you this, but I don't have any money. Grandma was going to give me the money for tonight, but she had to buy groceries so she she didn't have it. I am so sorry." Keith said, "That's okay." I said, "You can take me home and then go somewhere nice to eat in a minute's peace." Keith said, "I think we can eat in a minute's peace right here. Don't feel bad, it's okay. We weren't going to let you buy anyway. We're paying for dinner." I said, "I don't think I can eat. I don't feel very well. This didn't work out tonight. Could you just take me home and go without me?" Lori said, "No, we can't take you home. We are all three going in, we are all three going to eat and we are all three going to have a good time, and that's an order." I said, "I'm really not hungry. I'm really not." Keith started laughing, not a mean laugh like he was making fun of me, just a nice laugh, and said, "If you don't come in and eat, you'll have the wrath of Lori on you and you don't want that." We went in and I ordered some fries and a coke, but I didn't want them, I felt like a bum. I was nervous, uncomfortable, embarrassed, humiliated and I just wanted to go home. Grandma was wanting me to stay away from them, so I decided to be real quiet and unresponsive to them. That way they would stop calling me or coming by to see me. I thought I better end this friendship, because if I didn't Grandma might not let me stay with her, and besides that, I really didn't want to upset her.

When I got back home, I had only been gone an hour or so, Grandma was still mad at me. Lori went in with me and said, "I talked with Trena, Frankie. I think she was having a bad day, I don't think she'll be sassy to you anymore. She knows how much you love her and care about her." Where did that come from? We had barely talked about me and Grandma. Oh well, it made Grandma happy, so whatever. When Lori left Grandma said, "I don't mean ta harp at you Trennie, but I'm a gonna tell you a few things! You're shittin' on all yer family over some friends that don't care nothin' about you. Just like you used ta not mind workin' for Georgie on your nights off so she could get some extra rest, but anymore you got yer nose up Lori and Keith's asses so far your nose is brown. And every time Georgie wants you ta work for her, you say ye can't so ya can go runnin' off with them son-of-a-bitches! Yer puttin' them ahead a your family, the only family you got, right here! We been good to you and you just drop us like a hot potato ever' time they call. I'm a gettin' tired of it!" I said, 'Grandma I won't ask them to go out anymore. I just asked them this one time, but I won't again." She said, "It ain't just that! Pay attention to what I'm tellin' you! You put them above us! We're the ones that let you in when that crazy bitch mother o' yours tried to fuckin' kill you! Now you act like we're second fiddle to that goddamned bitch!" She was referring to Lori. I said, "That's the only way I can get to the prison to see my dad." She said, "I'm tellin' you that there's somethin' funny about that bitch. I can tell by the way she does 'er mouth! She's a goddamned queer! And you'd rather spend time with that than ta go to work and help me!" I said, "I'm gonna start avoiding them. I won't even clean their house anymore. If they call just tell them I'm not here. And I'll be at work every night so they can't bother me there." That made Grandma happy and she calmed down. She said, "Well, that's more like it. That's the Trennie Grandma knows! That's the way it ought ta be."

After about a week of avoiding them, Lori and Keith figured out something was not right. Maybe they figured it out before then, I don't know, but they had to have had a feeling that I was deliberately avoiding them. I went back to the restaurant I had worked at before, and took Georgie with me, that way I could work for her when I was supposed to be off. Also, if Lori and Keith tried to find me at work, they would go to my old job and I wouldn't be there. By then, it had been around two weeks since Alcee had tried to kill me. I was back on track, working all the time, going to school very little and being loyal to Grandma. One night Lori came into the restaurant and said, "How ya' doing?" I could feel my face light up, I didn't think I'd ever see her and Keith again. I said, "Fine.

Did you know I work here?" She laughed and said, "Yeah, you can't hide from me!" I don't know if she really knew I had been hiding from her or not, but I sure was glad to see her. She said, "I wondered if we could talk sometime. Maybe when you get off work?" I said, "Well, as soon as I get off work I have to get home." She said, "How about if I call your grandmother and tell her I'll give you a ride home." It was winter and Grandma was now living a good distance from the restaurant, and we were in the middle of moving even farther away. I said, "If Grandma says it's okay with her, it's okay with me." She was there when I got off work, and I was so happy to see her. That meant Grandma said it was okay. She bought us a coke and we talked in her car. She started asking questions again about school, Grandma and work. I told her Grandma was just upset because Alcee kept having the utilities shut off, school was fine and so was work. She went in with me when we got to Grandma's. She acted so sympathetic to Grandma. She said, "Frankie, I don't know how you do it. It's horrible what Trena's mother is doing to you. And how do you take care of all these teenagers living here? You're amazing." Basically, she was making friends with Grandma, she thought. Now, as long as she was telling Grandma how much she felt sorry for her, and how amazing she was, Grandma didn't seem to think she was so bad. But if she wanted to take up any of my time, she was a queer. Grandma could tell by the way she 'did her mouth.' Uh-huh, okay, whatever.

Within days of thinking she made friends with Grandma, Lori picked me up at work again. She said Grandma knew she was picking me up and that I was going to her house for a while. She said she and Keith wanted to talk to me about something. On the way to her house she said they wondered if I would like to move in with them and that's what they wanted to talk to me about. I told her I didn't think Grandma would like that. I remember thinking, "How would I explain being broke all the time when I give Grandma all of my money. They will find out what goes on in our house. I better not even think about it. Anyway, if they started babying me, like they did that Friday night I stayed there, they would ruin me." Lori said she could deal with Grandma. She said, "Oh, I don't think your grandmother will be a problem. I'll talk to her and I'm sure she will agree that it is probably the best thing right now. She has so many others to take care of and you need the protection against your mother. Keith and I can protect you." I really wanted to do it. I knew those things Grandma said about them were not true, she was just jealous of the time I had spent with them. I told Lori, "You guys don't want me hanging around all the time. You don't know me, I'm pretty bad. You might not realize it because you haven't lived with me, but I'm nothin' but trouble. I would drive you guys crazy! Trust me, you don't want me." She said she'd take her chances.

When we got to her house, we continued the conversation with Keith. I told them both, again, that I was a lot of trouble and I better not. I said, "I think I was only put on earth to aggravate people. I'm not much. You guys just don't know me, I'm nothin' but trouble." She asked me if I knew a lot about pregnancies. I said, "I'm not like that. I'm not *that* kind of trouble." They both laughed and that's when she told me that she thought she was pregnant. I said, "Well, congratulations, is Keith happy about it?" They both laughed and she said, "Well of course he is! We both have discussed it and we want you to come live with us. We can make a deal. You can help me with my pregnancy, the house and the baby, in exchange for living with us. You don't have to pay us anything." Oh, so I *would* be earning my keep. I wouldn't be just taking something for nothing. Lori said her mother died when she was a teenager, she was an only child and she knew absolutely nothing about pregnancy or babies. She said I would be a big help to her. She and Keith were both very busy attorneys and she was worried about being pregnant and them having a baby. She wanted the baby, but she was really scared. I believed I really would be paying my own way by helping out with everything. I knew how much work pregnant women and babies were, and they had a big house to keep up, that was a lot of work too. I wouldn't be sponging off of them, I really would be earning my room and board. But what if they decided they didn't like me. I still hesitated. I asked, "What's the catch? Nothing can be that easy, what do you want from me besides helping you?" She said, "The only catch is that you *have to go to school* everyday. No more missing school, that's it. And you have to quit your job. You work too many hours for someone your age." I said, "Oh, I can't do that, I have to have my job. I have to have money." Keith said, "You will have money, you will be getting an allowance." An allowance? No way! I heard about allowances from the kids at school, an allowance was only a few bucks a week. I had to have five dollars to send my dad every week, ten dollars to send him for holidays, and what if Grandma needed money? No, I had to have my job. I couldn't move in with them and live like that. I would be dropping the ball on too many people who needed me. I told them I really wanted to, but I really believed it would only turn them against me when they realized how bad I really was. I wanted to stay friends, so I better not. I said, "Look, I'm not what I'm cracked up to be. I'm no prize out of a Cracker Jack box." Keith chuckled and Lori said she was going to talk to my grandmother and give me a few days to think about it. They both told me to keep in mind that almost everything was negotiable, *except school*, no negotiating about school.

She approached Grandma about it, and it was not what Grandma even wanted to think about. Lori told her that if I moved in with them for a little while, maybe Alcee would stop harrassing her. She also said that Grandma had more than she needed to handle anyway. She told Grandma, "Let us help you out by taking part of your load off you. We just love Trena and we would love to have her with us for awhile." Grandma was definitely against it. Lori might have *thought* she made friends with Grandma, but she hadn't. Grandma said, "Uh-huh, I been half way expectin' you to bring this up. I'll just have ta think about this for a few days." After Lori left, she said, "That bitch is just wantin' ta use you as a goddamned maid! She's a goddamned sneakin' bitch and that youngin' she's a carryin' ain't even her husband's! I heard all about her goin' down ta the cab stand and fuckin' one o' the drivers! I know who that little bastard she's a carryin' belongs to and it ain't Keith!" I told Grandma I wanted to go with Lori and Keith. I said, "I know you can stop me if you want to, but I want to try it. I want to live with them for awhile. And maybe Mom will leave you alone." She said, "Don't act like you're a doin' it for me! You ain't wantin ' ta go to save me from yer goddamned crazy mother! You think they really like you, but you ain't got sense enough ta know when somebody's a usin' you! You go with them and you'll find out they're just wantin' a goddamned maid and babysitter! You'll find out! And when you do, don't come crawlin' back here, goddamned you! You ain't any better than the rest of us and you need to stay right her with your own kind, by God!" She went on and on about how good she had been to me and said, "If you go with them, you ain't comin' back here! Next time yer fuckin' mother tries to kill ya, I hope they wanna keep ya 'cause you ain't never comin' back here, Trennie! You are tearin' my heart ta pieces! I been good to you and you stab me in the back!"

Lori, in the meantime, had gotten the court to appoint her and Keith guardians of me, she didn't even need Grandma's signature. I think with my dad in prison, and criminal charges pending against my mother, it was pretty easy for her to get it done. I didn't say anything to Grandma about when I would be leaving, I didn't know yet, but it would only be a couple of days. We were in the middle of moving again, and this time Grandma was moving outside the city limits, and it would be next to impossible for me to walk to work, especially since it was winter time. Lori told me to get off work no later than seven o'clock one evening. She said she would pick me up and we would go to Grandma's to get my things. I got off at eight, that was the best I could do. Lori picked me up and took me out to Grandma's new place. I went in to get my stuff, which was not enough to fill a banker's box, and Grandma wasn't there, she had gone out drinking. Her husband and one of my uncles were there. Her husband said, "I wouldn't do that if I was you. Yer grandma ain't gonna like it." My uncle said, "Yer a little fuckin' cowardly ain't 'cha? Why don't 'cha come back when Mom's home?" Lori said, "Get your stuff and come on." I did. She told my uncle that Grandma could call her if she wanted to, and we left. And I was so worried. I don't know why, but I was.

As we were driving to Lori's house, she said, "Well, I guess you need to start checking in with me after school." I got that lump in my throat again, like I had when they tucked me in that time. Just because she wanted me to check in with her after school! That was so nice, I thought I was going to cry. I wasn't supposed to just get out of school and run to work? What was I supposed to do then? I said, "Well, I'll be at work right after school." She said, "I don't think you should go to work tomorrow. Your family knows where you work, I think you need to come home, or to the office, after school." Then she said, "The three of us will sit down and talk this weekend. We need to set some rules on how we're going to do everything." She wanted to make some rules, there would be some guidelines and structure? I could follow rules! Maybe I *won't* mess this up. Maybe this *will* work out! I was starting to feel some confidence that this could work and we weren't even to her house yet. Then I told myself to calm down, I thought, "There still has to be a catch somewhere, don't get to excited until you find out what it is. You'll find a way to screw it up, you've screwed up everything else." Lori said, "We can talk more this weekend about getting settled in and how we'll work everything out." I thought, "Maybe I'll find out what the catch is then."

That weekend the three of us did sit down and talk about what was expected of me and what I could expect of them. The biggest emphasis was on school. I was still on a half day schedule, and until that week, I had been going from school to work. Lori and Keith said I was to quit my job and concentrate on school. The plan was for me to finish the year on the half day schedule, get plenty of rest and then, in the fall when school started again, I would go back on full days of school. I was a sophomore and there was time for me to catch up if I worked extra hard at it. The problem was quitting my job. I said, "I have to have a job. I have to pay my own way, I can't just mooch off someone. You said everything except school was negotiable." Lori was also a judge in a lower court, so she said I could work ten or eleven hours per week in her court, but no more. She was going to pay me the same hourly rate I had been earning at the restaurant. Okay, I would have around ten or twelve dollars per week, after taxes. I could still send my dad five dollars per week and have a few dollars left. I didn't need lunch money because I still got out of school by lunch time. I never ate lunch anyway. What about clothes and cosmetics? They said I could buy my own cosmetics, but they would buy my clothes. Really! They were going to buy my clothes? I remember thinking, "This is getting better all the time, there must be a ***giant*** catch somewhere." First I said, "I can't let you buy my clothes! I would be mooching and taking advantage. If you let me work a few more hours I can buy my own, I don't need very many clothes anyway." Keith said, "You won't be mooching, you will be part of our family and that's what parents do for their kids. It's our responsibility to provide housing, food and clothing. We want to do that for you. You're going to be like our little girl." Oh get real! I didn't think I had been a little girl since I was four years old. I said, "Why? You don't even know me that well." Lori smiled and said, "Oh, we know you just fine. *You* don't know *me* very well, but you will." Keith started laughing and said, "When Lori decides something's a rule, it becomes a rule." Lori said, "Yeah, and here's the rule. You work for me ten or eleven hours per week, you keep all of your money for yourself, and we will provide food, clothes and housing." I said, "Okay, I can try that, what else?" Lori said, "You keep the house clean, the laundry done and cook two or three nights a week." I thought, "That's it? I can do that standing on my head. There has to be more than that. They still aren't telling me what the catch is." I said, "This is really nice of you to do this, but there are a lot of kids who need a deal like this more than I do. Why did you pick me? There a lot better kids than me to take in." Keith said, "We can't help ourselves, we fell in love with you. Please give us a chance to prove it to you."

I thought, "Okay, let me get this straight. They want me to clean the house, do the laundry and cook a few nights per week, help Lori however I can with her pregnancy and help with the baby when it gets here. I am only allowed to work ten or eleven hours per week in Lori's court, *and* I keep all of my money that I earn. *And* they claim they *love me*. Me. Of all people, they think they can love *me*." I figured I could use this opportunity to catch my breath, get my bearings and get strong again. I just knew it would be a matter of time before they found out I wasn't even loveable, there was no way they could really love me, it wasn't possible. As soon as they saw my despisable side, they would throw me out. But I figured I could beg my way back into Grandma's when that happened. But then on the other hand, I would be eighteen in less than three years. What if I could make it until then? I wouldn't have to beg anyone to let me back in. What if I did catch up at school and graduate? Maybe I could go to college. I could help the kids more after I was eighteen than I could now. But three years is along time, there's no way I can hide what I am for three years. Well, I could still get myself together and gain some strength back before they pitched me out on my butt. Then I told myself, "No, no, no. Where in the fuck is your head? Look for the catch! If you find the catch, and you think you can do it, then maybe you can make it. You *have* to know what the catch is or you'll get sucker punched, idiot!" I said, "I don't know why you guys are being so nice to me, but I'll try to earn your kindness and not let you down. But I want you to know up front, I'm not much. Just remember I told you that up front."

The next thing Lori brought up was my bad checks. She said, "We need to make a list of all your bad checks, how much they are and where you wrote them. Can you remember where all of them are?" I said, "I think so, but I'm not sure. How many do *you* think there are?" She said, "I know about the bad check scheme at your grandmothers. I know you have more than a few to pick up, it's okay. You don't have to be afraid. I want you to make a list, and I will take you around to each place so you can pick them up." I couldn't remember every single one, but there were quite a few and

I was embarrassed. Grandma was supposed to pick them up, eventually. I said, "You don't have to do that, Grandma will pick them up when she gets the money." Lori said, "No, you will pick them up today. I'm not doing anything except loaning you the money, you're going to pay me back. You wrote the checks, you pay for the checks." When Grandma had them picked up she sent her husband to do it. He used to tell the merchants that we were young and just hadn't learned to keep a check register yet. Anyway, I made the list, the best I could remember, and she did drive me around to each place to pick them up. She gave me money, and except for a couple of places, made me go in alone to pick them up and give her the bounced checks. She said I could have them when I paid her back. It was embarrassing to pick them up. She wasn't being mean, but she was being stern. I think she just didn't want to make it too easy for me to get out of the bad check business. I think she was just trying to make sure I didn't *want* to do that again. I don't think she understood that I didn't write bad checks for the sport of it. I think she knew I did it for my grandmother, but maybe she thought I didn't see anything wrong with it. I did, though. I hated doing it, but there was no way she could have known that because I didn't tell anybody how I felt about anything. After I picked them all up, and made arrangements to buy them back from her, she didn't harp on it. She never screamed at me about it, didn't call me any names and didn't lay a hand on me. I was still waiting for the other shoe to drop, but I guess this wasn't where it was going to drop. So I'd just stay on my toes and watch out for it somewhere else.

It was fun living there. I had fun watching Lori go through her pregnancy. She really didn't know the first thing about babies, or having one. She asked me so many questions and I knew most of the answers. I felt really smart until I caught myself feeling it, then I put myself back in my place. I didn't want anyone else to have to, I could do that myself, too. They were both nice to me, but Keith was the warm, fuzzy one. Lori wasn't mean, but she didn't believe in spoiling kids either. She had a stern demeanor most of the time, and sometimes said no just to show me she could. Like one time, I asked her if I could use her hairspray because I had run out. She said, "No. Not because I care about the hairspray, but because I want you to know that I can say no." I didn't get it, I still don't, but she was nice, and it was a huge undertaking to let a strange kid come into her house. And God knows, there was no kid on earth stranger than I was. Keith told me that her dad had been very strict on her after her mother died and that's all she knew. She loved her dad very much and thought the way he raised her was the right way. He obviously thought she was too strict sometimes, but neither of us challenged her. I certainly would have never challenged her, I thought I had died and gone to heaven. I felt like I was being fattened up for a slaughter. I just wanted the other shoe to drop so I could pick it up, put it on, and try to salvage my relationship with them after it fell.

Within a week of me moving in, they asked me to go with them to pick out paint for my room. I couldn't believe it, they wanted me to pick out my own color! They were giving me a huge bedroom upstairs, I had been sleeping on the couch until then, and I got to pick the color. I thought, "When it comes time to pay the piper for this deal, I'll never be able to come up with the price. I wish I could figure out the catch *before* I get sucker punched. It's not a sucker punch if I see it coming, but I can't figure it out. I wish I was smarter." Not only did I pick out the color but I got to paint my room myself. I also got to pick out curtains and a bed spread to match. Keith made me a dressing table. He *made it* with his own hands, *for me*. He went out and bought wood, spindles and paint and made me a dressing table. He even put little curtain rods around the edge and put a skirt around it with curtains that matched my window curtains and bedspread. Then after all that, they found a record player for me and let me put that in my room and go buy some records! This is the stuff I heard other girls at school talk about. Then they let me put an old typewriter in my room to play around with. Now, Keith wasn't the handiest man in the world, he was more an intellectual, but when he carried my dressing table up to my room, I thought it was the most beautiful thing I had ever seen. It just made my room come together. I said, "It is so pretty, I can't believe it's mine." He smiled and said, "All little girls need a vanity." There I went again, I felt like crying, but I didn't. I finally finished getting my room in order on Saturday, I was going to start sleeping up there that night. I was so excited. I had already made friends with the girl who lived two doors away, she came over almost every day, and I couldn't wait to show off my room. *My room*! It was so beautiful. And so peaceful. I had a place I could go to and call it my refuge. Keith and Lori said so, they said my room was my private little world and I could count on it not being invaded. At least, they said, as long as I didn't do anything illegal. They were just teasing me.

The next thing I knew, Lori said she was taking me to buy some clothes. This was getting to be too much, I didn't deserve *any* of this, let alone *all* of this. When we went shopping I was, at one point, embarrassed and appalled, because she took me to an expensive clothing store and actually had me measured to see what size bra I needed. I said, "Look, I can just get this one. It will fit, I know what size I need." But she insisted I be measured and get the right size according to the expert at the store. It was nice of her, but I was still embarrassed. I was fifteen and I didn't want anyone to measure me for a bra. I didn't even want anyone to know what size I wore. She wasn't mean, she knew I was embarrassed and she was very comforting to me about it. She put her arm around me and called me by a pet name they had already given me and said, "I just want the best for you. You're worth it, whether you think you are or not." She bought me a bunch of clothes that day, including five or six bras. Thank God, I didn't have to be measured for my underwear! I think I would have *died* of embarrassment if that had happened, and I remember worrying about it until I saw we could buy that without measuring. I kept thinking, "Wow, Keith is gonna have a fit when he sees what all we bought. I hope he knows I didn't ask for anything. I hope he knows Lori is the one who picked all this stuff out and insisted I try it on." When we got home he was so nice about it. He said, "So do I get to see what my girls bought or is it a secret?" I thought, "Uh-oh, here we go. Wait until he sees all this." Lori said, "Let us put a few private things away and we'll have a fashion show." We took all the bras and underwear out of the bags so Keith wouldn't see them, I appreciated that, and I told Lori thanks. They had me to put on each outfit and show Keith, Lori had already seen them. He didn't even get mad. He was smiling and happy for me, I could tell. I said, "I haven't worn any of these yet, so if you want me to take some of it back it's okay." He said, "You will not! Lori bought all those things because we want you to have them." And they hugged me! There I went again, I felt like crying. I remember telling myself, "You gotta stop being such a cry baby. What the hell is the matter with you? Get it together and stop the emotional bull shit!" I was pretty hard on myself by the time I was fifteen. I can see that now, but I couldn't then. Looking back now, I wish I had fallen into their arms and cried my eyes out. I know they would have held me and made everything okay. But I was too worried about getting strong and tough again so I could protect myself. Looking back now, I wish I had been strong enough to let myself be weak, even if just for a little while. But that's looking back now. Back then I didn't know which end was up when it came to emotions.

I was so busy getting my room in order, settling in, getting new clothes and learning a new routine, that I had almost forgotten about the kids. I did think of them every single day, but not as much as I should have. When I did think about them, I told myself that they would be okay. I figured with criminal charges pending against Alcee, she couldn't push her luck. Lori had made sure three different law enforcement agencies were aware of what she did. And she had been arrested, that had never happened before. But then I started coming to my senses. I felt guilty about deserting the kids and Grandma. I always knew that Grandma and Alcee would make up and start talking again, they always did, and I eventually would have had contact with the kids if I had stayed there. Now, I probably wouldn't see them again until they were each eighteen.

How could I have done that? How did I get myself in such a position.? I started hating myself. I told myself that I was in such a position because I was a selfish, self centered, worthless, twisted little bitch. I loved where I was, but I hated myself for allowing myself to be there. I told myself that I was no better than my brothers and sisters and I didn't deserve any more than what they had. On the other hand, I had made a commitment to Lori and Keith and they were counting on me. And they were *nice* to me. But then on the other hand, they could get someone more deserving than me to offer refuge to. I told myself, "Any idiot could do what you do. You're just the idiot they picked, you moron!"

After I was there a few weeks, and we were all getting used to each other, I felt more comfortable. I still felt guilty for having it so easy, but I was more comfortable. I still waited for the other shoe to drop, though. In fact, I felt so guilty I *wanted* it to drop. I deserved for it to drop, I was just taking care of myself, being selfish. Like the selfish little bitch I had been called so many times in the past. I worked extra hard when I cleaned the house, did laundry or cooked. I tried to make sure there was nothing left for Lori and Keith to have to do around the house. After dinner, I did the dishes and carried mixed drinks to them, while they watched TV or listened to the Fifth Dimension album that Lori loved. No matter how hard I worked, I still felt guilty about having such a break. They were so good to me, that it was impossible to work off the guilt I had for letting myself accept the life they were offering me. I worked harder and harder and harder, but I still felt guilty. I didn't deserve this nice of a life. It wasn't perfect, but it was very nice. Lori was strict about rules, even the ones she made up on the spur of the moment, but she was usually fair. And Keith was like a big warm fuzzy teddy bear. They were both affectionate and were constantly hugging me, rubbing my arm or just touching me. *They* didn't think I had cooties. I still hadn't figured out what the catch to all this was, but I was still watching for it. Actually, I was praying for it.

One night I was in my room asleep, it was the middle of the night, and Lori woke me up and said, "Come downstairs, your mother is outside shining a spotlight on the house." I started shaking, all the familiar feelings of danger, fear and vulnerability came rushing back. Actually, they hadn't really been gone, I had just put them on a shelf or something. Lori was terrified, she worried that Alcee had a gun and that she might shoot through our windows. Here she was pregnant and she had to be up in the middle of the night, terrified, shaking like a leaf, afraid to turn on the lights and trying to protect me. She told Keith and me to pull the sofa away from the window because she didn't want me to sleep in front of it. We pulled the sofa away from the window, almost to the doorway of their bedroom, and made it into a makeshift bed. I slept there that night, and many other nights when Alcee came to shine the spotlight in our window. Lori said she thought Alcee knew which room was mine because of the flowered curtains on the window. She was afraid to let me sleep up there. Sure enough, Alcee started shining the light in my bedroom window. She did know which room was mine. Now, I felt even more guilty than I did before. Lori and Keith were being terrorized because they had me living in their house. I was the only one to come out ahead in this arrangment, the *only* one. Everyone else lost, I was the only winner. The kids lost because I couldn't be there for them, Grandma lost because I had deserted her, now Lori and Keith were losing because Alcee was harassing and scaring them.

I had stopped eating for the most part. I was five and a half feet tall and my weight was down to under one hundred pounds. It was driving Lori crazy. She kept trying to get me to eat. I kept saying, "I'm not hungry. When I get hungry I will eat, I'm okay. Stop worrying." It went on until she got to her wit's end. I didn't know anything about eating disorders back then, but now I really believe I was anorexic. I don't think anyone had heard about anorexia at that time, so I can't fault them for not recognizing it. Lori and Keith both tried everything to get me to eat regularly, but I ate only enough to keep me alive, no more than that, and I didn't believe I deserved that much. I did the same amount of work everyday, if not more than I had always done. In my mind, the price for what I did eat went up, I had to work harder for less. Lori was worried and she demanded that I eat dinner or I was grounded. I didn't care if I was grounded, I loved being home, I was safe there. Then she started demanding that I sit at the table and eat what she put on my plate, or go to my room. I went to my room, but that did bother me. If I was stuck up in my room, I couldn't be with them. Even though I knew I didn't deserve it, I was starting to like sitting with them in the evenings, watching TV or listening to albums. They called me a pet name and talked to me a lot, but I still never told them any details of my past. They didn't know about my first paying job, what happened to the dogs with mange, the games Gordon played or any other details. Lori ordered me to eat, Keith begged me to eat, but I couldn't or wouldn't. I thought I was eating more than I earned anyway. This went on almost the entire time I lived there. Lori got so frustrated and worried that she called Georgie and asked her if I had ever done that before. She asked her what my favorite foods were, she said she was desperate, that she would try anything. The only thing her call accomplished was giving my relatives the satisfaction of knowing that there was trouble in paradise. They loved it, they even laughed about it. My grandmother called me one night and said, "I heard ya don't wanna eat? There ain't nothin' like Grandma's cookin' is there? I'll bet you miss that!" She laughed and said to call her if I changed my mind about living there.

I was almost sixteen and Lori and Keith said they would teach me to drive. I said, "It doesn't matter, I don't have anyone to sign for my license." Lori said, "Why do you say that? We're your guardians, we can sign." I couldn't believe my ears! Not only did they provide a nice home, clothes, and more food than I would allow myself to eat, they were willing to sign for me to get my drivers license! She said, "After you get your license you can drive the little car to school and Keith and I will ride to the office together. That way we won't have to take you to school and pick you up. It will be better for all of us." Oh, my God! Somebody pinch me! No way! They were going to teach me to drive, sign for my license AND let me drive to school! I was absolutely beside myself. I already thought things were too good for me and they just kept getting better. I said, "You're kidding me right? Are you teasing me? You don't have to do that. It's okay, I would understand if you didn't want to do that." Keith started giggling again, like he did so many times when I was in disbelief. Lori laughed too, and shook her head, like she did so many times when I didn't believe I was really awake. They both put their arm around me, and Keith said, "You poor baby, you don't know that this is how it should be for you, do you?" There I went again, I had gotten this 'lump in my throat thing under control' and now they were yanking the controls again. It wasn't the drivers license that made me get choked up, it was the affection, and that was killing me. When ever they got affectionate with me, I wanted to give in and spill my guts and cry like a baby and tell them everything that had happened to me. Then, *after* they found out about *everything*, I wanted them to hold me while I cried my eyes out, and I wanted Keith to say, "You poor baby," and looking back, I bet they would have done that. But I wouldn't have bet on it then. I don't think the problem was that they wouldn't have been there for me, I think the problem was that I couldn't *allow myself* to *let* someone be there for me. Anyway, I couldn't tell them, I still couldn't or wouldn't tell anyone, maybe because that other shoe that I kept looking for, still hadn't dropped. If it ever did, I could pick it up and put it on, and ***if*** it fit, then *maybe* I could tell. But until the other shoe dropped I couldn't do it. Until I figured out what the catch was, I had to protect myself so I wouldn't get sucker punched.

My sixteenth birthday was coming up and I didn't want anything. I had more than what I needed or would have ever asked for. But Lori and Keith said every girl should have a sweet sixteen party and I was going to have one. I had worked all the time, before coming to live with them, and I didn't even know enough kids well enough to invite them to a party. Lori said, "Then we'll invite the whole sophomore class and you can *make* friends. Our girl is going to have a sweet sixteen party." I said, "Well okay, but I'm not going."

They knew I was being funny and they both laughed. I could easily make them both laugh, and I loved doing it. I loved it when we all three sat around and told funny stories and made each other laugh. One of their favorites was when ever I got into trouble for something and got grounded, I almost always typed a petition for leniency or clemency. It used to crack them up. I took one of their petitions and copied from it so the format looked like a legal document. I would plead my case as to why I should be let off the hook. It was really funny, they got a big kick out of it. It worked a couple of times, too. Anyway, they did have a birthday party for me, the first one I had ever had in my life, about ten kids showed up and Lori didn't like some of them. Neither did I. After Lori ran one girl and her boyfriend off, because they were 'little hoodlums,' the rest of us went out into the field with a Ouija board and had a seance. It was too funny. I ended up having fun, but I felt sorry for Lori and Keith because they were stuck with a lot of food. And we all knew what the chances of me eating it was, slim to none. They were so good to me, *too* good to me, and I still couldn't figure out why. Now I was sixteen, and they were still tucking me in at night, but I was starting to get used to it. In fact, I was starting to look forward to it every night. That felt dangerous. One time I made myself go to sleep before time for them to come up and tuck me in, so I wouldn't know it, but the next day Lori told me how cute I looked sleeping when she came up to tuck me in the night before. That was dangerous too.

That summer I got my drivers license and they let me drive a lot. It was so much fun, but they were both afraid Alcee would catch me out somewhere and hurt me. Lori issued an arrest warrant through her Court for Alcee's arrest, and had me carry with me at all times. She said, "If you are ever out and she starts chasing you, scream, run, do what ever you have to do to get a cop. Show them this warrant and they'll take her away." That helped ease their minds, but they still worried because they knew, as well as I did, that a warrant wouldn't stop a bullet. Alcee was still driving by their house in the middle of the night and shining the spotlight in my bedroom window. The three of us talked about it and decided as long as she had that to harass us with, she might not advance to other things. We all three decided not to try to have her arrested for harassing us with the spotlight because it might antagonize her and cause an escalation of her threats.

Lori was getting farther along in her pregnancy and she was also getting very irritable. It seemed like I couldn't do enough to please her, but that was okay, she was pregnant and I knew that came with the territory. We went to the lake almost every weekend, Lori had grown up on a lake and she loved the water, we went to church once a week, went to movies, went shopping, went on weekend trips and we played a lot. That summer Lori took me to the dentist, that's right, she took me, as in, she went with me. She sat out in the waiting room while I had some teeth pulled. A few days later I was in a lot of pain and she took me back to the dentist. I had formed dry sockets and it was very painful. She was waiting out front when she heard me groaning in pain and came back to the room I was in to see what was going on. The dentist and his assistant told her I was being a cry baby. The assistant said, "It gets uncomfortable to pack a dry socket, but I think she might be putting us on a little." Lori got really angry. She said, "You know, I had a dry socket once and I remember it being more than uncomfortable. You could be a little nicer. You don't have to be so rough." She actually argued with this dental assistant, and the dentist before it was over with, because they were hurting me. When we were finally leaving, the assistant made a snide remark, and as we walked out, Lori called her a bitch. It made me feel so good that she took up for me. I used to go to doctors by myself, but even though I was sixteen, I was so glad she was there. That night they had me to sleep downstairs, so they could keep an eye on me, and they bought me a dozen roses because I was sick. That was the first time anyone had given me flowers.

The summer passed and Lori took me shopping for new school clothes. School started, and shortly after that, Lori had her baby. It was a little girl and she was beautiful, she looked like Keith, and we all fell in love with her at first sight. She was a good baby, too, easy to take care of. Lori started acting funny within a couple of weeks of coming home from the hospital. She was depressed and kept saying that she didn't know if she would go back to work. She said maybe she would just let Keith be the bread winner. But she didn't seem happy about it. She seemed sad all the time and she was on me about something constantly. She had never had any complaints about the way I kept the house clean, and now, all of a sudden, she did. I was still driving them both crazy, because I wouldn't, or couldn't eat. It seemed like the more they did for me, the less I ate. Lori went from being worried to being pissed. She started threatening to send me to a boarding school that was about an hour away. That hurt my feelings and scared me. I started getting real clingy and didn't want to go anywhere at night. I just wanted to be home with them all the time, I was afraid it was going to end, and I would be right.

Lori and Keith started arguing a lot. Keith didn't drag me into it, but Lori did. She said she was a better lawyer than Keith, that if she counted on him support them, they would starve. She told him that to his face, too. She started saying that Keith hid her clothes just to make her think she was crazy. She was even more terrified than she had been before, when Alcee drove by with her spotlight in the middle of the night. She told me that she thought Keith wanted to rape me and I should agree to go to the boarding school. She was depressed, paranoid and mean. She started yelling at me a lot, she didn't call me names and say I was stupid, but she yelled. One night she called me downstairs and set a plate on the table, she screamed, "Eat it or wear it!" I ate it, but I threw up later. I didn't make myself, I just did. I think I was anorexic, but I don't think I was ever bulimic. I knew about the 'after baby blues' and I thought this would eventually pass, but this was the worst case I had ever seen. One night she said, "One of us has to go! Which one of us has to go? There's only room in this house for three of us." My obvious answer was me, after all, I was the one who didn't belong. I was hoping that was the right answer, but I was afraid to answer the question. Keith was standing behind her and signaled me to say him. I said, "Keith?" She got really angry and said, "No! She has to go! Out in the snow with you!" And she reached in the crib for the baby. I jumped in front of the crib while Keith pulled her back. I reached in for the baby and she broke lose from Keith and lunged at me. I pushed her back towards Keith and then she really got mad. She said, "I will not tolerate physical altercations with you!" I took the baby upstairs to my room and Keith, somehow, got her calmed down. It was like that for months. Sometimes Keith cried, Lori only cried when she got drunk. She did drink a lot before the baby was born, but not like I was used to seeing from my relatives. She was drinking even more now that the baby had been born. One night, she said I mixed Keith's drink too strong because I was trying to kill him. I know now that she had severe depression, maybe even post partum psychosis.

I wasn't exactly an angel, and I started skipping classes. One day a bunch of my friends and I left school and went to a pizza place where one of them worked. We sat there most of the day eating pizza and playing the juke box. On the way back to school, we stopped at a four way stop, and directly across from me was Keith. We even made eye contact, there was no doubt that he saw me. That night when I got home he didn't say a word about it, but he gave me a 'we love you' present. It was pajamas and a robe. I felt awful. I knew he saw me and he didn't even yell, what's more, he obviously didn't tell Lori or she would have been ballistic. He was so sweet, he knew how to make me feel guilty. That same week, he and Lori were going to 'meet the teacher night' at my high school. I didn't know, until I got home after school that night, that they were going. I hadn't even told them about it, but they knew, obviously. I was so scared one of the teachers would tell about me skipping class that day when Keith saw me. As soon as they left the house I called the school and asked for my teachers, one by one, to make a deal with them. I said, "If you don't say anything about me not being in your class that one day, I will be there everyday for the rest of the year." I pleaded with them one at a time until I felt pretty sure that Lori wouldn't find out. She did find out that night, but I didn't know about it until about a month later. I was doing pretty good in school, but I was so sleepy all the time. I could hardly stay awake in class, no matter how much sleep I got the night before. I think I was getting depressed, too. I was afraid they would keep loving me, and I was afraid they wouldn't.

Things started to get a little better, Lori went back to work and she and Keith took the baby to the office with them. When I got out of school in the afternoon, I picked her up at the office and took her home with me. She was an easy baby to take care of, she was a happy baby, she smiled a lot, and was fun to play with. Then Alcee called Lori and said, "So you've got a daughter? You took mine, maybe I'll take yers." Lori was almost hysterical. She was terrified. I didn't blame her, it scared me too. I could feel it coming to an end. Between Lori's depression, Alcee's harassment and my emotional retardation, it had to come to an end. It was just that nobody had said it yet. I could tell Lori was pushing me away, and I could tell that it hurt me. I was starting to feel. That was my fault, I knew better. I felt desperate to save what I had fallen into with them. One day I asked them, "Do you think I could call you Mom and Dad?" I thought Keith was going to cry, and I almost did too when Lori said, "I don't think that's a good idea. It wouldn't be fair to our own child if we allowed that. Maybe we will allow Aunt Lori and Uncle Keith, but we'll have to think about that." The thing about Lori was that she could be as sweet and loving as anything, but if she was going to be a bitch that day, she was going to be **one hundred percent** bitch.

Lori started going down hill again, she fired people at the office because she said they were talking about her. She hid a bottle of liquor in her desk drawer and drank while she worked. She picked at Keith all the time. She was mad at me about something everyday. She was so scared of Alcee that she had a totally separate phone line ran into the house. It came into the house on a different wall, and the phone was installed in the staircase that went upstairs from the bathroom. One night she jerked the bathroom door open while I was taking a bath and said she thought I was trying to kill myself. It was really bad. I think she hated all of us, even herself, and the baby. And being the mental midget I was, I still drove her crazy by not eating enough. She got mad because I told her I didn't believe Keith wanted to rape me, so she took me to the doctor for a pelvic exam to see if I was sexually active, I thought I would die of embarrassment. One morning Keith was driving me to school, and on my way out the door, Lori grabbed me and said to tell Keith something. She said, "I'll know if you told him and you better tell him." I tried to get my nerve up all the way to school and I finally did. Right before I got out of the car I said what Lori told me to say, and Keith got teary eyed. I said, "Don't tell Lori I told you, but she told me I had to say that. I didn't mean it, those aren't my words." He smiled at me and said, "I know." Instead of getting better, things were getting worse again.

One night she said if I wanted to stay there, I had to change my ways. She said she read all about a controversial treatment for kids like me and we were going to try it. I didn't like the sounds of that, and neither did Keith, but Lori said, "You can go through the sessions or get out." Keith usually signaled to me so I would know the right answer, he signaled to say yes, so I did. But I was worried. Sessions? What were the 'sessions' like? Who lead these 'sessions'? As it turned out she did. It went on all night long. It was gruelling for Keith and me, but I don't think Lori even got tired. Keith looked helpless and got teary eyed a few times. Sometimes he said, "Lori, stop it. Let her go to bed." But Lori said, "Get out." So he dropped it and so did I. I could deal with it, I knew how to dissociate, so I did. I just left, at least I thought I did. Finally about six o'clock in the morning, she let me go to bed. I laid down for about an hour and got back up at seven to get ready for school. I thought she kept me up all night so I would miss school and then she would use that as an excuse to throw me out. So I wanted to make sure I didn't miss school, and so did Keith. Lori had locked me in my room from the outside, and Keith let me out so I could get ready for school. He had to drive me that morning because I wasn't allowed to drive that week.

About an hour after I got to school, I felt like I was going to fall apart. When the bell rang, instead of going to my next class, I went to the cafeteria. There was a boy there, who I knew, and he came over and asked me if I was alright. I started crying, and I couldn't stop. I couldn't talk, all I could do was cry. He got scared and went to get help. The principal, who everyone in the school feared, came to get me and helped me upstairs to his office. He kept asking me, "Oh now, what can be so bad?" I couldn't talk, all I could do was cry. I just kept sobbing. He said, "What is it, sit down and tell me what can be so awful. What ever it is will be okay. Nothing is hopeless." He told a secretary to call my guardians and tell them to come and get me. I kept sobbing and sobbing. Then Keith and Lori came in, she was in her pajamas, they led me to the car and took me to a doctor's office. They pulled around back, took me in the back door, still sobbing uncontrollably, and the nurse gave me a shot. I barely got back into the car and I was asleep. I don't even know how I got in the house when we got home. Later that day when I got up, Lori was still mad at Keith for taking me to school. She said, "I had no intentions of you going to school today, Keith shouldn't have taken you. One of you should have asked me first." I said, "You were asleep, we thought you needed to rest." She said, "Like I said, one of you should have asked me."

I said I wouldn't participate in any more 'sessions' and Lori said, "Then you are out of here." Keith tried to reason with her but at the time she had no reasoning power. She was still threatening to send me to the boarding school. They owned rental property near the campus and there was an empty sleeping room in one of the houses. Keith talked her into letting me go there temporarily, until we could come up with an agreement or solution. He took me over there, and he cried when he left me there. Looking back now, I think he must have been on the verge of his own nervous breakdown. Anyway, I had been there before when we went over to do cleaning or repairs, so I wasn't scared of staying there alone. What I feared was the end of what had become my paradise. I stayed there and made it to school every morning. Lori had agreed to let me use the little car to get to and from school, for a little while. There was a kitchen at the end of the hall so I could cook if I wanted to, but I mostly ate stuff that didn't have to be cooked. The kitchen was shared with the students who lived there and it was pretty dirty. I cleaned it a couple of times, and they were grateful for it, but it didn't last. Most of them were pretty nasty creatures when it came to the kitchen. But I made out okay.

The holidays were coming up and I thought Lori would surely let me come home so we could spend them together. I was wrong. I spent Thanksgiving in my sleeping room alone. But that was okay with me because I hated Thanksgiving, I had since I was a kid. Even today, I like to spend Thanksgiving day alone. My son and I have Thanksgiving dinner on Wednesday evening and then he goes to his dad's house for Thanksgiving day. Keith, Lori and the baby went out of town for Thanksgiving and Keith wanted me to go, too, but Lori said no. The college students had gone home for the holiday, so I had the whole place to myself. It was okay, I did fine. I had peanut butter and crackers and I loved it. It was peaceful and quiet. Before they left town, Lori had taken the little car home, so I couldn't run all over town while they were gone. That was okay, too. Remember how I said I wasn't an angel? On Friday I went to the house, found the car key that Lori had hidden and took the car for the weekend. I didn't run all over town, but I did go to the store and the laundramat. Then Saturday evening I took the car back to the house and put the key back in Lori's hiding spot. I don't know if they ever found out about that or not.

Christmas was approaching and I was worried about spending it alone, not very worried, just a little worried. I knew I could handle what ever happened. I knew I could play any hand that was dealt to me. I just didn't want to have to play any hand, I wanted a good hand. Lori said I could come home Christmas morning for a little while. Keith picked me up and took me home. As soon as I walked in the door, Lori started screaming, "Get her out of here! Take her back!" So Keith took me back to the sleeping room, but that was okay. By then almost everything was okay because I was strong and tough again, or so I thought.

Right after the holidays, Keith came over to the sleeping room and told me to gather my things as fast as I could. He said, "Lori is sending you back to your mother's. I can't reason with her. I contested it, but the judge is signing the order as soon as they get your mother's consent. Gather all of your stuff and I'll be back to pick you up. I won't let them send you back there, but I need some time." He told me to wait until I heard from him, but to be ready to move as soon as he called. He came back hours later and we put my stuff in the car as fast as we could. He took me to their secretary's house. He said, "I have a plan but Lori is looking for you and I don't want her to find you. Sara will hide you until I come back for you." Sara had always been nice to me, and as soon as I went in, she said, "Lori has flipped. None of this is your fault. Keith won't let them send you back to your mother's. It will be okay, you can trust him." The phone rang and it was Lori, she asked Sara if she knew where I was. She said she went to the sleeping room and all my stuff was gone. Sara told her she didn't know anything about it. Right after Lori called, Keith called to say Lori was coming to Sara's to look for me. Sara told me to take my suitcase and get in the closet. She hid me behind some boxes in the living room closet. A few minutes later we heard a knock at the door. It was Lori, and Keith was with her, Sara opened the door immediately and acted surprised to see them. Lori asked her again, "Where is she? If you know where she is and don't tell me, I'll fire you." Sara said, "I have no idea. What's going on? Why would she be here? Do you think she would come here?" Lori looked around the house, she even opened the closet door, but she didn't see me. I wasn't scared, but Keith was terrified. Before they left, Lori reminded Sara again about her job being in jeopardy. After they were gone, Sara said

Keith was shaking like a leaf. She said she felt sorry for him, so did I. That afternoon Keith came by and picked me up. He took me to the bus station and sent me to his mother's house, in another state. He said he talked to his mother and she would not tell Lori I was there. He said, "Mom will meet you when you get there. You're going to enroll in school and I'll try to make sure Lori and your mother don't find you. I'll be in touch with you in a few days. I love you. I said I would protect you and I will. You have to trust me." When I got on the bus he hugged me, kissed me on the forehead and said, "You poor baby," just like he had said so many times before. The thing that worried me the most, was that I had only met his mother a couple of times. She might not even like me. I hoped she could at least tolerate me because I was on a bus headed to her house.

A few days after I got there Lori called to see if I was there. Keith's mother acted like she didn't know a thing, she was great. She had saved the Christmas presents they had bought for me, and gave them to me when I got there. She said Lori wouldn't let her send them to me, but she still had them. I enrolled in school, when it reconvened after the holiday break, and I hated it at first. It was a very small town, actually it wasn't even a town, it was like a little burg or whistle stop. Keith's mother was a nice, doting grandmotherly type, but his stepfather, Willard, was creepy. She insisted that I go to the Presbytarian Church with them on Sunday mornings and I hated that, too. I was used to a Catholic mass and this was very different, and it was a lot longer. I had been there for about two weeks when Lori called one evening. She said, "Hi, it's me Lori. Keith told me he sent our little girl down there and we want to come and get her. I feel just terrible about everything that has happened." Keith's mother said, "Well we just love having her, but I'm so happy you kids have worked everything out. I know she'll be glad to come home." I knew right then that Lori had tricked her. I was amazed that a grown woman could be so easily tricked. I guess I shouldn't have been, but I was. It was a lot harder for anyone to trick me. Lori said, "Put her on, I want to talk to her."

When I took the phone she started laughing and said, "Keith's mother isn't very smart is she? How do you like it there? Has Willard bothered you yet? He will, ask Keith's sister, she'll tell you." I said, "Is Keith there? Can I talk to him? I wanna come home." She said, "Your mom wants you to come home, too, she has guardianship now." By then Keith's mother was in tears because she knew Lori had tricked her. I kind of felt sorry for her, but I also thought she was way too easy to trick, and I was kind of ticked off at her. Lori let Keith take the phone, he said, "I'm so sorry for you. Lori and your mother have formally changed your guardianship back to your mother. They had you declared incorrigible by the court. You can't come back into the state, if you do they will have you picked up." He asked to speak to his mother and they talked for a few minutes. She was crying and apologizing for screwing up. After they hung up Lori called back and told Keith's mother that she should put me on a bus and send me back. She said, "The police will use long arm statutes to come and get her. You are hiding a fugitive, and I won't bring your grandchild there to visit as long as you are harboring a fugitive." Keith's mother was so upset because his baby was the only grandchild she had and she was afraid the police would come and get me. A few days later she put me on a bus and sent me back. I think she did the right thing. I shouldn't have become her responsibility. I could go back and do what ever I had to do standing on my head, I would be eighteen in less than two years, but she was not used to such chaos and anxiety. And she needed to be sure she could see her granddaughter without a fight. She hadn't raised Keith, she had him out of wedlock, and his grandmother had raised him. Keith's baby was very important to her, and I didn't like it there anyway.

While riding the bus back home I had hours to think. I thought about the way I got a lump in my throat when they tucked me in, the way they laughed when I filed my petitions for leniency, how they told me I was smart enough for college, the way they touched me and smiled at the same time, the way I felt when Keith said 'we couldn't help ourselves, we just fell in love with you,' and I realized that I had fallen in love with them too. I didn't know how I let it happen, but I knew I had, and I wished I hadn't. Even after I left, I would still wonder, for years, what the catch was that I couldn't figure out while I was there. I would figure out, after it was too late, that there was no catch. But it would be after I became an adult that I realized I was looking for a phantom. The reason I couldn't figure out what the catch was, I believe now, is because there never was one. The whole time I was waiting for the other shoe to drop, I was merely being suspicious and fearful of the only people who had truly fallen in love with me during my whole life, up to that point. I was just too close, or too scared, to see it and believe it. I should have known that Lori and Keith never had the other shoe, Alcee still had it. And when she dropped it, I would go spiraling back down into the bowels of helplessness, hopelessness and defeat. And this time I wouldn't know if my own strength could pull me back out.

I believe that Lori and Keith were sincere in their efforts to make me part of their life. That was the first time I realized that everyone didn't live like my family. All people didn't beat their kids and spouses. Some people nurtured, protected and loved them. They touched them and kissed them and told them how much they loved them. Keith is by far, and will remain so to me all my life, the most wonderful father image a kid like me could have had. I have no idea where he is today, but if I did, I would go to him and tell him how he changed my life forever. I would love to hug him, let him hug me, and hear him say 'you poor baby' one more time. I think the harassment and threats from Alcee, Lori's post partum depression and drinking, and my twisted emotional state made a fatal combination for our relationship. I believe if any one of those elements had been gone, we could have survived the others. I don't believe they were using me, I believe they really loved me and wanted me, and that was too much for me to believe or comprehend. I believe if we had gotten professional help, things might have worked out. I think my inability to believe anyone could love me caused a great deal of our problems. But, not to give myself a break or be a cry baby, I also believe a kid like me should have been given more than one chance to *learn how* to be loved. But I *didn't know how* to be loved and I was on a bus headed back to square one.

CHAPTER FOURTEEN

Superman And The Wicked Witch

The ride back on the bus wasn't nearly long enough. I knew what I was going back to, and the bus brought me back to it sooner than I ever wanted to return. When I got back home what would turn out to be the happiest part of my life, until the birth of my son, would be ripped away, torn to shreds and tossed to the wind like a million pieces of confetti. I would never be able to find all the pieces, and even if I did, I would never be able to put it back together. But the effect Keith and Lori had on my life would last forever. As I traveled through so many transitional stages, from childhood to adulthood, I would ask myself what Keith or Lori would tell me to do. I strived to live by what I thought their guidance would have been. I don't know whether or not I would have made it out sane, or even alive, if they had not passed through my life. They were the only break I had during my childhood. Even though things got really bad after Lori got sick, and even though it was brief, I will forever love them both for the break, and the love, they gave me. Even today, I strive to follow what I believe their guidance would be, as imaginary as it is, I feel like it's still there.

I was almost seventeen, so I had less than two years until I could escape forever. My dad, if granted parole, would be out of prison in a few months and I still had hope that he could help save me. I would find out how stupid I was to hope for that, too. Knowing Alcee had control again, I thought about how to soften my upcoming situation. I was older now, and I was wiser thanks to Lori and Keith. He picked me up at the bus station when I got back. He took me to pack all my things and get me out of Lori's sight. Keith and I were both emotional, him more than me, I had to be strong and tough so I could get my things together and get out. He at least got Lori to agree to let me go back to the sleeping room for a few days. I asked them for another chance to prove myself. Lori said,

"It's a done deal, you're out of here. Your mom is taking you back, and if I were you, I would learn how to make friends with her." She was still sick, I can't hold it against her, even now. I told Keith I was going to miss all of them, even Lori in her currently twisted state. Keith said, "You didn't do anything wrong. We will always remember you, and love you, in our hearts. I am so sorry this didn't work out." Lori was cold, she just wanted me out of her sight. Keith was teary eyed and shaking. I was feeling a lot of things inside, but I kept myself together and I didn't even cry. I can't even identify all the emotions I was feeling, but my exterior demeanor reflected none of them. It was time for me to go back on *high* alert, stay on my toes more than ever and expect the worst because, within a few months, the worst would come. And it would be one of Alcee's finest games. A victory like even ***she*** couldn't believe she could have.

As soon as I got to the sleeping room I started paving the way for going back to Alcee and Gordon's. I came up with a plan to make it look like I had wanted to go back there for a long time, but I was just too stupid to know how to get back in. The first thing I did was call Alcee and tell her I would refuse to testify against her for the still pending criminal charges, if she let me back in. Nothing had changed with her, she started telling me what I would and wouldn't do ***IF*** she decided to let me come home. She said, "You ain't foolin' me, you little son-of-a-bitch! I already know they revoked their guardianship and yer ass is mine." I said, "That may be, but unless I refuse to testify, you still have to go to court." She said, "They ain't gonna believe nothin' you got ta say anyway. I don't know if ya know it 'er not, but you been declared incorrigible. Lori's gonna get the charges dropped. Whatta ya' think o' that?" She kept laughing her same mocking, threatening laugh that I knew all too well. I knew I had to let her feel victory, but she wouldn't feel it if I didn't put up some resistance. She had to win a fight, she had to be a real victor, she had to feel like she conquered me. She said, "Yer gonna refuse ta testify anyway, even if Lori cain't get the charges dropped. Yer a minor and I ain't lettin' ya go ta court. Whatta ya' think o' that?" You know, I might have been stupid, but even *I* knew the prosecutor's office would have me testify whether she gave her permission or not. I said, "Well, I don't know why I even try to stay ahead of you. I'm just gonna call the prosecutor's office and tell them I'm not testifying against my own mother. I know you can make me come home, but if things are like they were before, I'll just keep running away." She said, "Oh yer comin' home alright! But don't tell me what you are er ain't gonna do! I'm yer boss, you ain't mine!" Okay, she wins.

So I was back to square one at Alcee and Gordon's, and nothing had changed. Gordon was still working out of town during the week and came home on the weekends. He and Alcee were as mean as ever and still delighted in sadistic behavior. For instance, one day Tim threw a rock at Dena and hit her in the temple of her head. One of her eyes started bleeding and we took her to the hospital. They admitted her and put pressure bandages over both eyes. The doctors said she might be blind, but we wouldn't know for sure until they took the bandages off in a few days. She had to stay in the hospital for, the best I can remember, about three or four days. A few days later they took off the bandages and she could see. When she was released, the doctors specifically said to protect her head where she had been injured. They said that spot was extremely vulnerable to re-injury because it wasn't completely healed. I had tried to impress upon Tim what he had done, but he didn't care, and he also didn't want to hear anything from me. I had deserted them and I don't think the kids trusted me anymore.

When Gordon came home that weekend we made him fully aware of Dena's condition and how she needed to be protective of her injury. I don't even remember what Dena did to make Gordon mad, but all of a sudden the familiar sounds of chaos erupted, and Gordon was going after her. He roared, "I'll knock yer fuckin' teeth out ya little bitch!" I said, "Leave her alone! You're gonna hurt her! You could cause her to be blind!" Dena ran into her room and locked the door. Gordon tore the door off the wall, hinges and all, and charged at Dena. He screamed, "I'll make sure ya use a fuckin' white cane the rest o' yer life, ya little whore!" I kept yelling for Dena to cover her head. Gordon kept yelling and hitting her in the head and face. Everything was the same as it was when I briefly escaped two years before. The only thing that had changed in that house was shoe sizes, everything else was the same. The screaming, the yelling, the fighting, the chaos, it was just like I left it, especially on the weekends when Gordon was home.

I went back on a half day school schedule and worked more than full time again. It was okay because I decided I could go to summer school and make up what I missed through the regular school year. I knew Lori and Keith would want me to graduate even if one, or both, of them hated me. But I had to put school lower on the priority list in order to keep Alcee happy. I didn't have a room, so I slept on the couch when I slept there. I stayed away as much as I could. Sometimes Alcee got 'pissed' at me and reported me as a runaway, so the police would pick me up. She called them and said I was a runaway and then told them where I was. How much sense did that make? Then she sat across the street from the jail and smiled at me as they took me in. Oh well, whatever. The two women who ran the girls probation department knew me, and they also knew Alcee. As soon as the police picked me up they had to call the probation department to let them know they had a juvenile female in custody. When they called and said they had picked me up, one of the two women who was on call told them to wait until my mother left and let me go. They knew I wasn't bad, and they knew my mother was crazy, so they didn't want me to have an arrest record. I wasn't even booked. As soon as my mother pulled away, they let me go, and I would go to grandma's, or any other place I could get into, and hide out for a few days.

It seemed like Alcee and I constantly circled each other, each of us waiting for the other to strike the first blow. Like two wrestlers, each waiting for the other to start the match. I said I wouldn't sign my paycheck and hand it over to her anymore. I told her I would cash it and give her most of the money, but I was keeping enough to make sure I had a few bucks, and enough to give the kids lunch money. And that's what I did. I even bought an old car to drive back and forth to work and school. I remember sensing, whether it was real or not, that Alcee was losing some of her power and control over me. That would prove to be another time that I was so wrong, because in a few months she would prove that she still had every ounce of power and control that she had ever had.

The two youngest ones, Tony and Denise, were still close to me, but the older ones often seemed distant, probably because I had deserted them. Tony still let me baby him and Denise was still like a little puppy following me around. Tony had remained sensitive and loving and he was about to endure one of the biggest heartbreaks of his life. He had bonded with Bear, the big dog my uncle had given us years before, and as far as he was concerned, Bear was his dog. One afternoon Tony fell into a lake. It wasn't deep enough for him to drown if he had just stood up, but Bear jumped in and dragged him by his shirt closer to the edge of the water. Tony liked to tell people, "Bear saved my life once." Now, years later, the dog was very old and sick. One night Bear couldn't stand up, he just layed on the floor and didn't respond to anyone, not even Tony. It was on a week night and, thank God, Gordon was out of town. Dena and I knew what was happening and we told Tony that we would take Bear to the vet. We carried him to the car and put him in the back seat. He was breathing, but his legs were stiff, and mucous was drooling from his mouth. Dena and I took him to the vet, who said the dog was dying. He said the dog might live a few more hours, or even another day or so, but he was dying. He said we could take him home and let him pass on there, or he could help us with sending him on his way and putting him out of his misery. Neither of us wanted to hear that, but we both knew it was true. We gave permission to euthenize Bear. I didn't want him laying there dying when Gordon came home that weekend. We talked about what we would tell Tony, we knew he would be devastated. We also knew he had a field trip at school the next day and we didn't want him to miss it. We decided to tell him the vet was keeping Bear overnight to do surgery the next day. He was so worried and scared about his buddy that the next morning he didn't want to go to school. We told him to go to school, and go on his field trip, and we would go sit at the vet's office while Bear had surgery. I said, "As soon as you get home, we'll tell you what happened." So he went off to school that morning worried about his dog, and I was already dreading what he would find out when he got home that afternoon. As soon as the school bus pulled up that day, Tony ran as fast as he could to the door. He was smiling and looked happy, I think because he expected his dog to be home by then. As soon as he jerked the door open he asked, "Where's Bear? What happened in surgery?" I thought Dena was going to cry, she got teary eyed and walked out of the room. I said, "Tony, he didn't make it. He died while they were trying to save him. The vet said he died in his sleep and didn't feel a thing. There was no pain at all, but he's gone." It was so sad, he said, "No, no, no." He started crying, actually he was sobbing, and didn't stop completely for several days. He grieved over Bear for a long time, but he did eventually bond with the other dog that was still living there. Unless Alcee, Dana or Dena told him, he still doesn't know that Bear was dead before he left for school that morning. I don't know if we did the right thing or not. Maybe we should have taken Bear home and let him die in Tony's arms, or maybe we should have just told him the truth the night it happened. The only thing I know for sure, and I knew it for sure then, was that I didn't want Gordon to handle that situation.

So, I worked full time and went to school part time, while I waited for my dad to make parole. When it was almost time for him to get out of prison, I sneaked around and found an apartment to rent for us. When I got caught, I told Alcee I was setting up the apartment for him, but as soon as he got out I moved into it with him. I picked him up at the bus station the day he got back into town and took him to our apartment. It was only a one bedroom, but one of us could sleep on the couch, he said he would. His first night home he went out drinking and brought home a prostitute. I couldn't believe it. I ended up on the couch, which I didn't mind, but I did mind being able to hear them in the other room. We moved to another apartment within a couple of weeks of him getting out of prison. The landlord at the first place found out he was a convict and told us to move on. Of course, no one knows who called them with that information. They didn't say that was why they wanted us to move, they said it was because there were two people living there and they only wanted one person in that unit. I'm sure him being a convict and bringing prostitutes home every night, also had something to do with it, though. The owner lived in the front of the house and she was very religious. She saw the police there a couple of times because Alcee decided to have me picked up as a runaway, again and again, because I wouldn't come home.

One night, I was sitting on the porch and I saw Alcee's car turn the corner just a couple of doors away. I went to the back of the house and saw my dad walking up the alley. I asked him, "What were you doing in her car?" He said, "Aw there ain't nothin' to it, she just gave me a ride home. Don't say nothin' about it." However, there must have been something to it, because that same week my dad moved in with one of his girl friends and said, "You oughtta go back to yer mom's house before she gits anymore pissed. I don't want 'er causin' me no trouble, I'm on parole." Well, I had to go back to Alcee's then because I was underage and it was illegal for a minor to live alone. So that didn't last long, and neither would the next time I tried to live with my dad.

The summer sessions at school had started, and I was still working and going to school. I changed jobs and started working from eleven at night until seven in the morning. Then, I went to school until about noon and slept in the afternoons. My dad had moved out of his girlfriend's house and needed a place to live. I told him there were sleeping rooms over the restaurant where I worked and he rented one. I didn't really live with him, but I stayed in his sleeping room sometimes while he was at work during the day. I used the excuse with Alcee that I couldn't sleep during the day at her house because it was too noisy. So, when I got out of school at noon, I went to my dad's sleeping room and slept there while he was at work. When he got off work in the early evening, I got up and did homework or went to Alcee's to see the kids. She was mad all the time, she said, "I'll never figure out what yer attraction is ta that no good son-of-a-bitch! He ain't never done a goddamned thing fer you! Yer gonna stay away from 'im er I'm gonna have yer fuckin' head examined! I worked three fuckin' jobs ta keep you when you was born and now you'll pick that mother fucker over me?" I told her I wasn't picking anyone over her, I just wanted to try to get to know him. She said, "There ain't nothin' ta know! Ask me, I'll tell ya! He's a goddamned jailbird, and you ain't hangin' around him! Yer gonna keep yer ass right here where I say yer goin' to!" Well, Alcee was about to prove that she did indeed have the other shoe, and she was going to drop it.

One day, I was asleep in my dad's sleeping room over the restaurant and the door busted open. It scared me because I was sleeping and it woke me up. I was disoriented and trying to get my bearings as to what was happening. I tried to jump up, but someone threw something over my head and pushed me back down. Someone was at my feet and somone else was at my head holding me down. I said, "Hey, who are you? What do you want? Let me go." I was fighting to get away, and the towel they had thrown over my head came off. It was Dana and Alcee trying to pick me up and carry me out of the room. I wondered how they got in. I found out later that Alcee told the owner of the building I was a minor and he let her in. He unlocked the door and they rushed me before I could even run. Alcee said, "Yer goin' with me, I got a surprise fer ya." I said, "No, I'm not goin' anywhere with you." By that time she and Dana had carried me out of the room and into the hall. I started screaming, kicking and making a lot of noise. The owner ran back up the stairs and said we had to quiet down and leave. I said, "I'm not going anywhere. My dad lives here and I'm waitin' for him to come home." Alcee told the guy that I was a drug addict and he should just stay out of it. There was an empty sleeping room at the end of the hall and I knew it was unlocked, because the night before I had shown it to a prospective tenant, and I had left it unlocked. I ran down the hall and into the empty room where I locked the door. Dana and Alcee kept telling me to come out, but I wouldn't do it. I didn't know where they were taking me. What if they were nabbing me to murder me and throw me in a quarry? What did they have on their minds? They just came charging into that room and tried to carry me out. There was no way they were just going to take me to Alcee's. I didn't know what they were up to, but the way Alcee said 'surprise' I knew it wasn't anything good. I thought I was terrified then, but little did I know that, before the day was over I would know what real terror was. Anyway, I refused to come out of the empty sleeping room and the owner called the police. When the police arrived I came out of the room. I told them I was sleeping when they busted in the room and tried to carry me out. I told them I wasn't going to leave with those two, Alcee and Dana. First Alcee told them that I was a minor, she had custody and she demanded that I go with her or they take me to jail. They said I hadn't done anything wrong, so they couldn't arrest me. Then she told the cops who my dad was and they knew him by name. Then she told them I was a drug addict, I was hanging around my jailbird dad, a doctor had diagnosed me with a Bonnie and Clyde complex, ***and*** I had been declared incorrigible by the court. Uh-huh, that should do it. The cops said I had to go with her. I lunged for a window and tried to break the glass, I wanted to do something so they would arrest me. The police said, "You can go with your mother or go to jail." I said, "I'll go to jail." I figured when I got to the jail they would call the probation department and be told to let me go. Alcee laughed at me and said, "That's okay, I still have a surprise fer ya."

By the time we got to the jail, Alcee was parked outside smiling, as usual. The police took me in and started booking me as a juvenile delinquent. I said, "Please call the probation department and ask them about me" but they wouldn't do it. The cops on duty that day were all new. I knew the sheriff and his wife, but I didn't know the cops who were booking me. They booked me and called the jail matron to search me and put me upstairs in a cell. I kept begging the jail matron to call the probation department, she told me to shut up. After about twenty minutes, the matron came back and took me downstairs. I thought they had called the probation department and they were going to let me go, but they hadn't and they didn't. There was a private ambulance in front of the jail and they said it was there to pick me up. I couldn't believe it. I kept asking what was going on, but everyone just kept telling me to shut up. The two guys in the ambulance got out and said, "You can get into the ambulance on your own, or we can restrain you and put you in anyway." Dana and Alcee were standing there smiling, more like smirking. I looked at Alcee and said, "How could you do this?" She said, "Do what? Have yer head examined?" I still didn't get it. I thought the ambulance was going to take me over to the local hospital where they would test me for drugs. I remember thinking, "Okay, this is embarrassing, but this could be a good thing. Alcee told them all I was on drugs. She's gonna look like a fool when they all find out I'm not." But I still didn't get it. I should have known it would take more than embarrassing me and a blood test for Alcee to feel a victory. I should have known that she would have to have much more fun with me than that. Maybe I did know, but I was too emotionally stunted to feel or acknowledge anything. Maybe I really was stupid, I don't know. I remember that I started getting angry and told myself that I would be eighteen in less than a year, and I wouldn't need any of the adults who had either tortured me or ignored my existence, for ***anything***, anymore.

The ambulance pulled away from the jail with me in the back seat, as opposed to being strapped to a cot. The hospital was only about four blocks away, but they didn't go in the direction of the hospital. I said, "Hey guys, where are we going? The hospital's the other way." They said, "We aren't taking you to that hospital. Just relax and enjoy the ride." I said, "Where are you taking me then? You can at least tell me where you are taking me can't you?" One of them said, "We were hired by your mother to transport you to a private mental hospital." I asked them where and they told me. They were taking me across the state line to be committed to a mental institution! I turned around and saw that Alcee was following us. Every time I looked back, she smiled and waved like she was mother of the year, like I was on my way to a track meet or something and she was following the bus that was taking the team to the competition. I knew there was no way these guys would believe she was up to no good. We had been driving for well over an hour, and I was starting to feel more scared and desperate. I started talking to them about why my mother hired them. I told them that she was in a dispute with my dad about me wanting to live with him. I said, "No one will know where I am. I will be totally isolated from my dad and he will be frantic. If I give you his address, will you please tell him where you took me?" They said they couldn't do that because my mother hired them and that would be a breach of confidentiality. I kept begging and said, "Look, just let me give you my dad's address, he doesn't have a phone. Just hang on to it and think about what will happen to me if I'm telling you the truth. He will worry and no one will know where I am. My mother is not what she appears to be. She is spiting my dad by making me disappear." One of them took the information, but I could tell he was just pacifying me.

As we continued driving, with Alcee following, she got rear ended in bumper to bumper traffic. It was rush hour in the city we were in and the traffic was heavy. The two guys jumped out of the ambulance and ran back to see if everyone was okay. They left me sitting in the back seat of the ambulance with the keys in the ignition and the red lights flashing. Now, I did think about taking off in that ambulance. I even looked for the button to turn on the siren. But I thought that would confirm what Alcee said about me needing my head examined, so I decided against it. While the two ambulance guys hovered around the accident, watching Alcee grow more agitated by the minute, I turned around and smiled at her. With those guys right there to see her, she got so mad she "flipped me off." Then she screamed, "You ain't got yer wish ya little bitch!

It's just a fender bender, it ain't like I broke my neck." The two guys looked at each other in disbelief. They saw her give me the middle finger, and they heard her cussing at me, but they had not seen me smile at her. That was a good thing for me. After the police came, took a report and calmed everyone down, we were on our way again. When they got back in the car I said, "You guys should be careful leaving people in here with the keys. Some people would have taken off." I told them my mother was a spiteful person who was trying to hide me out away from my dad. I begged them again to just tell him where I was. The driver said, "Your mom was pretty upset back there." I said, "No, not really. She wasn't even really mad, you should see her when she really gets mad. A couple of years ago she pulled a gun on me. It was in the paper. You can check it out and then you'll know I'm telling you the truth." It wasn't that week, but one of those guys did eventually find my dad and tell him where I was.

We drove for a little while longer and the ambulance pulled into a driveway that led to a big, dingy, drab, cold looking building. I can't find the words to illustrate how terrified I was. I couldn't believe she was going to go all the way with this stunt. I had so many thoughts racing through my head. How did she pull this off? How could someone do this to another human being? How could someone do this to their own kid? Does Grandma know where I am? Was she in on it? I would later have reason to believe that she was. Will these guys tell my dad where I am, and if they do will he come and help me? What is this place like? Grandma would say I was marked because they named me after a woman in an insane asylum. Is this place like the ones they show in movies? I will never get over this. Is she going to have them do a lobotomy? She had threatened to several times. She has gone too far this time. I will find a way out of this, and when I do I'm going to disappear for the rest of my life. I hope I never have to see her again. What about the kids? What will she tell them? When the two guys escorted me into 'admissions,' Alcee and Dana were sitting there smiling like caring, loving relatives. Alcee was giving the 'admissions' clerk quite a history about me, none of it true. She told them I was on drugs, that I insisted on obsessing over my father who was a career criminal, hence the earlier diagnosis of the Bonnie and Clyde complex *and* she told them that I was violent and dangerous to myself and others. She was using all the keywords to accomplish her goal. She filled out some forms, signed some papers and they said I was 'admitted;' although, I believe the appropriate word would have been "committed.' In fact, the psychiatrist that was assigned to me insisted, years later, that the hospital was a private institution which only accepted voluntary 'admissions,' no one was ever 'committed' against their will. However, when you are seventeen you are a minor, and I believe that if someone else 'voluntarily admits' that minor to an institution against her will, then that minor has been '***committed***' not '***admitted.***' ***Alcee*** signing voluntary admission papers does not constitute ***my*** voluntary admission. I don't care who wants to split hairs over the terminology, I was there and I didn't walk in voluntarily. Anyway, an employee approached me and said, "If you'll just come with me, we can get you settled in." She held my arm and started walking towards an elevator. I looked at Alcee and said, "Please don't do this. You have gone way too far with this one." She didn't respond to me, but she looked at the woman about to take me upstairs and said, "My gosh! I just told you she was dangerous! Yer not gonna get in that elevator with 'er by yerself are ya? I wouldn't even consider myself safe in that elevator with two people to hold her back." Well, I ended up with three escorts to take me upstairs, two women and one male orderly. As they led me away Alcee sneered and said, "Good luck."

Now, stop and think about this. If someone really needed to have their child involuntarily committed to a mental institution, wouldn't they probably be upset? I certainly would be. Wouldn't you think the parent would be tearful, instead of cheerful, while signing the papers? Wouldn't you think something was out of the ordinary for the parent to be so smiley and say 'good luck' to the child on their way out? That would be a red flag for me, how about you? I cannot imagine myself ever deriving pleasure or satisfaction from my child being terrified. It would break my heart to think he ever felt that much terror or hurt. Sometimes, to this day, I just want to scream, "Where in the hell was everybody while Alcee and Gordon were having fun with their baby factory kids?"

Upstairs was a maximum security ward with some seriously ill people there. Some of them had been there for years, and if what I heard was true, some might still be there or maybe even have died there. They took me to a room that had two beds, mine and one with an older woman who sat in silence and rolled the lit end of a cigarette on her fingers. They showed me which dresser was mine and said I could put my clothes in it, but I didn't have any clothes to put in it. The only clothes I had were the ones I had on. They told me my mother would be bringing some of my clothes soon. 'Soon' turned out to be the next day. There was a TV room and a dining room on our floor at the end of the hall. They brought the meals up from downstairs and served them at tables in the dining room. After my 'tour,' I ventured into the hallway and saw some obviously very disturbed people. There was a young woman who I think had St. Vitus Dance. She walked back and forth, like she took a few steps forward and then took a couple of steps backwards. She was mostly quiet and kept to herself, but she did talk to me a little bit later that day. There was an old woman, who they referred to as Old Miss, and she kept raising her dress above her head and clucking like a chicken. There was a young man there, who kept grabbing imaginary threads or hairs from the air, then he played with them like they were streamers. There were a lot of people in there, and most of them scared me. That afternoon, even though I had not seen a doctor or any other mental health professional, a nurse brought me my medication. I said, "I just got here today and I don't have any medication." She said, "Well, your doctor has ordered this, and you need to take it. It will make you feel better." I said, "Look, I don't even have a doctor and I don't feel bad, so I don't need that to make me feel better." The nurse said, "Swallow this for me and I won't have to call for help." I said, "I don't belong here. My mother put me here to hide me from my dad, it's a spiteful thing, she doesn't want me to see him." I could tell from the nurse's attitude that she heard this story every day, the "I don't belong here story." I took the pill and tried to hold it under my tongue, but even my tongue wasn't private there. The nurse said, "Let me see under your tongue." So I swallowed the pill and let her look under my tongue. I could tell this was going to be one of my worst nightmares, but as bad as I *thought* it would get, it would turn out to be even worse. I watched the other people in that ward most of the afternoon and thought, "How could they possibly believe I should be in here at all, let alone medicated? Even if I really am stupid, despisable, hateful, lazy and worthless, that's not why they put people in a place like this, is it?" Could it get any worse? Yes it could, and it would.

Early that evening I was herded down the hall with the other females on that ward. We went to a room that had ***a*** shower in it, literally. In one corner there was a little raised edging on the floor to keep the water from running all over the room, but the shower head was just mounted on the wall, there was no curtain or stall. There was no privacy to it at all. We were all forced to line up, and while one person was showering, or being showered, the next one in line had to strip completely naked and stand there like that while waiting in line. As soon as that person got out, or was taken out, of the shower the next person was already nude and told to shower. We stood in line, naked part of the time, and one by one we were each told to get under the shower and bathe! While people were showering, everyone else in line was watching! I was seventeen! There was a nurse sitting in a chair next to the shower area and she watched us bathe. Some of the people didn't cooperate and were bathed by the staff. Like Old Miss, she kept fighting them and clucking like a chicken. There were several staff members in there, I don't know which ones were nurses and which ones weren't. I just know that they were there to keep the people in line "in line." I don't know how to describe how awful that was. It had a devastating effect on me, that I don't think I'll ever be able to erase.

I felt so humiliated, degraded, mortified and I don't even know what else I felt. While writing this I feel like screaming from frustration because I can't find the words to communicate to you the degree of degradation and humiliation I felt. After my shower, they gave me a gown to wear, it was like a hospital gown, but it wasn't open in the back. They took all our clothes and locked them in our closets in our rooms. It was maximum security and they thought people wouldn't try to escape without their clothes. But I'm telling you, most of the ones I saw in there would have. Then they locked us in our rooms for the night. I kept thinking, "This is a nightmare, this can't be real." But it was real. And it was terrifying. Remember my roommate, the older woman who rolled lit cigarettes on her fingers? I watched her and thought, "How could they let her have matches?" I called a nurse and asked her to unlock the door, I told her I was afraid of the woman in my room. She didn't care, she said the woman was harmless and wouldn't bother me, she told me to be quiet and go to sleep. I sat on my bed and watched the woman light cigarette after cigarette and roll the lit end on her fingers. I don't think it hurt her because her fingers were yellow with nicotine and had thick callouses. I tried to get her to speak, but she wouldn't. She just stared at me for a few seconds and looked away. I thought if I could get her to speak, I could get a feel for whether or not it would be safe for me to go to sleep.

I sat on the edge of my bed thinking all night and watching the old woman in the other bed. The girl who I thought had St. Vitus Dance had told me earlier that the woman in my room had been there seventeen years. That's how old I was, and I thought about that. I thought, "My God, if they keep me here seventeen years I'll be thirty-four when I get out of here. But she's been here seventeen years and she isn't out of here yet. She's been here all my life! What if nobody finds out where I am? I can't survive this, I'm not gonna make it." I remember feeling more helpless, hopeless and defeated than I ever had. I just knew I couldn't live through this. So Alcee is playing her ultimate game, short of murdering me, and basking in her victory. How could she do this to me? How could she do this to anybody? How could anyone do this to anyone? I looked at the closet where they had locked up my clothes, the steel cages over the windows, the locked door with steel mesh in the glass and the woman in the next bed. I had been medicated twice by bedtime, and the more I tried to convince people that I didn't belong there, the more they acted like I did. Several times I caught myself falling asleep. I was so afraid I'd fall asleep and the woman in the next bed would hurt me or start a fire.

The next morning Alcee did show up with some of my clothes. She seemed happy and content, like there was nothing wrong with what she was doing. I said, "Mom, do you know what you did this time? Do you have any idea what you've done? Do you have any idea what it's like in here? You have to get me out of here! Today!" She said, "I'll get ya outta here when I'm ready and I won't be ready 'til you learn ta mind." I said, "What do you want? I want out of here, I'll do anything." She said, "Well, so I guess you ain't as fuckin' smart as ya thought 'cha was are ya?" Then she stood there smirking at me. She acted so nonchalant or something. She said, "***IF*** I decide ta get you outta here, I ain't puttin' up with no more o' yer shit! You ain't seein' yer goddamned no good daddy fer one thing! And ye ain't hangin' around yer grandma's either. Yer gonna keep yer ass at home where ye belong! That's all ya have ta do is learn ta mind and I ***might*** get you outta here." I stood there and watched her smirk and laugh at me. She had no heart or soul for anyone, not even the children that shared her body for nine months. I kept looking at her and thinking about all the nightmares she had brought to every one of her kids, every single one of us. I just wanted out of there and I said, "What ever you want. Are you gonna get me out of here or not?" She said, "I said I'd think about it when ya learn ta mind, and I don't think you've learned yet." She just kept mocking me and making fun of me and taunting me. She said, "How was yer night? Mine was fine." I didn't say anything, I just stood there and watched her. I wondered how she could be the way she was. I used to never wonder, I used to think everyone was like that, but after living with Lori and Keith, I knew she wasn't normal. I knew there was nothing normal about our household or anyone in it. As I watched Alcee mock and taunt me, I thought, "If I get the chance, I just might tell everything I know about her. I'll be eighteen in less than a year, they'll have to let me go then. What ever comes, I'll do it standing on my head, and when I'm eighteen I'll get away." She acted like she was bored, she stretched and said, "Did ya sleep good last night? I sure did! I slept like log! 'Course I knew where all my kids were last night, so I slept easy." She just stood there looking so satisfied, like there was nothing wrong with what she was doing to me. I thought, "She's crazy, she must be." She said, "Well, I gotta go. Let me know when ya decide ta mind. I might get 'cha outta here." I said, "When are you coming back?" She said, "Which - fuckin' - word - did - you - not - understand? I said when ya decide ta mind! That's when I'll be back! That's when I'll ***think*** about lettin' you outta yer cage!" She just stood there waiting for me to beg her like I did when I was little. I remember feeling enraged. I wanted to kill her with my bare hands. I wanted to kill her while she begged me not to. To her surprise, and actually mine too, I looked her right in the eye, and said, "Fuck you!" That infuriated her and she said, "You stupid, fitified, little mother fucker! If ya think I'm kiddin' ya, yer wrong. I'll leave yer ass in here 'til yer older than I am now! You call me when ya see things my way." I looked her right in the eye again and said, "Fuck you. I'll stay here 'till I'm eighteen, and while I'm here, I'm gonna tell these doctors everything that you and Gordon have done to all of us."

Now, you might think that I must not have been as scared as I said I was, or I would have agreed to anything to get out of there. Well, you would be wrong. As bad it was there, and as scared as I was, I couldn't hold it inside anymore. I don't know if it was anger, fear or stupidity, but I felt like I would explode if I didn't say what I said to her. And there was still the possibility that my dad would save me from the hell I had already lived for seventeen years and the hell that was coming, but if he didn't, I would be eighteen in less than a year. I decided to roll the dice, tell my mother to fuck off and take my chances. It was not easy, one option was as scarey as the other, but at least the one I chose that day kept me out of her reach. I looked at her and thought, "If I can survive you for seventeen years, I will somehow get through this." As scarey as it was, in my mind, it was the lesser of two evils. Within the next few weeks she would come close to convincing me that I made the wrong choice, but she would only come close, she wouldn't convince me. It wasn't really my choice or option anyway. I knew she wasn't getting me out of there that day. She was having too much fun with it to give it up that soon. It would also become very obvious that she was worried about what I might tell. That would only help me, because I wasn't going to tell anything, but if she thought I was, she would go on and on trying to refute to the doctor what she *thought* I was telling. For instance, one day she called to tell him, "If Trena tells you her step-dad touched her breasts, she's lyin'. The only reason I'm tellin' ya' this is 'cause I know she's told that same lie before ta other people. But it's a lie." The thing is, when the doctor asked me about *anything,* even that, I said, "What ever my mother told you is fine. Just go with whatever she tells you." She told him a lot of things to not believe if I told him, but I never told him anything. I really didn't have much faith in a guy who would order medication for me without even seeing me. He had never met me or talked to me and he ordered drugs to be forced on me for three days before he did. I had trouble trusting *anyone*, and this guy would be near the top of my list of people not to trust.

Finally, on the third day, the good doctor would find out what I looked like and sounded like. He was an older man, tall, gray hair but balding, nice smile and pleasant, but my instinct told me not to tell him anything. I remember thinking, "Gee, I hope you had a nice weekend while I was being drugged at your whim." I might sound bitter about this guy, that's because I am. I wonder how many public showers he had to take in his lifetime. I wonder if he ever had a clue, in all the years he practiced, how absolutely terrifying it was to a seventeen year old girl to be ***committed*** to a place like that. I really got the impression that compassion was not his long suit. He made rounds at the hospital a few days per week, spending five or ten minutes with his patients, and billed the insurance companies for full sessions. I honestly don't believe this guy knew, or even cared, about the feelings of his patients. I know after being in therapy with a dedicated professional like my therapist, that this guy was *not* dedicated to his profession. It's not by anything she has ever said, but by the differences I have seen with my own eyes, heard with my own ears, and felt with my own emotions. Anyway, he ordered more drugs for me, a 'fatten me up shake' for every evening and told me he would see me again. I told him I wanted to be moved to another floor so I could take a private shower. He agreed to have me moved to the other end of the floor I was on as soon as I adjusted to my medication. I asked how long that would be and he said maybe a week. I asked him why I couldn't get used to my medication on a floor with private showers. He just smiled and said, "I guess there is no real reason." So, he had me moved that afternoon, but I still didn't trust him. I figured I would just keep my mouth shut and let my mother drive this guy nuts. If we both tried to talk to him, he would probably believe her anyway, she's the one who payed the bill. Why put him, or me, in a bad position? I told myself to just let it go.

That afternoon I was moved to the other end of the floor. It was high security, but not maximum security. I could take a shower in a private shower stall, without an audience. I couldn't leave the floor or use the phone, but I was still better off than I was the day before. And the nurses' said after I got used to my medication, probably in a few days, I could 'earn adlibs' with good behavior and be allowed to leave the floor for so long at a time. I could go outside, go to the pool, the bowling alley or just sit in the lobby. Well, doesn't it sound like a nice place? I still didn't think so. The first room on that floor that they put me in upset the woman who was already in there. I don't know why they put me in there to start with. I found out later that she did not want a roommate. They had tried before to put people in her room and she had a fit every time. She was crude, intimidating and threatening, but I would only be in her room for a few days. I looked around at the people on that floor and thought, "My God. Is there anyone even remotely coherent around here? Is there any floor in this entire place where people know who they are? Am I really that deranged? Were they all like that when they came in, or are they all over medicated? Did this place make them the way they are now? Am I gonna end up like they are?"

I watched Laura for hours, a foreign woman, who had a husband and several children. She cried all the time and I wondered why. I would find out later that she was one of them who had shock treatments and sometimes, afterwards, she didn't know her name. Although she spoke English she sometimes didn't seem to understand what people said to her. I wondered if her relatives, from her home country, knew where she was and what she was going through. I wondered if she had been put there like I had, 'admitted' against her will. There was Midge, a small woman who laughed all the time, except when the orderlies came to get her for shock treatments. I don't mean laughing because something was funny, she just laughed out loud to herself. As small as she was it still took three orderlies to carry her away for her shock treatments. At first I didn't recognize her, but I kept thinking she looked so familiar. I watched her for a while and then I remembered where I had seen her. She was a friend of my grandmother! I remember thinking, "So that's how Alcee found this place. Grandma told her about it." I would later ask Grandma about it and she would swear to me for years, and I'm sure even today if given the chance, that she knew nothing about my mother hauling me off to that 'asylum.' What a coincidence! To this day, I believe she did know, because right before Alcee 'hauled me off,' Grandma was so mad at me she couldn't see straight. She was still mad about me moving out of her house to go live with Lori and Keith. I believe she was in on it, and I still remember how hurt I was when I put two and two together and realized it. There was Sandi, who I met in the TV room, she had suffered a nervous breakdown and she, too, took shock treatments. She also tried to fight the orderlies off when they came to take her for her shock treatments, all of the people did. She was married and had a baby, and she wasn't too far out in left field. She definitely had problems, but not what would, in the eyes of a seventeen year old, qualify her as crazy. I wouldn't use the word crazy today, but I'm trying to relate what my thoughts were at the age of seventeen, while I was stuck in a mental hospital. Not what my thoughts are or would be today. I don't know what caused her nervous breakdown, but she told me that's why she was in there. She didn't have a roommate in her room, and the woman I was rooming with wanted me out, and I wanted out, so we talked one of the nurses into helping me switch my room to Sandi's. She was one of the younger ones in there, probably mid twenties, but I'm just guessing. She was pretty coherent most of the time, but the days she underwent shock treatments were a little strange. Sometimes at night she sleep walked and didn't remember it the next day. She frequently got up in the middle of the night, walked over to my bed, shook me awake and said, "Take this. Take this and don't let anybody find it. Hide it! Hide it! Hide it!" I pretended to take 'it' and said I would hide 'it' and she went back to bed. Sometimes she did that several times during the same night. But she seemed coherent and appeared to know where she was. Sandi was nice and we became friends, not close friends, but friends.

I think the mornings were the scariest, because there was a lot of loud chaos when the orderlies came to carry people out for their shock treatments. The people cried, screamed, begged and fought, all in vain. Some literally got on their knees and begged the orderlies not to take them downstairs. Sometimes I just went in my room and shut the door, but I could still hear the terrified crying and begging. Sometimes I couldn't get down the hall to my room, because the orderlies were dragging the kicking, screaming people down the hall and I couldn't get past them. Those people sounded so scared and desperate, and the orderlies just smiled and carried them away. I can understand how someone might get desensitized in a job like theirs, but did they have to chortle and wink at each other like they thought it was amusing? It wasn't like they were really mean, but they were in no way comforting to the people who were trapped there. They just seemed cold and indifferent. Some of the nurses were kind and tried to be comforting, but the orderlies just seemed like bouncers at a bar. I tried not to make eye contact with them, because I was afraid of them. I was one of very few who had not been taken for shock treatments and I was terrified that it was just a matter of time until they came for me. I remember hoping that someone would find me and save me before Alcee's game went that far, maybe my dad.

There was a girl named Brenda there, and she was so mean she reminded me of Dana. I don't know why she was there, other than maybe being so mean, but she picked on me like a six year old bully would pick on a new kid on the playground at school. She called me names, hit me and pushed me up against the wall and made me say I was afraid of her. I said it, too, because I was afraid of her. It was kind of like having to let Alcee feel victory, Brenda had to feel it too, and I let her. I couldn't go crying to the nurses because Sandi said the first sign of violence and I would be sent to shock treatments. She said it didn't matter if I hit back or not, the staff could shock me with or without my doctor ordering it, if I was involved in *any* confrontations. I don't know if I believe that now, but I know I believed it then. Brenda was already taking shock treatments, so she had nothing to lose. What else could they do to her? I tried to avoid her, but I swear, sometimes she tracked me down just to pick on me. She didn't just do it to me, she did it to other people too, but most of them didn't know it because they were so unaware of what was happening. Some of them thought she was playing and laughed when they told her they were afraid.

Every evening they gave me the nasty, thick, slimy shake that my doctor ordered because I was underweight. I think they wanted to fatten me up, so it would look like I was getting physically healthier, and that would make people think I must be getting mentally healthier too. It would make it look like the hospital was doing a great job. I don't know if that's true, but that's what I believed then and that's what I believe now. They weighed me every morning. Every morning! How much can your weight change in twenty four hours? The doctor increased my medication to the point that I could hardly stand up by mid afternoon. It made me so sleepy and tired that I couldn't walk down the hall without leaning on the wall. That caused the nurses to restrict me to my room because they didn't want me to fall in the hallway. I told the nurse the drugs were too strong. I said, "What ever that stuff is would kill a horse. Are you sure that was ordered for me?" She said, "Oh, it will level off and you'll be fine with it. It might take a week or two." I was thinking, "A WEEK OR TWO?" I was supposed to be that out of it for a week or two? I was getting very frustrated with these people because I had been there long enough for them to know I was not a drug addict. Yet, they kept treating me like I was. I knew Alcee told them I was on drugs, but they hadn't done any blood or urine tests to find out if I was or not. I had been there long enough to have withdrawal symptoms if I was a drug user, and I hadn't had any. It just seems to me, that as soon as they figured out Alcee had lied about me being a 'junkie,' they would have considered that maybe she lied about other things too. Like for instance, why she *really* put me in there. So, I decided I would have to come up with my own plan to avoid being drugged. More times than not, the slimy shake went into the toilet, and Sandi showed me how to hold the pills under my tongue and then roll them to the top if the nurse asked to see under it. It worked, and I was more comfortable not taking the drugs. I remember thinking, "If they keep pushing these drugs in my face, I really will be a junkie by the time I get out of here!" I wondered if that's why most of the people in there were so incoherent, maybe they were all over medicated.

Pat, another patient, came in after I had been there for awhile, I don't remember how long, but it was the week I learned to hold the pills under my tongue and get away with it. I was still trying to 'adjust' to my medication so I could get adlibs and go downstairs to use the pay phone. Pat came into the hospital on our floor instead of the maximum security floor. Now, I figure Alcee had to really convince these people I was dangerous since they started me out at maximum security but they were starting this junkie at only high security. Anyway, Pat befriended me the day she got there. She had signed herself in there to avoid jail, a place she had seen many times before. She was a drug addicted professional criminal, committing mostly burglaries and drug dealing crimes. Pat got adlibs almost immediately after coming into the hospital. I guess it made a difference whether or not you were voluntarily 'admitted' or voluntarily 'committed.' The staff was satisfied that I had 'adjusted' to my medication, and I finally got adlibs too. I could sign out for an hour at a time and just walk around the hospital grounds. Better than that, I could use the pay phone. The first day I signed out, I was going down the stairs and ran into Brenda. She pushed me against the wall and said, "Say you're afraid of me." I said, "I ***am*** afraid of you." Pat was coming down the stairs behind me and, like lightning, she grabbed Brenda. She pushed Brenda against the wall and said, "I'm ***not*** afraid of you." She didn't hit her, but she threatened her and told her to leave me alone. I don't know why Pat took a liking to me, maybe she didn't really like me, but felt sorry for me. Whatever it was, it kept Brenda at bay, and I was grateful for that. Pat started hanging around with me, or I started hanging around with her, and I gave her all the medication I held under my tongue. She wanted it, I didn't. It made sense to me.

I really liked Pat because, what ever her motive was, she was nice to me, and I felt protected when I was with her. She rarely called me by my name, usually calling me Kid, but sometimes she called me Baby. Okay, call me a big baby, but I loved it, I ate it up like candy. I was a frightened seventeen year old emotional wreck. I don't know, maybe I did belong there, but I ***still*** don't think so. I did sense something about her that reminded me of my grandmother. She had that Fagan like personality, but I was going to take the kindness and affection until I had to pay for it, or give it up. Pat frequently called her husband and asked him to go 'boost' what ever we wanted, like tennis shoes, clothes, anything we wanted, including what Pat wanted most, morphine. We signed out for adlibs and met him on the grounds, usually near the parking lot.

They had me to watch out for anyone approaching. Pat called it "pinning" for them, while they shot up with drugs. They kept trying to talk me into trying it, but I kept saying no. I couldn't believe how easy it was. They actually shot up right there on the hospital grounds! I was from a college town where drugs were rampant in the sixties, but it was easier to get drugs at that hospital than it was on the college campus back home. At least it seemed like that to me because I saw more illegal drugs at that hospital than I ever saw on the streets at home. I couldn't believe the irony of it all. I was supposedly there because I was on drugs, which was a lie, and the people there were pushing drugs right in my face! Junkies and staff alike! None of it made sense, but nothing Alcee did ever made sense, so I guess my situation was not out of the norm for my life. Pat carried her radio around with her all the time and sang along with the music. To this day, when I hear the songs Candida or Groovin' On A Sunday Afternoon, I think of her. She used to sing Candida to me when it played on the radio, almost every day. She also walked me up the street to a bar where she hung out when she wasn't in jail or in a hospital avoiding jail. We walked up there several times and Pat drank liquor while I drank cola. Eventually, I did have a couple of mixed drinks at Pat's urging, but not both in the same trip. We just walked off the hospital grounds, up the street to the bar, drank and walked right back. Nobody ever said a thing. It was unbelievable! I did worry a little that we might get caught, but it was okay because I was with Pat. I felt safe with her.

Sandi, my roommate, and I were still friends too. She had been depressed and crying a lot because she wanted to see her baby and somebody wouldn't let her. I don't remember for sure, but I think her husband wouldn't bring the baby to the hospital to see her. I do remember that she was very sad. Sandi arranged for a friend to pick her up and take her to see her baby. This 'leave' she had arranged was not authorized by the hospital. One evening we were herded outside to some sort of baseball game, I think it was a staff softball game, but I don't remember for sure who was playing. We were supposed to be closely supervised because the ball diamond was so close to the road. Sandi asked me to help her sneak closer and closer to the road. We were sitting in the grass watching the game, and we kept inching up the hill a little at a time. Every time the nurses turned their backs, we scooted a little closer to the road. We knew the nurse sitting closest to us had asthma because we had seen her have asthma attacks, that's why we sat closer to her than one of the others. The nurse came over and told us we had to move back down the hill closer to our group. When we stood up Sandi ran for the road where her friend was waiting, and I 'accidentally' blocked the nurse when she tried to chase her. I kind of felt sorry for that nurse because she was one of the nice ones. But Sandi got away and went to see her baby. She came back to the hospital that night around eleven, just like she said she would, and she wasn't as sad. That really was all she wanted to do, just see her baby. I was glad she came back because I didn't want to lose her as a roommate, but I lost her anyway. When she came back they put her on another floor with more security for a couple of weeks. I still saw her in the arts and crafts room in the mornings, but she couldn't walk around anymore because she lost her adlibs. By the way, in the arts and crafts room they really did have basket weaving. I refused to weave a basket though. There was just something too cliche about weaving a basket in that place. I couldn't do it. I wouldn't do it. I remember a painting that was hanging on the wall in the hallway right outside the arts and crafts room. I found out that a former patient had painted it and left it there. I fell in love with it and if I knew where it was today, I'd try to buy it. The picture was of a sad, desperate looking teenager, wearing a blue shirt, slouching in a straight back chair. There were a lot of blues and grays in it. It might sound like a depressing picture, but for what ever reason, I really liked it.

Alcee decided that my spirit was only bent and not broken yet, so she stopped coming to see me. She had only been there a couple of times anyway, I didn't miss her, but if it made her happy to think I did, so be it. It had been at least two weeks, maybe three, since I had seen anyone from home, and as far as I knew she was still the only one who knew where I was, except for the strong possibility that my grandmother knew. My dad didn't have a phone. I had called the restaurant below his sleeping room to leave messages for him, but I still hadn't heard from anyone, except Alcee. It was Wednesday evening, and as other patients relatives started arriving to visit, I started feeling bad. I sat out front on a bench with other patients watching for someone familiar to show up. I started wondering if I would really be stuck there until I was eighteen. As it got later and later, I knew I was waiting for nothing. I must have looked pretty sad because Harvey, an older man around fifty, said, "Hey, let's go for a ride and get a sandwich." I didn't know him very well, but I had talked to him in the dining room and at the canteen. He had his truck parked at the hospital, which was against the rules, but he did it anyway. He told me that after he signed himself in, he had a friend park his truck in the lot and give him the keys during visiting hours. I remember thinking, "My God! Is anyone watching us here?" It didn't look like it. He seemed friendly and safe, so I got into his truck and we pulled out of the hospital with no problem. When we were a good distance from the hospital, Harvey pulled out a bottle of liquor from under his seat. He took a drink and then told me to take a drink. I said, "No, I can't. I don't want any." He yelled at me to take a drink and that's when I got scared. He said, "I said take a drink! Take a drink!" He kept shoving the bottle at me and screaming at me to take a drink. I wouldn't do it. He put the bottle between his legs and started grabbing at me with his right hand. I kept pushing him back while he drove and he eventually got behind another vehicle that caused him to slow down. We came to a traffic signal that was red, and as he stopped the truck, he lunged at me, but I had already started opening the door, so I jumped out and took off running up the street.

I ran to a gas station and told the attendant I was in trouble. I said, "Look, I'm supposed to be at the mental hospital. I got into a truck with another patient and he scared me, so I jumped out. I need to call the hospital." He let me use the phone to call the hospital, but they didn't answer the main number. They had an answering service or something, I don't really know who answered, but I couldn't get them to understand what was going on. They just kept saying, "We can't pick anyone up. You can call the admitting office tomorrow." I was scared and I didn't know what to do. I didn't want to try to walk back. I was too far away and didn't know the city. Besides that, I was afraid Harvey might be driving around there looking for me. There was a man in the station wearing a security officer uniform. I went to him and told him what happened and he seemed nice. He told me he worked at a children's hospital near the mental institution and said he would give me a ride back to the hospital. I was pretty scared to get in the car with another stranger after what had just happened with Harvey, but this guy had an identification tag on his shirt with the children's hospital name on it. I got into his car and he took me straight back to the hospital, just like he said he would.

The next morning I saw Pat at breakfast, and she was livid about what Harvey had done. She had already heard about it the night before. Some of the others we hung around with told her I left with Harvey and he came back without me. Two of the guys in our little circle of friends, Bill and John, said Pat went after Harvey the night before, when she heard about it. They said she was screaming and cussing at him and that the staff broke up the fight before Pat could get a good kick in on Harvey. They didn't do anything to Pat, but Harvey was drunk and they put him in maximum security. Pat also told them about his truck and they had it towed. Once again, Pat was being protective and I couldn't get enough of that. It was like someone was watching over me instead of me watching over them, or *me* watching over *me*. I hadn't had that feeling since I left Lori and Keith's house. I knew this would be short lived, so I soaked up as much of it as I could get. And for what ever reason, the staff didn't move me to another floor, I got to stay where I was. That afternoon Pat's husband brought her some morphine. I pinned while they shot up. They both kept trying to talk me into shooting up, but I just wouldn't or couldn't do it. Pat gave me some powdered morphine and a little cup of warm water. She said, "Okay then, try it this way. Drink it fast because it tastes real bad!" I didn't really want to do it, but I didn't really not want to do it, either. I took it and it tasted bad, just like Pat said. I thought if I was ever going to try somehting like that, I should do it while I was there. If anything went wrong, I was already at a hospital. I have to admit that part of my reasoning was that Alcee had put me in there saying I was a drug addict, and I had never even tried drugs. I thought it was kind of poetic justice to do an illegal drug there, the only time in my life I had ever done that or would ever do that. Looking back now, I wish I hadn't even done it then because after that I couldn't say *I had never tried a single* illegal drug. But I can honestly say that that's the only time I did. It was scarey, I didn't like the way it made me feel and I told myself I would never do that again. Since that day I have never understood why someone would purposely make themselves feel as bad as I did then.

The following week one of the nurses told me my dad was coming to visit me on Sunday. I said, "My real dad?" She didn't answer and I was afraid she meant Gordon so I asked her again. I said, "You mean my real dad right?" She said, "I don't know." I said, "Well, what's his name?" She told me his name, and I was really excited because she told me my real dad's name. So he found out where I was, and he was coming to see me! I was looking forward to Sunday and it seemed like forever until it finally arrived. My dad really did show up with one of his girlfriends, and I think before he could even sit down I said, "What took you so long? How did you find me?" He said the ambulance driver came by his sleeping room one evening and told him. The driver told him he had been by there about three times, but he could never catch my dad home. I couldn't believe how lucky I was, this guy kept going back until he found my dad! After my dad found out, it took him a while to get permission to leave the state, actually even the county, because he was on parole. He had to get his parole officer's permission before he could come and see me. My dad said, "Man, yer mom is nuts! I'm gettin' an apartment an' you can live with me when ya get outta here. I'm tryin' ta find ya a little car, too. Did ya know that crazy bitch sold yer car? I called 'er and told 'er I knowed where ya was and she started cussin' me fer no reason at all. I'm tellin' ya she's nuts! Has she always been like that ta you kids?" I was so hopeful that day, it wouldn't work out like my dad and I had said it would, but it sure gave me hope at the time. I thought, after all these years, my dad was finally going to save me, and he did for a little while.

I don't know if the hospital called Alcee and told her about me leaving with Harvey, or if she was mad because my dad had been there, but I believe it had to be one of those two things that set her off. The week after my dad was there on Sunday she came barrelling into the hospital one afternoon, demanding that they 'do something' with me or she would sign me out of there that day. She was far from calm, in fact, she was ranting and raving. The good doctor said he wanted to speak to me alone and we went into a small meeting room that was near the lobby. He asked me if I wanted to leave with her. I said, " No, I don't want to leave with her, especially when she's like this." We walked back to the lobby and he said, "I won't sign a release for her to leave today. I can't stop you from taking her, but the insurance won't pay for her treatments without me authorizing her release." Alcee became agitated and argumentative. I stood there listening to them argue back and forth, actually the doctor was calm, Alcee was the only one being argumentative. She looked at me and said, "Go get yer stuff, yer leavin' now." I stood there for a few seconds and then went to my floor, but I didn't get my stuff. I knew she couldn't personally get to me because it was a locked floor. I sat upstairs and looked out the window waiting for her car to pull out or for someone to come and get me and my things for me to leave. After a few minutes I saw her car leave, she left without me, and even though I was where I was, it had to be a blessing. It was ironic because her situation had gone from me begging her to get me out of there to me refusing to leave with her. One of her favorite sayings was, "The worm always turns."

I don't know how many days had gone by, but one day Pat told me she and her husband were going on a crime spree in another state and they wanted me to go with them. There were several jewelry stores they were going to rob and they needed a minor, just like my grandmother used to need minors. As much as I loved the feeling of someone caring about me, whether it was sincere or not, I couldn't do it. I believed if I got into trouble the little ones would follow my path. I told myself I had to make it out of the hell hole we were raised in, and then try to get them out. I told myself that I couldn't let them down again, and I couldn't let myself down either. *Myself* was really all I had. I really knew all along that Pat wanted something from me, I was just taking what I could get for as long as I could get it. She hugged me every day, like people pet their dogs everyday, and she bragged *about* me and *to* me every day, to make me feel like I mattered. She was grooming me to be her "super good pin," so she and her husband could use me on a crime spree. They did have a little boy, maybe she just wanted me to be a babysitter, I don't know. I didn't care if she was trying to turn me into their little stooge, I loved the affection and love, albeit fake, while I had it, but I wouldn't go bad to keep it. I had lasted seventeen years through all the hell at home, and I was not going to blow it then. First I told Pat I was just too scared, so she would keep trying to talk me into it. I did that because I wanted to hang on to the connection I had with her for as long as I could. The afternoon that she and her husband took off, I didn't go with them. I knew I would miss her, and I also knew she had been using me. But that was okay because I had been using her, too. She had been my tourniquet. It was like I was hemorrhaging emotionally when Pat came to the hospital and she became a tourniquet for me. But, by the time she left, my emotional bleeding had slowed to that of a paper cut. By then all I needed was a band aid and I could be my own band aid, in fact, I preferred it that way.

One day I called Alcee's to talk to the kids and she got on the phone and said, "You think yer real fuckin' smart don't 'cha? We'll see how smart 'cha are when I sign the papers fer fuckin' shock treatments! Yeah, we'll see how smart 'cha are then! Oooo weeeee!

You won't even know yer own fuckin' name by this time next week." She sounded maniacal, threatening and angry. I had no doubt in my mind that she would do that. I had already wondered why I was one of very few who hadn't been shocked. The thought terrified me, and I knew if they started shocking me I would never be the same again. I didn't know if that would be a good thing or a bad thing, but I didn't want to find out. That day I said I wanted to see my doctor, but he was busy, so I had to wait until the next day. I remember thinking, "With my luck the papers she signed will come in today's mail, and I'll be downstairs getting my brain fried by the time that old codger finds time to talk to me." I was a nervous wreck anyway, but I was way beyond that after I talked to Alcee. The next day, after being there over a month, I told the doctor that school was about to start, and if I didn't get out so I could start with the other kids, I wouldn' t go back at all. I told him I wanted him to release me to my dad. I didn't tell him anything about Alcee and Gordon. I just told him I got along better with my dad, and I would be living there when I got out. After talking to me longer than he ever had in a single visit, maybe ten minutes, he said he would sign a release authorizing my being released to my dad on Sunday morning. He gave me a prescription for the medication I had miraculously 'adjusted' to weeks before and I could hardly wait for Sunday to get there. I could hardly believe my dad was finally coming to save me.

Sunday did get there, and my dad showed up like he said he would. He and his most recent girlfriend helped me load my things in the car and we were out of the there! My dad was funny and made me laugh almost the entire ride home. He acted like he was glad I was with him, he looked happy. As I watched him and listened to him, I realized how similar our senses of humor were. We also had favorite foods in common. I remember thinking about the environmental verses genetic arguments regarding personalty traits and likes and dislikes. For ten years I had imagined my dad saving me and today he was. So what if he was a jailbird? I didn't care. At least he wasn't mean spirited, he was pleasant, and *very funny*. So what if he was a convict with a criminal record 'as long as your arm?' He was saving me, and that day he was my 'superman.' But we would soon find out that the wicked witch of the west, Alcee, had kryptonite, and she would use it. To say she was livid would be an understatement. There was always a big price to pay for beating Alcee at one of her own games. The price this time would be her using her kryptonite to take my 'superman' out of the picture. She was infuriated, because she had dealt me a hand that she *thought* I couldn't play, and I had trumped her ace.

CHAPTER FIFTEEN

Save The Others Or Save Yourself?

I really believe that my dad wanted to try being a dad to me, but he didn't know how. He had been in and out of jail since he was eleven years old, starting with reform school and escalating to the state prison. By the time he got out of prison, the summer we tried to live together, he had been incarcerated more than half his life, each time for two years or less. I have often wondered, because he had been incarcerated from such an early age, if maybe he felt safe in jail and subconsiously caused himself to be sent back repeatedly. It must have been like home to him. I met his father a couple of times and got the impression he didn't care much what happened to my dad, nor had he ever. I'm not making excuses for my dad because he knew he had kids and should have been there for them. But he did go by my grandmother's frequently over the years to ask about us, and he had Dana and my names tattooed on his arm. He had more kids than just Dana and me, he had three other kids and he hadn't been there for them either. But I do think he was trying to turn over a new leaf that year, and in a way he might have done that. As far as I know he has stayed out of jail since that summer more than thirty years ago. That wasn't easy for him to do considering Alcee tried everything she could think of to have his parole violated. She started her mission the day my dad picked me up from the 'asylum' and took me to his place.

We pulled up in front of the apartment my dad had rented for us and there was a little car parked in front of it. He said, "Who in the hell parked in front o' our house? I'm gonna talk ta the landlord and get that damn car towed." After we got inside he said, "Hell, I don't wanna get that car towed. I forgot, that's the one I picked up fer you. Why, I forgot about that! Here ya go, these keys must be yers." He was so proud of himself, I could tell. I was so thankful and excited about him doing that for me. It wasn't the car itself that meant so much, it was that my dad had not only saved me, but he was doing what other dads did for their kids. I told him how much I loved the car and how grateful I was that he did that for me. He chuckled and said, "Yeah, yer nutty mom cain't sell that one. Her name ain't on it so ya don't have ta worry about that. ***I*** got ya that." He said, "Yer mom's always been nuts, but I couldn't hardly believe she done that ta you. I'd a never thought she'd go that far. When that guy told me where ya was and I called 'er she went crazy. I never know'd it was that bad fer you kids, yer Grandma Frankie never told me none o' that stuff." I told him I was just glad he was letting me stay with him until I turned eighteen. He said, "She ain't gonna do nothin' while yer here with me." He was barely literate and very crude, but he was my superman that day, and I think he loved it.

The apartment was another one bedroom, but there was a sofa sleeper in the living room, so I slept there. His girlfriend had four or five kids, but they didn't live there, she left them alone at her house most of the time. From what I saw of her and her kids, she wasn't abusive to them, but to say she was neglectful would be an understatement. My dad's nephew, a cousin I had never met until that summer, was there a lot of the time. There were people in and out of our apartment all day, every day, but that was okay because I was at school or work most of the time. When I was home I cooked. My dad loved that because my cooking was much better than prison food. His girlfriend either didn't know how to cook or didn't want to. My brothers and sisters were old enough to call me if they needed me, so I didn't worry about them as much as I had in the past. I really thought I could get through my senior year of high school, graduate and maybe even go to college. I wasn't sure I could do it, I was still making that my goal, but there was no way I would bet on anything for sure. I remember thinking, "Just go for it, and if it happens okay, and if it doesn't that's okay too." I had less than a year to go until I hit the magic age of eighteen, but Alcee couldn't wait that long. We hadn't been back an hour when she called and said, "Ya might think yer real fuckin' smart today, but just wait and see what tomorrow brings." I was instantly scared because I knew there was no limit with her. There never had been, so why should there be now? She started the day I got back threatening and harassing my dad and me. Because of her “kryptonite,' which consisted of lies and false accusations, my living with my dad would last about a month. She did everything she could to get his parole violated and everything she could to humiliate me at school.

Less than a week after I went back to school, two of my classmates approached me about buying drugs. They wanted to buy them from me! I said, "How would I know where you get that stuff? I'm not into drugs!" One of them said, "C'mon man, we know your mom had you dried out last summer. Help us out, be cool. Where can we get some good shit?" Alcee had told my cousins that I was addicted and she had to 'put me away' that summer, so I could 'kick the habit.' She was going to make sure I couldn't stand to go to school. The fact that the kids at school knew I had been put in a mental institution that summer was more humiliating to me, than them thinking I did drugs. Alcee didn't want anyone to know where I was when she kidnapped me and had me committed, but now that I was out she wanted to make sure everyone knew where I had been. The stigma was almost unbearable. Even high school aged kids can be cruel, and some of them were. I just tried to keep to myself and ignore the few true idiots who saw my situation as gossip fodder for their entertainment. Alcee made sure my cousins and Georgie spread information about me all over the school. I remember one class when we were discussing the prison system in this country in a class discussion format. I brought up a few issues about the system and said I thought the system was more punishing than rehabilitating. I was so embarrassed, when two boys in that class joined together to verbally beat me to a pulp. One of them said, "I guess if my dad was in prison as much as yours' is, I might see it that way too." Then they both continued on about the criminals being treated like vacationers instead of criminals. It was humiliating, and I just shut up and let them have their fun. That doesn't necessarily reflect my view today, but at the time I was seventeen and thought my dad was superman for saving me. I had never told the kids at school anything about my dad, Alcee or Gordon. So within weeks of going back to school it seemed as if everyone there knew my dad had been in prison, knew I had been in an 'asylum' and believed I was a drug user. I remember thinking, "This is so hopeless and useless. Just quit and go to work somewhere." Then I talked myself into hanging in there for a while longer. Every time I wanted to quit, I talked myself out of it. I don't know how, but I did. But I could only do it for so long, and so long would last less than two months.

While sowing seeds of humiliation for me at my school, Alcee was also busy trying to get my dad's parole violated. She called his parole officer and said, "He's usin' drugs and he's givin' my daughter drugs, too. I even had to have her put away last summer because he was givin' her drugs." Then she filed phone harassment charges against him saying he called her house "all hours of the day and night" and cussed her out. A man with a criminal record like my dad's didn't stand much of a chance when it came to a 'he said she said' court case. Alcee was the one making threatening phone calls and driving by the apartment all hours of the day and night. It wouldn't have done much good for me to stand up for my dad and go against her, though. After all, I had just been released from a mental institution and had been declared incorrigible less than two years before. My dad's girlfriend was afraid of Alcee, so she wanted him to move in with her and her kids. She thought, if he wasn't in the apartment with me, that Alcee would back off and leave him alone. She would be wrong, Alcee had a score to settle and wouldn't stop until ***she*** said it was settled. My dad came home one night and said, "I'm gonna move in with her. The rent's paid through the end of the month, after that I don't know what ta tell ya." I said, "You're caving in! What about her not bothering me while I'm with you! You said you'd hang around 'till I turned eighteen!" I was so upset that I was yelling at him. He said, "Look, goddamn it, I ain't goin' back ta jail. If I stay here yer mom's gonna have me in trouble. Ya know how she is." His girlfriend got mad because I yelled at him, so she started putting her two cents worth in. I gave it back to her and they left in what was supposed to have been my car. I had been back about a month and I was being forced to Alcee and Gordon's again! I was seventeen and could get away in less than a year, but that didn't make me feel any better that night.

My dad called Alcee and told her he had moved out, and she could go get me if she wanted to. She did. As soon as we got to her house, she started in on me about all I had done to her. She said, "The only mistake I made by puttin' you away, is not havin' 'em give ya shock treatments! I told you that ya ain't gonna outdo me! You give me any more trouble and I'll put 'cha some place where nobody will ever find ya! Do you hear me? Ya deaf? Answer me, goddamned you!" Everything was the same. She said, "Yer gonna apologize ta Gordon fer showin' yer ass the last two years, and yer gonna tell him yer thankful fer him treatin' ya like yer his own! Do you hear me? I don't know why ya ever thought you could outdo me! Especially over that son-of-a-bitch! Where's yer daddy now? Huh?" When Gordon got home I kissed him on the cheek and told him I was sorry I had been so much trouble. I told him he was a big man to take me in like I was his own kid. I would quote my words, but to this day I gag when I think about having to say those things to that brutal, sadistic, maniacal fiend. He said, "It's about fuckin' time ye stopped bitin' the hand that feeds ya." Alcee was happy watching me cower until I had reduced myself to a sniveling nothing. She said, "Just so ya know, there ain't no hard feelings on my part, as long as ye don't start showin' yer ass again. Just don't start any shit and there won't be any!" I told them I knew I was no good, I didn't know why I acted the way I acted towards them, I didn't know how lucky I was and that sometimes I believed I inherited my dad's bad genes. This made them both so happy because I was nothing and I was even willing to say so. They won again, totally and completely. I was just an empty headed baby factory doll, no sense, no emotion, no feeling, no nothing.

I kept trying to go to school during the day and work at night. My school work left a lot to be desired, I would have probably flunked out anyway, if I hadn't quit. I still gave Alcee almost all of my money, some weeks all of it. The factory near the alley where we used to live started hiring seventeen year olds because they were so busy they needed more workers. Normally you had to be eighteen to hire in there. Alcee and Gordon started hounding me to quit school and hire in at the factory. Alcee said, "You'd be a friggin' idiot not to get in there while ya can. They pay good money." Gordon's logic was, "Ya git in there now as young as ya are and ya could retire at a young age after thirty years. There ain't no college that'd let you in anyway. Ya might as well face it, ya ain't got the smarts fer college." Two months after I had gone back to school, I quit and hired in at the facotry. I stayed at Alcee's for a while longer, but like she used to frequently say, "The worm always turns." I worked at the factory and I did make decent money. I gave most of it to Alcee and bought school clothes and other things for the kids. The kids loved it, because I could really spend money on them then, even after giving most of it to Alcee.

Alcee was as mean as ever, and I tried to run interference between her and the little ones as much as I could. One night she got mad at Dena because she hadn't folded the towels. Dena had gone to a drive-in movie with some friends. Alcee called the movie theater and had Dena paged as an emergency. I tried to stop her. I said, "Don't do that. I'll fold the towels, she just forgot, leave her alone. I'll jump her ass when she gets home, just leave her alone." But Alcee had to humiliate Dena by having her paged as an emergency and then demanding she come home right that minute. The whole car load of kids had to leave, so Dena could come home and fold towels. A few years later Alcee would pull a similar stunt with Tim at a drive-in with his girlfriend. Tim had been giving Alcee his money too, only he told her it was a loan and she had to pay it back. When he asked for his money back, he and Alcee argued about it. That night, he picked up his girlfriend and went to the drive-in. Alcee went to the drive-in and parked a few rows behind them, unbeknownst to him. I knew she was going and I said, "Do you know what that will do to him if he sees you spying on them?" She said, "The little bastard's gonna learn not ta fuck around with me!" That night Tim came home shortly after Alcee and she started taunting him. She said, "I saw you at the movie tonight crawlin' all over that little whore ya took. I wonder how her mother would like ta know about you two makin' out at the drive-in? Yeah, maybe her mother would like ta know what a nice guy you really are. I saw ya pawin' her all over. I'll bet her mom would like ta know about that, don't you?"

I tried to stay at Grandma's part of the time, but I heard her say that she had become afraid of me. One day I heard her ask Alcee, "Ain't you afraid to lay down down and go to sleep with her in the house, after havin' to put her away?" Alcee said, "No, she ain't gonna start no shit with me, 'cause she knows if I have to put her someplace again, she ain't never gettin' out. And her goddamned daddy don't want nothin' ta do with her." Grandma said, "By God, when she was here the other night, I made the boys take turns sittin' up to watch her. I cain't lay down and rest when she's here. I'm scared to death of what she might get up and do in the middle of the night." I just stayed away from Grandma's after that. I didn't want to scare her or anything, and I was really of no use to her with Alcee cashing my check, was I?

I became friends with a woman I worked with at the factory. She was a widow with several kids and lived in a mobile home near where we worked. She had left her kids with her mother in another state, while she came to make a new start for all of them. Her plan was to get set up and then bring the kids back to live with her. While she was trying to make a home to bring them to, she needed a roommate. The roommate she had was going back to their home state, and she didn't want to live alone. She asked me if I was interested in moving in and sharing expenses. I wanted to jump at the chance, but how could get around Alcee? The plant was offering overtime, actually some of the overtime was mandatory, so

I was making a lot of money. I told Alcee that my friend, Carolyn, was living alone and was scared at night, so I was going to spend the night there. She wouldn't know for sure how much I made when I worked overtime, so my plan was to cash my check and pay half the expenses and still have enough left to satisfy Alcee. It sounded good to me at the time, but remember I was only seventeen and known by my family to be stupid. This was okay for awhile, but Alcee was getting suspicious because every week I told her I lost my paycheck stub. I mostly stayed at Carolyn's, but frequently Alcee got on a power trip and came over to demand I go home with her right then.

One night, Carolyn and some of the others were going out drinking and I went with them. Most of them didn't know how old I was, and I looked so old for my age that I didn't even get carded. While we were at the bar, a waitress brought me a drink, she said, "That guy over there sent it to you." I looked over and saw my dad smiling at me. I told the waitress to take it back, I said, "Take it to him, I don't want it." I was drinking coke anyway, I didn't like booze, I had seen too much of its effects throughout my life. Those women from work did get me drunk one night, but for the most part, I just didn't like to drink. My dad came over and asked me to dance and I danced with him. While we were dancing, he tried to fix me up with one of his drunk buddies sitting at his table. I said, "Ya know what Dad, you're a pervert and a coward. Tell your friend I'm not interested." It had only been a few months since he bailed out on me, and I think I was still mad or hurt or whatever about it. That's the last time I saw my dad until I looked him up when my son was around six years old. He and I got together several times and we called each other every week. After a few months, I still couldn't seem to bond with him. I liked him and thought he was funny, but I just couldn't get close to him. He was married to a woman who had three kids. She was very suspicious of me, to the point that she asked me what I wanted from my dad. I told her I didn't want anything from him. She said, "Then why, after all these years, are you just showing up out of nowhere?" One day we were all together and he said, "Ya gotta admit, I never mistreated ya." That comment stirred up a lot of unidentifiable emotions in me. I felt *something,* but I don't know what it was. I looked at him and said, "Yeah, but you know what? You didn't stick around and make sure nobody else did either." That's the last time I saw him.

So anyway, Carolyn had seen my dad and my mom, and it wasn't hard to figure out that my life wasn't exactly a model for a TV series like Father Knows Best or something like it. Carolyn started talking to me about my mother. She said, "You know, something just ain't right here. She comes by and gets your money and acts like it's your job to take care of your brothers and sisters. Those are not your kids, they're hers." I made excuses for Alcee because I knew if Carolyn showed any signs of not liking her, I would be in a bad position. Pretty soon Alcee sensed that Carolyn had no use for her. She said, "That fuckin' ignorant bitch, you like to hang around with so well, has got yer ass in a real sling! You been givin' her money to stay there, I know ye have. I know about the overtime ya been workin' and I wanna know where yer goddamned money went." I told her Carolyn was a widow, and all I did was pay my half of the expenses. She said, "Ya told me you was just spendin' the night there. It sounds ta me like ya ***think*** you moved in. Well, yer movin' out! Yer gonna have yer ass right here at night, so I know where ya are! You proved ta me that 'cha cain't be trusted any farther than yer goddamned sneakin' no good daddy! I'll take ya ta work and pick ya up from now on." Just like old times. She didn't want me to talk to Carolyn at work anymore, but she couldn't really stop me, so I did anyway. She called Carolyn and said, "I just wanna let ya know that I just got her out of an asylum last summer. She probably didn't tell ya that did she? I ain't gonna be responsible if she does somethin' ta you or yer kids. She's considered dangerous, and you know that now, so what ever she does you brought it on yerself." Carolyn asked me about it, and I told her what happened. She said, "There is something wrong with your mother." But even with her reaction, I was still so embarrassed and felt so worthless and humiliated. I remember thinking, "The rest of my life is going to be like this." I also remember thinking, "So make it a short one, you idiot!"

When Carolyn tried to move her kids to their new life in a new state, they resisted, so she decided to give up on a new start and go back home. She said, "If you move where I live, I guarantee your mom won't get to you before you're eighteen. It will take her longer than that to get the paper work done to cross state lines." I was only a few months away from turning eighteen and really wanted to go, but I had to think of a way to pull it off. I told Carolyn she would have to help me trick Alcee, if she was serious about me moving back home with her. I told Alcee that Carolyn was moving back to her home state, and that I would miss her because she had been nice to me at work. I said, "I hate to see her move back where she's from. You should hate it too, because she really likes you. She thinks your funny." That week Carolyn helped me find an old car, and I bought it with money she had been hiding for me, about a hundred dollars. I told Alcee I was going to help Carolyn move all her things back that weekend, and I would be back late Sunday night. I didn't come back Sunday night though, I stayed with Carolyn until I was about eighteen and a half. Alcee called me at least once a week to threaten me. She said, "You ain't as smart as ya thought 'cha was! I got the fuckin' papers to put you where nobody will ever find ya! You'll think twice before ya ever fuck with me again!" She mailed me a bathing suit top with a note that said, "I didn't figure you'd need the bottom, since you'd have 'em off most of the time whorin' around, anyway." Then she started sending papers for me to sign for loans. After I turned eighteen she started getting loans in my name. Carolyn told me not to sign them, but I did anyway. I thought turning eighteen would make a bigger difference than it did. I thought I wouldn't be as afraid anymore, but I was still afraid of her. I was still terrified of her. Then she called and said, "I can understand ya turnin' yer back on me, but I cain't believe the way ya turned yer back on these kids." Carolyn's boyfriend was getting mad about her calling and raising hell all the time. He also didn't understand why I wouldn't just go home.

I was causing trouble by being there, and I was several months beyond my eighteenth birthday, so I decided to go back home. I sold my car and took a bus home, so I wouldn't be broke when I got there. I found a job as a night clerk at a local motel. I had known the manager since elementary school, and his sister owned the place. He had an apartment at the hotel, and I stayed across from his apartment in the boiler room. It wasn't too bad because they stored old furniture in there, so I had a couch to sleep on. When he got up and went to work in the mornings, I went across the hall to his apartment and used his bathroom and kitchen. After working there for several months, we got married. That marriage didn't last long, but at least there were no children involved. We separated after about three months, and I found a different job. I rented an old trailer in a run down trailer park and stayed there most of the time. Gordon was working out of town, and Alcee often went to visit him in the middle of the week. When she was gone, I stayed at her house with the kids. I went to their parent teacher conferences, bought their school clothes and gave them lunch money. I was still more like a parent than their sister, but that was okay, except for the fact that I couldn't pay my rent half the time and I had to move. I moved back into Alcee's. She was gone part of the time, and Gordon was gone most of the time. One weekend Gordon came home and started yelling and screaming at everybody. The boys were getting bigger, and I told them if he laid one hand on anybody, they should carry him outside and pin him. They did. Things were starting to turn around a little then. Alcee and Gordon were out numbered, and none of us were little kids anymore. Denise was still pretty young, but she was verbal and she could run. But the abuse would continue for years, and the kids wouldn't have me there to run interference for them much longer.

A few months after my first marriage ended, I met my second husband. He was nice to the kids, and we took them places they had never been, like amusement parks and the circus. We dated for a year or so and got married. I had bought another car, which Alcee didn't want me to take with me when I got married. She said, "Well, you don't plan on takin' that car do ya?" I said, "Well, yes I do. I'm still making payments on it and since I'm paying for it, I'm gonna drive it." She said, "What the fuck am I supposed ta do fer a goddamned car? Mine ain't worth shit! I cain't believe you'd take that fuckin' car and strand me with this bunch o' kids!" I said, "Believe it, because I'm taking my car. I need it to get back and forth to work." She said, "That mother fucker you're marryin' has got a car, use his." I said, "No, I'm taking my car with me. I'll loan it to you if you need it some days, but I have to take it with me." The morning after I got married she totaled my car in front of her house, right smack in front of her house! I paid her the premium every month to put me on her insurance as a rider because it was cheaper for me. The insurance company declared my car as totaled and made the insurance check payable to Alcee. She kept the check, and I had to pay off the loan. So that's what I got for saying, "If I'm paying for it, I'm gonna drive it," because Alcee showed me that wasn't so. I paid for it, but I didn't drive it because it was totaled. Right in front of her house, so she didn't even have to find a ride home. No one was injured. Not only did she make sure I didn't take my car with me, she wouldn't let me take anything that was mine out of that house, like school pictures, record albums and very few clothes. The day I married and left there, I didn't have enough stuff to fill a medium sized suitcase. She wouldn't even let me take school pictures with me. But years later, when my husband asked for a childhood picture of me, she gave him my second grade picture. It's the only picture I have of myself as a child.

I still took care of the kids as much as I could. I bought their school clothes and let them spend the night a lot. A few times Alcee and Gordon fought, and she decided she was going to leave him. I even let her stay with us for a few days, until she decided to go back to him. The kids had a place to run, because they knew I would hide them out, and I did. One time, Tim ran away, and Alcee came to my house looking for him. It reminded me of when my grandmother used to come to our house looking for my uncles when they ran away. One night she came in the front door as Tim went out the back door. I said, "Mom, do you know where he was last night? He saw you coming up the street and crawled under a parked truck. That's how scared he was. If the truck had pulled away, he could have been killed." She said, "That's okay, if he was in his grave, at least I'd know where the little mother fucker was all the time." I said, "You mean to tell me if he was dead it wouldn't bother you?" She said, "If he keeps tryin' ta outdo ***me***, I'll fuckin' kill 'im myself, and his big sissy won't have ta worry about him crawlin' under trucks." She mocked me and made fun of me for worrying about him. She said, "I know ya know where the little son-of-a-bitch is, and I'm gonna have the little fittified bastard picked up if ya don't send 'im home." Tim eventually went home because he knew what she was capable of. She threatened to put him away and have his head examined too.

My husband and I moved away, not far, but to the next town. I went to a career center and obtained my G.E.D., which made Alcee livid. She said, "Aw, so I suppose ya really think yer better than the rest of us now, don't 'cha? You just had to get yer high school diploma so ya could rub it in my face didn't ya? Well, I'll tell ya somethin'! Yer the reason I couldn't graduate! I had ta work three fuckin' jobs ta keep you from being adopted!" I was ashamed to tell most people that I didn't graduate high school, and I was ashamed to tell Alcee about me obtaining my G.E.D. I later went to a trade school, and she went ballistic about that, too. She said the same things and more. She said, "Well don't ever forget that 'cha never fly so high but what 'cha don't fall. Every dog has it's day and you'll have yers!" It seemed like the more education I wanted to obtain, the more angry Alcee got. She couldn't stand for me to even talk about education. The night Tim graduated high school, she and my husband made fun of him and his commencement. I said, "I can't believe you two are ridiculing him. This is a big deal. I'm proud of him." They both taunted me for taking his graduation so seriously. I have heard over the years, that she bought a dictionary and thesaurus. I believe that to be true, because her letters to the editor sound much more articulate than she ever did when she talked.

She still liked to make me look like the bad seed, even in front of my husband. One evening she showed up at our front door and presented us with a cute little dog for our anniversary. I made her take it back, I couldn't accept a dog from her. My husband couldn't understand why, and I wasn't going to try and explain it. He didn't like Alcee unless we were arguing, but whenever we did argue, he went to Alcee's and they sat and made fun of me together. She told him that I had 'never been quite right in the head.' One night we were arguing and he said, "It's no wonder your mom had to put you in a funny farm! Sometimes, I think you're fuckin' nuts!" I never told him many details of my childhood because after trying to tell him just a few things, he said, "Jesus Christ! That's when you were a kid! It's time to get over it." I knew he couldn't or wouldn't ever comprehend the lasting effects such abuse has on children. He would never understand how permanently crippling it is emotionally. When we went to Alcee and Gordon's for dinner, she always fixed my husband's favorite food, even though I hated it. I soon saw them as friends, and I was just getting by again. I had a signal to warn my husband if Alcee or any of my other relatives grabbed me and carted me off. He thought I was being absolutely crazy, he said so. I said, "Okay, say I'm crazy, but if you ever come home from work and I'm missing, look for broken glass. If you find any that means they got me." He probably did think I was nuts, he had no concept of the fear I still had and would have for a lot longer. He wasn't raised like I was, how could he even have a clue? I tried to tell him about some of it, but he said, "Just don't tell anybody about it, or they'll think your nuts." He just couldn't comprehend the scars, and I'm kind of happy for him that he couldn't. If he couldn't comprehend it, then he must not have lived it, and I'm happy for him.

Alcee took advantage of us all the time, especially the friendship she had forged with my husband. Several times she had loan companies draw up loan papers, and instead of asking, she just told us, "I need you ta sign some papers," and we did. We even co-signed for her to buy Gordon a new truck for his birthday. She gave him the truck and told him she paid cash for it, so there were no payments. I found out that Gordon had been demanding to know where all his money had gone. He claimed he had given her a lot of money and she was supposed to be putting it in the bank. She hadn't put any money in the bank. Not only that, she had borrowed a lot of money in my name, my husband's name and I don't even know who else's names. She had taken money from all the kids who were old enough to work. She had made the older kids go to Gordon's relatives and play on their sympathy to borrow money for her because they wouldn't secretly loan her any more money. So she explained the money being gone by telling Gordon, "I was bound and determined that you were gonna have a brand new truck for yer birthday. That's where all the money went, I paid cash for it." A few months later she called me and said, "I just want 'cha ta know, that cock sucker got drunk and totaled that brand new fuckin' truck! He was drivin' drunk and they threw his ass in jail. I gotta go get 'im out." I said, "Mom, the insurance probably won't cover the accident if he was drunk." She said, "There ain't no insurance! That's why I called, ta let ya know the finance company is gonna be comin' after you, not me, 'cause I cain't pay it." I said, "Well, we're not gonna pay for that truck that he totaled because he was drunk! We're just not." She said, "Yer gonna have to 'cause I ain't got it." I said, "No, if you don't have it then I'm telling Gordon he can pay it. How did you get away with no insurance on a financed vehicle?" She said, "It don't matter how I did. All that matters is the fuckin' thing is totaled and there ain't no insurance and I cain't pay it so you're gonna have to." We argued back and forth and I said, "If I get one single call from the finance company, I'm goin' to Gordon and telling him he can pay it, not me." About a month later I would find out how mad she really was about that. She didn't even work any more and hadn't for years. She didn't have to, Gordon made good money and all of her kids worked and gave her money. Her kids amounted to a hive of worker bees for her, and she just sat there like the queen bee benefiting from all their work. And she wanted me and my husband to pay for that truck?

My husband and I moving to a different town made it better for us, but it made it worse for the kids. Alcee still went out of town to be with Gordon some weeks, and Dana was left in charge of the others. She was as cruel and abusive as Alcee and Gordon. She always had been, and would continue to be even to her own children years later. About a month after the truck was totaled, Alcee went to the town where Gordon was working through the week. She was supposedly begging the judge not to send him to jail. She was giving him the 'we have a houseful of kids to support' story. One night, while she was out of town taking care of Gordon, Tony called me and said Dana pulled a knife on him. He said he was afraid to go to sleep because she kept laughing and saying she was going to cut him up when he fell asleep. I drove over to pick him up and bring him to my house for the night. The next night Alcee and Gordon were supposed to be home, and I figured I would take him back home then.

That following night, after my husband got home, we drove Tony home. As soon as we walked into the house, Dana looked at me and said, "Yer in a world of shit with Mom! I told her ya didn't take Tony with ya, that ya just said ya was goin' to so he could get out and do his drugs." I said, "Why did you tell her that? You knew he was with me?" She started laughing and said, "Alls I know is, I saw him at the pool hall today talkin' to a known junkie." I said, "No, you didn't. He wasn't even in town, and you know it. You know he was with me." Gordon was passed out drunk in his urine soaked chair when Alcee came in screaming and said, "I don't know who in the fuck you think you are, but these kids are mine not yours! Don't even bother ta lie fer the little cock sucker 'cause Dana already told me where he was all day!" I said, "I don't care what Dana told you, Tony's been with me since last night. I have known where he was every minute since I picked him up last night. Did Dana tell you she pulled a knife on him?" She said, "Well fuck a goddamned duck! Now it's Dana's fault the little bastard took off, huh?" I said,

"He didn't take off, I made him leave with me last night, so the fighting would stop and nobody would get hurt. I made him go with me last night, and he's been with me the whole time." She said, "Oh that's right, I forgot you've got a fuckin' diploma, so you know what's best fer all these kids now!" She started mocking me and said, "I forgot about you bein' so fuckin' smart! Can you ever forgive me, you fuckin' fittified graduate?" She deliberately mispronounced the word graduate, she was making fun of me. She pronounced it gra-gee-ate. All of her screaming and cussing woke Gordon up. He jumped out of his chair ready to fight. He started yelling, "What the fuck is goin' on?" He grabbed for Tony and said, "So ya been causin' trouble ya little son-of-a-bitch? Com'ere and I'll show ya what trouble is, ya little mother fucker!"

I don't know where I got my guts, maybe I was braver because my husband was there, but there was no guarantee he would be on my side. I said, "Get your fuckin' hands off him, Gordon! Don't touch him again!" He was instantly enraged at me and came towards me with his fist pulled back to hit me. I felt my husband move and stand behind me. Gordon shook his fist like he could hardly hold himself back, but he didn't swing at me. I told Tony to get his clothes and come with me. Alcee said, "He ain't fuckin' leavin' here 'till I say he is! I'll tell ya when he's leavin'! He's leavin' Monday morning when I send 'im off ta have his fuckin' head examined! That's when he's leavin'!" I don't know where I got my nerve, guts, courage or what ever it was, but I said, "No! You are not going to send him anywhere to have his head examined! If you even think about it, I will not stop until you are somewhere having your head examined!" Alcee said, "Well ain't you just the bravest mother fucker in the whole goddamned world? I don't know when you ever got the idea that these kids are yers, but they ain't! They're mine! And don't you forget it!" I said, "Well, don't you forget this. If you ever put any of these kids in nut house, like you did me, I will see ***you*** put somewhere! I will get them out, and I will have you put somewhere! Whether it be a hospital or a jail, I will have you put away." Gordon told me to get out of his house. He said, "This is my house ya ungrateful mother fucker, and I want 'cha out of it! Get out!" I couldn't help myself, I said, "Your house? I've made more payments on this house than you have. Why don't you get the mail someday and find out what you own and what you owe? I have so much money tied up in this place, I could put a lien on it." Alcee was more than livid. She grabbed my shirt and started to hit me, but I pushed her away and said, "You know what? I'm not a scared little kid any more, I'm a grown woman. You might want to think it over before you do anything stupid, like touch me or send any of these kids anywhere!" She opened the door and said, "I'm fuckin' through with you!" I said, "I'm leaving, but I want you to know, if any of these kids disappear I will make it my life's work to put you away. You told me once there were no hard feelings on your part, there damn well shouldn't be. You have tortured and used six out of seven of us since the day we were born. The jig is up and there ***are*** hard feelings on ***my*** part." She said, "I should have smothered you at birth, ya ungrateful little bitch!" I said, "I heard you tried to." She came back with, "I evidently didn't try hard enough, you ugly fittified son-of-a-bitch!" I knew it wasn't lack of effort on her part, my great uncle told me he caught her and my grandmother trying to suffocate me when I was a few days old. Gordon picked Tony up with one hand and literally threw him against a wall. I tried to get Tony to leave with me, but he just kept crying and said, "I'm okay, just get out of here. I'll be okay." I waited out in the road for him for a few minutes and he came out and told me to go on. He said, "You know how they are. If you don't leave, it will just get worse." I left Tony there that night, bruised, bleeding and crying. He was only sixteen. I guess that was the cowardly part of me shining through again. I remember thinking, if Alcee and Gordon could feel their victory that night, maybe she wouldn't have Tony carted off somewhere. In a way, I do feel like I was cowardly that night for leaving him. I didn't feel like that then. I felt like it was the best thing to do at the time. I don't know what emotions, if any, I felt that night. But the fact is, I did leave him there.

The kids called me collect from school or their friends houses when they needed something; money, gym shoes, clothes, books or anything else they needed. I drove over, picked up lunch for us and met them at school on their lunch hours. That's how I got their money or their stuff to them. I kept waiting for Alcee to have me banned from their schools, but it never happened. After a couple of years one of them told me whenever they asked for money, it was because Alcee made them do it. That's why she never had me banned from the kids' schools. Whenever she needed money, she made them ask me for it. It might sound like the kids took advantage of me, but they had to do it. If they didn't, their lives would have been even more miserable and I knew that. They only did what they had to do in order to get by and make it to the age of eighteen. I did eventually have to stop meeting them at their schools. One morning I received a call from one of Denise's friends. She said, "You don't know me but I'm a friend of Denise. I know she would want me to call and tell you that your mom is headed for your house with her gun. She said she's going to blow your fuckin' head off." I asked her what happened to set Alcee off. She said, "Some people from the youth center picked Denise up at school and won't let your mom have her back. She thinks you had something to do with it." I swear I didn't have anything to do with it, but I couldn't have been any more scared if I had. I kept my lights off all day and sat on the floor behind a chair, so I could see her first if she approached my apartment. I was in my mid-twenties and was hiding like a scared rabbit in my own house. I didn't turn on the TV or radio, I just sat there waiting for her to show up so I could crawl into a closet and hide. There was only one door and I couldn't get past her if she showed up. My only option was to hide, and maybe she would think I wasn't home. It makes me so sad to talk about being that scared when I was that old. I didn't know if she would shoot me or haul me off and hide me somewhere. I sat there all day watching for her so I could break what I had told my husband I would break as a signal and hide. I was in my twenties!

Years later Denise told me that she decided to go to a school counselor and tell everything. The counselor contacted local authorities and they picked her up at school the next day. Denise wasn't expecting it and she was terrified. She said she begged them to call me, but they wouldn't do it. She also told me that she was raped at the youth shelter the night she was taken there. She was only twelve or thirteen years old when that happened. The next day there was a preliminary hearing and she told the judge she wanted to go home. She said she told the authorities she made it all up because she was angry about being grounded. She did that so she wouldn't have to go back to the youth shelter. She said Alcee and Gordon were both in court that day and they looked so smug and sure of themselves. They told the judge that she was the youngest of seven kids and she was very spoiled by the older ones. Denise said she just let them say what ever they wanted to say, she let them win. She said she was sorry she ever opened her mouth about what went on at home because it got even worse after she did. After that ordeal, she had an affair with an old man who drove her school bus. He was the same age as her grandfather. Years later she told me, "What the hell, the damage was done after I was raped. The bus driver took me to his house during the day, while his wife was at work, and we had sex all day. He gave me money every time I asked for it, so what?" She ended up black mailing that bus driver for several thousand dollars over the next fifteen or twenty years. I was afraid he would kill her if she didn't stop it. Where in the hell was everybody? Where in the hell is everybody now? Where in the hell is the newspaper staff that prints Alcee's self righteous editorials thirty years after reporting her arrest for pistol whipping one of her kids? Does anybody know what went on? Does anybody care? Maybe it's just easier not to notice. It's been over twenty years since I left there and didn't look back, and I still have to ask myself if I really made it out.

While I was growing up, and trying to help the kids grow up, I really believed I was doing the best I could. I still believe I was doing the best I could, it's just that my best wasn't good enough. I really did want to save all the kids from any hell I could save them from. Looking back I realize that I couldn't save us all, but sometimes I feel like I didn't save any us. I believe if we had all been trapped in a burning building, I would have died trying to get them out, I would have kept going back in until they were all out, or I would have died with the ones who didn't get out. But what we were dealing with was not a burning building. It wasn't as structured as a burning building. Our souls were surrounded by fire, but we never had a framework for the fire to burn in a pattern, like a building would have framework. It was more chaotic than that. We didn't have a front door, back door or even a window to try to get through. It was like we weren't even in a building. We were in space, wide open space where flames shot up suddenly with no warning, then rapidly danced from one of us to the other, burning us. There was no where to run in the open space, there was only more open space with dancing flames hiding and waiting, daring us to try and find the windows and doors that we weren't even sure existed so we could escape. If we went for what we thought was a perimeter, the flames shot up quickly and violently to hold us prisoner. I was faced with saving the others or saving myself. It pains me to think I have one selfish bone in my body, but what other explanation is there? Weakness? I suppose after so many years I may have gotten weaker instead of stronger, not exactly a positive attribute to my character. But I won't take one hundred percent of the blame for the way I, or the other kids, did or didn't make it. Any part of each one of us that did make it, made it because we had what it took inside of us. If I helped the others at all, I'm proud of that. Any part of each one of us that didn't make it, didn't make it because we were too overwhelmed with hurt, fear and badly damaged self esteem, if we had any left at all. If I had anything to do with the other kids feeling lost or hurt, even by deserting them, I am sorry. I guess after so many years of overwhelming abuse, if your options are to save the others or save yourself, basic instinct kicks in and you save yourself; maybe not everyone, but I think most people would. I couldn't stand the fire anymore, and when I finally made it to the perimeter, I found a river and jumped in to douse the flames, only to find out I couldn't swim. But somehow, I made it to the edge of the bank and crawled out, I saved myself. My soul, ***myself***, was badly scarred, but the flames were doused. I jumped out of the fire and into the river over twenty years ago and I haven't looked back. If you don't save yourself, if you let yourself drown, how can you pull someone else out of the river? I don’t even know for sure if any of the others made it to the river.

One of the problems with trying to save my brothers and sisters was that we were all so close in age. By the time I got completely free, they were already headed down their own paths, each of them in a different direction. Each one of their souls as charred and damaged as mine. How many different directions could I have gone all at the same time? How fast could I have ran to catch them? What could I have said that would have made a difference in what they had suffered? I'll never know, because I obviously chose to try to save myself. But you know what? It is still overwhelming, it is still terrifying, it is still painful and it is still tragic. I still have nightmares about my childhood, including a recurring nightmare of being grabbed by intruders and hidden away where no one can find me. And because scars last forever, and because kids don’t ‘get over it,’ I think for the rest of my life I will have to say.....

I am ***still*** *trying to save myself.*

CHAPTER SIXTEEN

Where Do Charred Souls Go?

I think charred souls go to a place only they themselves know. There are as many places for charred souls to exist as there are charred souls. That's one reason why I didn't try to tell my brothers' and sisters' stories in detail. As sure as I am that our childhoods had adverse effects on each and every one of us, I am just as sure that no two of us exist in the same place. In a way, each one of us exists within ourselves, alone. No matter how many people are with us, we still have our own space, an inner space that is only known to each of us, individually. We don't tell about our space because 'you just don't.' It's been over twenty-five years since I left Alcee and Gordon's house of horrors, and I have seen very little of the other kids since that time. I have heard that the others don't see much of each other, either. I can't really explain why, but I believe it will always be that way. Maybe it's a form of denial. Maybe we all like to believe that it wasn't *really* that bad. Maybe we like to believe that "it might have been that bad for some of the others, but not for me." Maybe we prefer to ***not*** remember most of it. Maybe we like to say, "I remember something about that, but I don't remember the details." If we all were as close as we were when we were kids, it would be harder to deny the atrocities that were inflicted upon us. Maybe just being in each others presence would allow our charred souls to silently confirm more than we would like remember or acknowledge. I don't know for sure where any of the others are today, right this minute, but I do have a little knowledge and some second hand information of where they are. I know more about how well the girls survived than I know about the boys.

Trena

As I said earlier, I dropped out of high school, later obtained a G.E.D., got married and divorced, then I remarried and had a son.

After sixteen years I got divorced again and enrolled in a two year program at a local college. After graduating, I started a business with another woman in my profession, who is also my best friend. The only arrests I have had are the ones Alcee arranged when I was a kid. I'm no angel, and I might have a couple of drinks a year socially, but ninety percent of the time I'm the designated driver. When I'm really tired or nervous, I like quiet, just plain old quiet. I've been accused of being a work-a-holic, and I may be. I do work more than anyone I know, it's hard for me to just do nothing. I have trouble relaxing. Maybe subconsciously I am still trying to prove that I have some value, that I'm not totally worthless. As recent as three years ago I couldn't believe that anyone, except my son, could *really* love me. I trusted almost no one. It seemed like I had only ***one*** emotion and I couldn't identify what it was. I didn't know how to react if someone complimented me because I didn't know if they were sincere or if they were making fun of me. I am a successful business woman, being president of my own company for ten years. I have accomplished much more than statistics would have predicted when I was a child. Until recently I was sure I was of below average intelligence and that my success must be attributed to pure luck, no one could have convinced me otherwise. Recently my therapist persuaded me to undergo testing to prove to myself that I was at least average. I found out that I'm not stupid, dumb or fittified. In fact, even with a learning disability, I am of above average intelligence. If she hadn't talked me into being tested, I would still believe I was stupid, dumb, fittified or at least below average. I think of the kids all the time. I think about how their innocence was destroyed before they were old enough to know the meaning of the word. I ***worry*** that they still believe they are worthless and stupid, and I ***pray*** that they have come to realize that they are neither.

Dana (Second born)

Dana dropped out of high school, eventually becoming an alcoholic, and has been on disability since sometime in her thirties.

She has been married and divorced at least twice and has two children, neither fathered by her husbands. She still lives in our hometown. One of her children passed through my life briefly several years ago, he was curious and wanted to meet me. He had dropped out of high school and married at seventeen or eighteen. The last time I saw him he had one child of his own. His little sister dropped out of high school and had her first baby when she was fifteen. It was very obvious that he and his younger sister suffered as much abuse, if not more, than all of us did during our childhoods. Charred souls recognize other charred souls, and I know that he has been so traumatized that he, also, has a place known only to himself. Dana tells people in town that she talks to me every day, but I haven't talked to her in over twenty years. She is as dangerous today as she was when we were kids. On my son's first birthday, my grandmother called to warn me that Dana was hunting me down to kill my son and me.

When Dana calls I hang up as soon as I realize it's her. She stalked me for a while, I don't know for how long because I found out after the fact. About nine years ago a woman came to my office and begged me for any old books I wasn't using anymore. I sensed a danger about her and persuaded her to leave by calling out to another person in the next room. There was no one in the next room, I was alone and scared, but it worked. I thought she was a homeless person rattling around the building from one office to the other. A few years later her son showed me a picture of her, it was the same woman who had come to my office. Denise told me that Dana knew my daily routine and how I went to and from work. She repeated very accurate details to me that Dana had told her. At one time she was involved in a cult. I know that because one of the cult leaders called to invite me to a meeting with Dana, I declined. Dana has been institutionalized several times over the years. I received a call from a counselor at one such institution requesting information about Dana, I declined to give her any. A few years ago Dana called me in the middle of the night and told me there was an emergency involving Dena. She told me she was with the local police department and demanded that I confirm some information for her. It was the middle of the night and I was a little disoriented at first, but after listening to her for about a minute, I realized who it really was and hung up. I did call the local police department to confirm what I suspected, there was no emergency. Over the last twenty plus years she has been arrested numerous times, I don't know exactly how many or what the charges were. Recently there was a newspaper story reporting her arrest for neglect of a dependent and battery.

Dena (Third born)

Dena dropped out of high school and got married when she became pregnant with her first child. She had two children with her first husband, and after four years of marriage, they were divorced. She also obtained her G.E.D. She was a wonderful, nurturing mother to her children, but she would lose them anyway. For seven hundred and fifty dollars her in-laws hired Alcee to testify against Dena in a custody trial. Alcee forced Tony and Denise to testify against her, too. Dana did it for free and voluntarily. With her mother, two sisters and one brother testifying that she was an unfit mother, Dena lost custody of her first two children. She lived with me or near me for several years after losing her children. I used to hear her crying in the middle of the night, just like she did when she was a little girl. She sounded so wounded that I couldn't even bring myself to get up and try to comfort her. There is no comfort, not anywhere on this earth, for what happened to her. The day the judge handed down the decision denying her custody, Alcee called Dena at my house to say, "Yer big sister didn't do much fuckin' good for ya this time, did she?" She became an alcoholic and drug user after that. She eventually remarried and had another child, she divorced again, but that time she retained custody of her child. Her drinking and drug abuse intensified over the years. She has at least five arrests for alcohol related offenses. Several years ago, when my son was a teenager, Dena moved into my house one day while I was at work. I didn't mind that at all, but she was strung out on something, and I didn't know what, I only knew she was out of touch with reality. She was paranoid and agitated. I told her she had to get some professional help and give up the alcohol and drugs, or get out of my life. I had protected my son from being exposed to that lifestyle and couldn't let anyone, not even her, bring it right into our house. She took her child, went back to our hometown and moved in with Denise. That's the last time I saw or heard from her. Two of her arrests occured after she left my house. She had one of her kids to call and ask me for a several thousand dollar loan, I wouldn't do it, though. I found out later she needed it for attorney fees. As bad as it may sound, Dena was still a good mother. She was very affectionate and nurturing to all three of her children, and she had the patience of Job. Instead of telling her toddlers to stay off the stairs, she taught them how to go up and down the stairs, scooting on their butts so they could do it safely. She was a pretty little girl and developed into a beautiful woman. She was so pretty that some people couldn't believe she was ***my*** sister. Dena was probably the weakest and most fragile of all of us. Out of all seven of us, I believe Dena's soul is the most charred and she is the most tortured because she suffered more hurt than any of the rest of us.

Tim (Forth born)

In the last twenty four years I have only seen Tim about three times. He got married the summer after he graduated high school and had two children within three or four years. He married the girl he was with the night Alcee spied on him at the drive-in. He went to a trade school and works in the same trade today. One of the times I saw him, he told me about taking his son hunting with him. The little boy was around eight or nine years old. Tim told me with pride, like it was really quality time, how he hid from his son in the woods until he became so scared he cried. I said, "Tim, why would you do that? Don't you remember how scarey it was when we took rides to the country and got dumped?" He said, "Hey, I love my boy, he knew I was just kiddin' him." He was so proud that he spent time with his kids. I don't think he was ever brutal or sadistic to them. I believe he ***was*** playing with his little boy, the only way he knew how to play, and just didn't know any better. Maybe because he was so beaten down as a child, he set up a situation where he could be a 'hero,' instead of a 'stupid little fittified bastard.' I don't know what he was thinking, I can only guess. He changed the spelling of his first name, I don't know why, I just know that he did. Maybe he no longer wanted to be the same person he was when he was little, that hurt angry mistreated little boy, maybe it's his way of escaping the past. I do know he was a much better father to his kids than the one he had. There was no doubt in my mind, as I watched him interact with them, that he dearly loved his kids. I don't know how many years after they were married Tim and his wife got divorced. He has at least one alcohol related arrest and lives in a town not far from where we grew up. Someone told me he does anything he can to please Alcee. I wonder if he is still trying to get her to like him. The few times that I saw Tim over the years, he displayed love and affection for his wife and kids. Although I sensed that there was still a hard bitterness about him, like he was struggling to keep his charred soul hidden away, he was as cute as he ever was. He grew up to be a handsome man.

Tom (Fifth born)

After graduating from high school, Tom went to a trade school and still works in that trade. He married, and later divorced, a drug addict with whom he had three children. After the divorce Tom obtained custody of all three kids. He lives near Alcee and Gordon and he, too, is still trying to please them. I don't have any first hand knowledge of an alcohol related arrest, only second hand from a questionable source. Another source told me he didn't drink at all. If I was forced to guess, I would guess that Tom doesn't drink or do drugs. I do know that he has sleep apnea due to obesity. I saw him about seven years ago, the only time in the last twenty four years I've seen him. He was still shy and had the same cute sheepish smile as when he was a little boy. He looked the same as he did when he was little, only bigger. He spoke kindly of his ex-wife and boasted about his three pretty daughters. I heard such gentleness and pride in his voice, that I knew his little girls were in good hands with their daddy. I believe in my heart that he is a good daddy. When Tom was a little boy, he was the one who seemed to always get the short end of the stick. For instance, if I went out and bought three identical toys for the three boys, if one of them was defective, it would be Tom's. He never whined or cried about it, though. He smiled his cute, sweet smile and said, "Oh, well. It's no big deal. It's not like I can't live without it" I wonder if that's what he said to himself when his marriage broke up. I felt his gentleness and kindness as he spoke of his little girls. His soul may be charred, but I believe it is still gentle. Sometimes I close my eyes and visualize his sheepish, pretty smile.

Tony (Sixth born)

Tony graduated high school and went into the military. He was given an early discharge from military service due to drug abuse. He spent several years in jail for car theft, possessing, using and dealing drugs. The last time I saw him was about seven years ago, when I saw Tom. He had been out of jail and released from house arrest for only a few months, and was going through a rehabilitation program. He told me he was about to get married to a girl he met in rehab and he was working in a factory. The last time I heard anything about Tony, he was married, happy and drug free. Denise said Alcee nearly kept a vigil at the jail when Tony was in there, and spent thousands of dollars for attorney fees. That was so out of character for her, we didn't understand it. He lives in our hometown, and I've heard he tries to remain close to Alcee and Gordon. I didn't sense the softness or gentleness he had when he was a little boy. He seemed strong, but shaky. He was just as cute, witty and smart as when he was a little boy. He had a beautiful smile too, but it was a mischievous one. He was the playful intellect when he was a little boy. He is also the one who let me pamper him the most.

Denise (Seventh born)

Denise dropped out of high school and got married when she became pregnant with her first child. I have seen her about three times in the last twenty years. She has had at least two alcohol related arrests. In fact, the first time I saw her kids was when the police called my house and asked me to come pick them up at the scene of her second arrest. I had never met them and when I approached Denise's car to tell them who I was, they had that same look some of us had when we were kids. The little boy was tough, showing no fear, and chuckling nervously, instead of crying. The little girl was scared and shaking. She was holding back her tears and ready to let anyone hold her. The last time I saw Denise she was physically and verbally abusive to both her children. She was holding her daughter in a head lock and repeatedly smacking her in the mouth. I asked her why she did that when she knows how that feels. She said, “It ain’t like we was done, this is different. I ain’t hurtin’ my kids! At least I don’t draw blood! Don’t start in on me!” I told her she couldn’t hit her kids at my house and that was the last time she was at my house. The last time I talked to her she was happy because her married boy friend was getting a divorce and moving in with her, he is her dad's age. She drinks daily and her kids are not nurtured or handled with care. She doesn't hold a job for more than a few weeks at a time and depends on welfare or what ever she can con people out of. She’s in her mid-thirties and has two grandchildren. The last time I saw her she told me that she waited for me to save her for years. She told me she used to sit by the window watching for me to come back and get her out of the hell. She said, "I knew you wouldn't just leave me there. I just knew you'd come back and get me, but 'cha didn't, did ya?" I never showed up to save her, and I think she hates me for that. As I watched her mannerisms and listened to her talk, I thought about when she was little. She is still as cute as ever, too. She's so pretty, but she is so tortured that most people will never see her beauty. Their vision will be so blurred by her drunkenness and hostility that they won't even know her beauty exists.

I don't know if all of us made it out of the hell or not. I don't know if none of us made it out. I don't know if some of us did and some of us didn't. But for those self righteous types who live amongst us in this world, and for those who viewed us as the 'kids in the alley,' please don't judge us. When you run into kids like us and pass judgment it isn't fair because you don't know us, and we all had enough unfairness to deal with the day we were born to Alcee. A lot of people were so quick to judge Dena after she lost her two kids, so besides grieving over her loss, Dena also had to cope with the stigma of being a mother who lost her children. Can you try to imagine how bad she must have felt about herself? They never took us away from Alcee, but they took Dena's kids from her. From Dena's perspective it must have looked like the authorities never thought Alcee was unfit enough to take us from her, but Alcee could cause the authorities to take Dena's kids from her. All seven of us will always be abused kids, no matter how old we live to be, because we can never get rid of the scars. I believe abuse not only stunts our development, but sometimes halts it altogether in certain areas. Even though we look like adults, act like adults and talk like adults, we are still abused children in our private little space where we keep our charred souls. If you knew any of the seven of us, it might look to you like we didn't get very far in life. I know how far we have come, and I know why every one of us is like we are. I don't condone my siblings alcoholism and self medication, or any of our emotionally crippled short comings, but I do understand it. If you feel compelled to judge kids like us, remember the words of Booker T. Washington, ***"I have learned that success is to be measured not so much by the position that one has reached in life as by the obstacles he has overcome while trying to succeed."***

.

.

.

.

.

.

.

.

As for Alcee and Gordon, they don't deserve to be mentioned in the same chapter with us kids, but they don't deserve their own either. I have symbolically made space between the paragraphs about us kids and the ones about them. This book is about *Charred Souls*, their souls are not charred, they are evil. They still lurk in our hometown. Gordon is disabled and has trouble getting around. I'll bet he doesn't go around hitting people now, huh? Alcee writes self righteous letters to the editor of the local paper and is involved in the 'Christian' faith. She is a pillar of the community, a pillar molded of mud. If anyone looked closely they would see that the pillar is riddled with cracks and pits. Her letters to the editor about child abuse are an affront to every abused child in the world. The letters are merely her instrument to publicly ridicule the agencies which she first baited into games and then defeated for decades, even playing the game using some of her grandchildren as game pieces. Her last letter to the editor was a 'Christian' testimonial about the sin of abortion. As I read it I thought, "God forbid a baby factory baby would be spared all the fun awaiting them in this world." I'm not stating my view on abortion, I'm just saying that if you are going to abort a child, do it ***before*** you give birth to it. Don't give birth to it and then slowly and fiendishly char it's soul beyond recognition, crippling it forever.

If you read this book and you think it's about you, what makes ya' think that?

QUICK ORDER FORM

Postal Orders: Oberpark Publishing Inc.
55 Monument Circle
Suite 1422
Indianapolis, IN 46204

Please send ______ copy(ies) of CHARRED SOULS A Story of Recreational Child Abuse.

Name: ____

Address: ____

City: __________________________ State: _____ Zip: ________

Telephone: ____

e-mail address: ____

Please enclose check or money order in the amount of $16.95 per book + $5.00 S&H for the first book and $2.00 S&H for each additional book.

Visit our web site at www.oberparkpublishing.com.